THE COMPLETE BOOK OF
CORVETTE

BY THE AUTO EDITORS OF CONSUMER GUIDE®

Richard M. Langworth

BEEKMAN HOUSE

Louis Weber, C.E.O.
Publications International, Ltd.
7373 N. Cicero Avenue
Lincolnwood, IL 60646

Printed and bound in Yugoslavia by CGP Delo
g f e d c b a

ISBN: 0-517-63673-5

This edition published by
Beekman House
Distributed by Crown Publishers, Inc.
225 Park Avenue South
New York, New York 10003

Library of Congress Catalog
Card Number: 87-61998

CREDITS

Principal Author
Richard M. Langworth

Photography
The editors gratefully acknowledge
Buick Motor Division; Chevrolet Motor
Division; General Motors Public
Relations; Floyd Joliet, GM Design Staff;
Charles M. Jordan, GM Corporate Vice
President, Design Staff; Dave Gooley;
Sam Griffith; Burt E. Johnson; Bud
Juneau; Vince Manocchi; Doug Mitchell;
Richard D. Spiegelman; Nicky Wright.

Owners
Special thanks to the owners of the cars
featured in this book for their
enthusiastic cooperation. All cars listed
are Corvettes, except as noted: Robert
and Diane Adams (Arctic White '57
roadster, Snowcrest White '59 roadster),
Kirk Alexander (Elkhart Green '72
coupe), Mark Alter (orange '74
roadster), Auburn-Cord-Duesenberg
Museum (1912 Ford Model T Runabout,
1935 Auburn 851 "boattail" Speedster),
Pat Bachrodt (silver '75 roadster), John
Baritel (silver '66 coupe), Paul Batista
(white '54 roadster), Blackhawk Auto
Collection (1936 Mercedes 500K Special
Roadster), Jim Blanchard (red '58
roadster, p. 79-85), Pete Bogard (red '57
roadster), Joseph E. Bortz (turquoise '57
roadster), Jeff Branson (white '56
roadster), Briggs Cunningham
Automotive Museum (1951 Cunningham
C-1, 1952 Cunningham C-4R), Frank
Capolupo (yellow '69 coupe), Richard
Carpenter (gold '61 roadster), Gordon
and Dorothy Clemmer (white '53
roadster, black over gray '68 Official
Pace Car), Thomas and Mae Crockatt
(red '60 roadster, p. 96-99), Paul Ellingsen
(red '69 coupe), David L. Ferguson (red
'55 roadster, p. 36-39), Dave Hill (1949
Kurtis), Melvin R. Hull (1954 Muntz Jet),
Ronald B. Irwin (1937 Cord 812
Supercharged Sportsman), Violet and
Bruce Jacobs (silver '63 coupe, p.
120-121), Jerry Johnson (1954 Kaiser-
Darrin), Bill Kitchums (blue '67 coupe),
Darryl E. Klock (Mosport Green '66
roadster), Tom Korbas (maroon '66
roadster), Rich Mason (1956 SR-2 racing
prototype), Michael D. McCloskey (red
'58 roadster, p. 86-89), Gerald McGregor
(1953 Nash-Healey), Marty and Itacque
Metzgar (maroon '67 roadster), Ben
Oliver (yellow '68 roadster), Edward E.
Ortiz (silver '82 Collector Edition), Ben
Rose (MG-TC), Santo Scafide (red '63
roadster), Tom Schay (silver '63 coupe,
p. 115-117), Dave Stefun (red '55
roadster, p. 40-44), Chuck Swafford
(Royal Heather Amethyst '62 roadster),
Charles A. Vance (yellow '70 coupe),
Carlos and Sherry Vivas (red '64 coupe),
Chip Werstein (red '60 roadster, p.
100-101), Rosanne Winney (brown '76
coupe).

CONTENTS

1957 Chevrolet Corvette roadster.

INTRODUCTION

That the Corvette is 35 years old with
the 1988 model hardly seems possible. Yet
it endures. America's only true sports car is
now, as ever, distinctive and unique. It captures
roughly the same number of sales as it always has, and
it's the *ne plus ultra* of thousands of car enthusiasts
who wish they could afford one, much as their forbears
had wished for one in 1953, or in 1970. Whatever
the fate of GM, the Corvette remains true to
its heritage—honest and uncompromising.

That the Corvette is 35 years old with the 1988 model hardly seems possible. But those three-and-a-half decades have passed, and through them the Corvette's manufacturer has undergone a lengthy period of crisis. Today, General Motors is facing what may be its most serious challenge yet. Despite five or six years of on-going prosperity, the company seems to be without direction. Its market share plummets. So many of its cars seem lackluster and dull—too much alike from make to make, with product offerings that have come too little and too late compared with their domestic rivals Ford and Chrysler. Ford leads Detroit styling for one of the few times in its history, and Chrysler is resurging with its best-built cars in years and is now the new owner of American Motors. Mass inertia—perhaps even mass hysteria—seems to prevail at The General's headquarters.

Yet the Corvette endures. America's only true sports car is now, as ever, distinctive and unique. It captures roughly the same number of sales as it always has, and it's the *ne plus ultra* of thousands of car enthusiasts who wish they could afford one, much as their forebears had wished for one in 1953, in 1963, or in 1970. Whatever the fate of GM, the Corvette remains true to its heritage—honest and uncompromising.

Of course, the 1988 Corvette is by a long measure the best Corvette ever. The marque has rarely gone backward. Arguments could be made that it did in 1968, but not in any other year. The 1988 model reminds us that somewhere within the halls of General Motors car enthusiasts are still alive and well, and they're doing their best for those who think like they do.

A sobering thought is that a good many of today's Corvette fans were not yet born when the first 1953 models burst upon the scene. Yet the younger enthusiasts have been no less affected by the Corvette mystique than those of us who grew up with the car. The mystique has many facets: the undeniably individualistic character of the cars, the colorful people who created them, the drama of the Corvette's troubled early years, the triumph of the later ones, and the allure of a proven winner on the show room floors, the race tracks of the world, and the main streets of America. The Corvette has endured, yes.

But it has also grown and improved, attracting an ever wider following whose interest and devotion has been swelling with each new model, each race victory, and each glamorous show car bearing the Corvette name. The car's charisma and the vast enthusiasm that it inspires make the Corvette unique in the annals of automotive history. It remains perhaps the best-known, best-loved single model ever to come from Detroit. And for millions of people around the globe, it is still the symbol of the brightest and best in American automobiles.

This book is primarily the story of the Corvette through its 35-year evolution and of the people who have played key roles in its development. But the story is as much that of the Corvette phenomenon and you, the many 'Vette fans who have made the car a legend in its own time. Capturing a legend is not easy, nor is giving a fresh point of view to a story so thoroughly documented elsewhere. However, we've tried to inject new information wherever possible and to show familiar events from a different perspective in order to make the Corvette saga come alive.

Other sports cars had been made before the Corvette, and some of them in America. Participants in the Roaring Twenties still remember the glorious Stutz Bearcat, and some may yet recollect the Bearcat's contemporary, the Mercer Raceabout. The Corvette was not the first quick two-seater built in the United States, even though the country somehow seemed to forget the two-seat concept during the Golden Age of the Classic Car—1925 through 1940.

Then came the Second World War, when most of us forgot about cars in general because we didn't have enough gasoline or rubber or ration coupons to keep them on the road. America's love affair with the automobile was temporarily sidetracked. But it came storming back after V-J Day, and with it came reawakened interest in the sports car. Tracing the Corvette's great history would be impossible without a look back at the development of the postwar sports car—first as an iconoclastic import bearing curious badges reading MG or TR or Jaguar and brought home by returning GIs and then, in the Fifties, by a host of imitations (some decent, some otherwise) produced by American manufacturers.

Among the latter-day domestic sports cars, the Corvette was neither the first nor, at least on paper, the most interesting. Initially, it was a six-cylinder car with an automatic transmission that couldn't hold a candle to a Jaguar. Indeed, the whole Corvette idea almost died two years after its birth. A significant turning point came in 1955 with the introduction of a lively new V-8 engine that would help save the Corvette from extinction. The brilliant second Corvette generation of 1956-57 is perhaps the most memorable of the early models, with sharp new styling, much improved roadability, and even more performance—courtesy of fuel injection and larger engine displacement. The basic Corvette design then had wider sales appeal in the third generation of 1958-62, which saw the Corvette become a profit-maker able to earn its keep for the first time. The last of the "four-lamp" cars, the 1961-62 models, are treated separately as a distinct bridge between the 'Vettes of the Fifties and Sixties. The fourth generation followed—the brilliant 1963-67 Sting Ray cars that seem no less sensational today than they did a generation ago. The fifth generation ran from 1968-77 with only minor alterations and then, with a restyled roof, from the 'Vette's 25th anniversary year through 1982. The sixth generation Corvette, which added a vibrant new chapter to the story in 1984, is with us yet, and it is probably destined to be around quite a few more years.

Interviewed herein are two key people who have made the newest generation Corvette possible—David R. McLellan, lineal successor to Zora Arkus-Duntov, the man behind the nuts, bolts, and computer chips of today's Corvette; and Jerry Palmer, head of Chevrolet Studio Three, who led the design team for today's extraordinarily aerodynamic new sports car. Three more men are also interviewed, those who were involved in the earlier part of Corvette history. No Corvette book could be complete without them—Zora Arkus-Duntov, godfather of the marque, who saw it through its early birth pangs and guided it through its development as a competition machine; Harley J. Earl, founder of GM Styling, design director for each Corvette through the 1961 model; and William L. Mitchell, GM design chief in succession to Harley Earl, who remade the Corvette's image during the early Sixties. It is unnecessary to elaborate our thanks to these people for the light that their candid comments shed on the Corvette story.

The production-line cars that rolled off the dealer lots are only part of the Corvette's tale. We'll take a look back in time to review the many Corvette experimental and show cars, and we'll look at the competition record—good and bad—from the early factory-supported efforts (including the assault on Sebring), through Bill Mitchell's personal campaign with his Stingray racer, and on through the hundreds of modified cars entered in all forms of motorsports.

Corvettes of all ages are supported today by a veritable army of professionals—businesses that provide owners of all models with parts, accessories, speed equipment, and printed matter vital to the maintenance of the breed. They, too, are reviewed here. And interspersed throughout this book is recent and original color photography of 50 different Corvettes from virtually every model year.

Admittedly, revealing something new about the marque is difficult nowadays. If information hasn't been presented by commercial publishers, then it has been distributed by the several car clubs—most notably the highly professional and expert-laden National Corvette Owners Association and the National Council of Corvette Clubs. But every epic story needs to be updated from time to time.

Here, during the 1988 model year, the Corvette celebrates its 35th year of production. Whether it is still "America's Only True Sports Car" largely depends on your definition of the term *sports car*. But of this there is no doubt—the Chevrolet Corvette is still the most recognized and respected American performance car on the road, and it has held that title for over 30 years with little sign of relinquishing it.

To borrow a phrase from the Bugatti people (something they probably won't like): Viva la marque! May we have Corvettes to write and dream about on the 50th anniversary in 2003 ...which undoubtedly will be here before we know it.

CHAPTER ONE

In the Beginning There Was an Idea

Although it will inevitably cause an argument, defining the meaning of the term *sports car* would be appropriate here, even for car enthusiasts, to put everyone on common ground. The most acceptable definition is that a sports car is a dual-purpose automobile, equally suitable for street transportation and for racing. A sports car usually—but not always—has two seats and a convertible top. It usually—but certainly not always—has some luggage space, if perhaps less than a *gran turismo*. A GT, by contrast, is usually a closed car, capable of carrying two people and an ample amount of luggage quickly and for long distances—but not all GTs are suitable for out-and-out road course competition, especially not modern ones.

Americans first experienced sports cars (though they weren't called sports cars) well before World War I, in the earliest days of the horseless carriage. The most crucial thing in them was the design of the chassis and drivetrain. A consensus on power did not exist by any means, with electricity, steam, and internal combustion all having their adherents. So the manufacturer first designed an engine, and then a chassis, and finally a body. Bodies were sparse, open affairs in the early years of this century, but large, closed sedan, limousine, and town car bodies followed quickly. The evolution of the automobile led to prestige cars like Locomobile, Simplex, Lozier, Chadwick, and the legendary "Three Ps"—

Packard, Peerless, and Pierce-Arrow. In due course, the adherents of these makes—moneyed types who could indulge their fetish for motoring—began trading the heavy, closed bodies for light, sparse, open two-seaters again. Even so, these cars tended to be heavy brutes and hellish cars to handle, with none of the agility that would mark the Corvette 40 or 50 years later. Speed runs, durability trials, and cross-country marathons were the main forms of competition in the early days. The two-seaters were certainly lighter, quicker, and better on twisty roads than the workaday closed models from whence they had evolved.

Inevitably, the lighter cars led to the concept of the dual-purpose, race-and-ride car—one of the earliest examples of which was the historic 1911 Mercer Type 35 Raceabout, from Trenton, New Jersey. Raceabouts were built from 1911 through 1923, but the T-head-engine models from 1911-14 are the best remembered. Here was a direct forebear of the Corvette to come. Within the context of its time, it was light, responsive, and fast. The big four-cylinder engine—designed by Finley Robertson Porter—produced 58 horsepower at 1700 rpm. Since the Raceabout weighed only about 2400 pounds, the car was a contemporary rocket. It could exceed 75 miles per hour off the show room floor, and racing versions came close to the magic 100-mph mark. In 1911!

The Raceabout gearbox shifted easily, though synchromesh was years away, and the whole car was relatively easy to drive. The chassis was quite modern, with a full-floating rear axle located by radius rods and semielliptic, vanadium-alloy steel leaf springs at each corner. It even had a pull-up handbrake for the rear wheels, supplementing the mostly ineffective foot-actuated service brake that operated on the transmission.

Priced at $2150—more than twice the cost of the most expensive Model T Ford, by comparison—the Raceabout was not the sort of car that everyone could afford, another characteristic of sports cars that persists to this day. But its jaunty air and jackrabbit quickness captivated the nation. It's still one of the most sought-after models among antique-car collectors.

The Raceabout quickly proved its mettle in competition, winning the important San Francisco Panama-Pacific Light Car Race in February, 1911. Later that year, two Mercers were literally driven onto the track from off the street and ran flat out to finish 12th and 15th in the first Indianapolis 500. The two Mercers averaged 63 mph and, according to many reports, were so trouble-free that their hoods weren't opened even once during the race. Afterward, in what would become traditional for sports car racing in a later era, drivers Hughie Hughes of England and Charles Bigelow (who'd won at San Francisco) simply

drove their Raceabouts off the track and on home. It was a spectacular showing for an unmodified automobile. The next year, a Raceabout driven by Hughes finished third at the Brickyard, averaging a little over 76 mph.

Though Raceabouts went on to score many more victories at the hands of speed merchants like Ralph DePalma, Eddie Pullen, and Spencer Wishart, production didn't continue long. The last ones were built in 1915. Just before that, however, a rival company introduced a new model that would be even more celebrated—the Stutz Bearcat, the car synonymous with sheiks and flappers and all of the other razzmatazz of the Roaring Twenties.

Designed as a "sportsman's car," the Bearcat was the road-going equivalent of the famous T-head Stutz racers that had scored many wins of their own against the Mercers. Its chassis and

four- and six-cylinder engines came from the Stutz F Series passenger models, a kind of "derivative" engineering that would be commonly employed for many later sports cars, including the Corvette. However, its wheelbase was considerably shorter and its stance much lower than those of the passenger model. Though it was far less graceful and more ponderous than the athletic Raceabout (which it resembled), the Bearcat had superior roadholding and thrilling performance overall.

The Bearcat progressed through an attractive restyle in 1917, when it also received a more powerful 80-brake-horsepower, 360-cubic-inch, four-cylinder engine with a 16-valve cylinder head. In this form it was capable of an astonishing 85 mph. The car was reworked again for 1920 and continued to sell well for another couple of years. The final 88-bhp model with

3.00:1 rear axle could hit close to 90 mph, but it wasn't enough to counteract a sales slide. The Bearcat was phased out of production in 1923.

America's automakers created a number of memorable sporty-looking models in the years between WWI and WWII. But, by and large, they were not the sort of compact, nimble, dual-purpose machines we now associate with the term *sports car*. To be sure, romantic roadsters and convertibles numbered among them, and some of them—like the elegant Auburn 851/2 boattail speedster and the futuristic Cord 810—have long been recognized as some of the greats from the automobile's Golden Age. But cars like these were more *gran turismo* than sports car—comfortable and fast, but too large and heavy to be entertaining over a challenging country road. Others, like the Millers and early Duesenbergs, were more competition

Some early sporting cars:
the 1912 Ford Model T Runabout (*opposite
page*), 1935 Auburn 851 boattail Speedster (*below,
owned by the Auburn-Cord-Duesenberg Museum*),
and the 1937 Cord 812 cabriolet (*above*).

car than road machine—too powerful, too unwieldy to be practical in everyday use for the vast majority of motorists. Besides, they were built in tiny numbers and cost a fortune. The same was true of the later SJ Duesenbergs, which were purely luxury tourers. America, it seemed, had given up on the sports car idea.

But not completely. In the late Twenties, certain enthusiasts were becoming known as "hot rodders." These backyard mechanics, blessed with dreams and a native intelligence but not much cash, began rebuilding old, worn-out wrecks into very personalized automobiles. Hot rods were supposed to look good on the street and to be fast on something called a drag strip. Model T and Model A Fords were the favored starting points because, even then, they were cheap and plentiful, and their simple basic engineering was amenable to all manner of modifications. The most common ones were to discard the fenders and running boards, lower the body, maybe bend some sheet metal, fiddle with the suspension, and, naturally, wring more horsepower from the engine. In a way, the early hot rodders were after the same things that the pioneer automakers sought in their racers—more speed, more agility, and more distinctive looks. Though their approach was certainly different—low-budget, one-of-a-kind machines built from a crazy-quilt of production car pieces—hot rods were nonetheless quite faithful to the "race-and-ride" ideal, sports cars in the best sense.

Meanwhile, the sports car idea was being pursued in Europe along several different lines. Bugatti in France put the emphasis on small, almost delicate, open-wheel racers and two-place road cars built unhurriedly, one at a time. From Germany came the imperious bellow of the heavyweight, supercharged Mercedes-Benz—the imposing S/SS/SSK roadsters of the late Twenties/early Thirties and the more civilized 500/540K sports tourers of 1935-39. Down in Italy, companies like Maserati and Alfa Romeo were building cars that combined race-bred performance and technical sophistication with curvaceous, open, two-seat bodies that marked a new peak in coachbuilding artistry. But England was left with the task of defining the classic sports car as we would come

to know it. The exemplars were lithe, lovely roadsters like the Squire, the four-wheel Morgans, the sleek SS 100 (forerunner of the Jaguar) and—most of all—the cars from Morris Garages (MG).

MG has long been credited as the marque that introduced sports cars to America. One model in particular kindled the fascination that swept the country in the early postwar years, the sports car fever that would be an impetus for the future Corvette: It was the MG TC, introduced in 1945. As American writer T. C. Browne explained, this car became "one of the most beloved British exports ever to reach these shores, rivaling Scots Whiskey in its popularity among Americans... [But the TC] was to become admired all out of proportion to its numbers (few) or its technical virtues (fewer). In fact, the TC was all but indistinguishable from its immediate prewar predecessor, and a typical British enthusiast regarded the earlier PB as a measurably superior motorcar. Legends are seldom born of logic."

Nevertheless, GIs stationed in England fell in love with this humble

little piece of ironmongery. They brought some of them home, and the word spread. What did the TC have that was so special? It had charm, for one thing. It was cute, but somehow it looked right—nifty and sporty. It was also appealingly quaint, with vintage Thirties styling, diabolical folding top mechanism, cozy two-seat cockpit, conveniences notable by their absence—the whole package. The flexible ladder-type chassis and crude solid-axle suspension were anachronisms a decade before, and the ride was stiff and joggly. Yet the TC's agility was a revelation to Yanks raised on workaday Fords and Chevys. With its implausibly small 1250cc four producing just 54 bhp, the TC was hardly fast—well under 80 mph tops—but it showed power-hungry colonials that a car need not have a big-inch engine to be fun. Plus, like the Model A Fords so popular with the hot rodders, the MG was about as simple as an anvil. But perhaps the TC's greatest contribution was that it combined all of the elements basic to the sports car idea that had evolved over the previous 50 years. That it had a folding top and

Two classic prewar sports cars:
a 1936 Mercedes 500K Special Roadster
(*top left*, from the Blackhawk Auto Collection)
and a Jaguar SS 100 (*bottom left*). An early
postwar effort was the '49 Kurtis (*above*).

only two seats seemed almost superfluous. The stage was set for the sports car revolution in the postwar era.

The revolution took a long time to get rolling, and none of the manufacturers immediately rushed to build sports cars in the United States. The end of war had brought the promise of a prosperity unknown since before the Depression, and the public's mood was an expansive one. Consumers had a pent-up demand for at least 15 million cars, and styling didn't matter much at first. Whether or not the postwar models looked like warmed-over 1942 models wasn't important. Independent manufacturers like Studebaker made the mistake of revealing their postwar plans before it was necessary.

Ken Purdy had a description for the early postwar production cars that summed up what might be called the first buyer backlash against Detroit, calling them "a turgid river of jelly-bodied clunkers." A small but sturdy

handful of Americans agreed with him. Most of them were sporting drivers who had brought back or at least experienced a European sports car like the MG TC. They knew that driving didn't have to be dull. But Purdy and his followers were a very small minority. In 1952, for example, the registrations in the United States of what by the broadest definition could be called sports cars added up to a grand total of 11,000 cars—0.26 percent of the total registrations of 4.2 million cars that year.

Another angle to sports car manufacturing was spotted quickly by Detroit. Although the average American couldn't afford a sports car or the garage space for one next to the family hauler, he could be *inspired* by one as it sat on the local Ford or Chevrolet or Kaiser-Frazer show room floor. Maybe that inspiration would lead to the purchase of one of the "turgid, jelly-bodied clunkers" that were making moguls of Detroit businessmen.

A number of American sports cars were built by non-mogul types who simply clapped a swoopy-looking two-seat body on a conglomerate of off-the-shelf production car parts and the hairiest engine they could buy. Most of these, however, never went beyond the prototype stage, if that far, while others saw only minuscule production. Examples would be the Kurtis and its derivative Muntz Jet, the Boardman and the Brogan, the Edwards and the Gadabout; they need no more than brief mention here.

One small company that did make a highly respectable effort was Cunningham. The most successful American onslaught on international sports car competition up to the early Fifties was made by California sportsman Briggs Swift Cunningham, and the cars that carried his name ranged from svelte *gran turismos* to all-out sports-racers. One of the latter, the 1952 C-4R, finished fourth at Le Mans. Its 1953 successor, the C-5R, finished

third behind two D-Type Jaguars, which had the main advantage of disc brakes. Cunningham had tried to buy disc brakes from their British manufacturer, but was stonewalled in his effort.

Cunningham automobiles were powered by hemi-head Chrysler V-8 engines that produced 180 bhp in street tune, and as much as 300 bhp for competition. The cars rarely sold for less than $10,000 each, which would be approximately $40,000 today—well over the price of a new Corvette. So the Cunninghams were produced in very limited quantities. Without a doubt, though, the Cunninghams were genuine American sports cars, able to compete with the best European entries on the racing circuits of the world as well as move fast on the highway. Briggs Cunningham, who quit building the cars when continued losses forced him to either give up or declare his business a hobby, deserves a vast amount of credit for proving the capability of American engineering on international racing circuits.

Most important and of direct influence on the Corvette were the efforts of two major manufacturers, albeit independents, much smaller than General Motors—Nash-Kelvinator, the imaginative producer of the Nash-Healey, and Kaiser-Frazer, which employed such men as Howard A. "Dutch" Darrin and Brooks Stevens as design consultants. Nash's forward-thinking president—George Mason—had a size 52 frame and felt more at home behind a Michigan duck blind than a sports car's wheel, but of all the independents, his company proved the most progressive. Nash ended up the only survivor of them all, through its takeover of Hudson and the founding of American Motors. In the Fifties, George Mason was looking everywhere to find a niche and to beat the Big Three to it. His direct influence caused Nash/AMC to bid for a merger with Hudson, Studebaker, and Pack-ard; to build the first successful sub-compact—the Nash Metropolitan; and to create the Nash Rambler, thereby establishing the compact car revolution. Along the way, George also fostered a very impressive sports car, the Nash-Healey.

To develop the Nash-Healey, Mason worked with England's Donald Healey. Healey had been considering a British roadster powered by an American V-8—until Mason bought him a few drinks on the *Queen Elizabeth* in mid-ocean and convinced him that a Nash Ambassador ohv six-cylinder engine was just what he needed. Even though they were powered by the sixes, the Healeys were competitive. A prototype finished fourth at Le Mans in 1950. An aluminum stock-bodied 1951 model ran sixth overall and fourth in class at Le Mans in 1951. The next year, when Cunningham placed fourth, a Nash-Healey ran third overall behind two much more powerful Mercedes-Benz racers. At that time,

The 1945-49 MG TC (*left*) was "The Sports Car That America Loved First," but the postwar styling and speed sensation was the 1948-54 Jaguar XK-120 (*above*).

America looked as if it was becoming a sports car power to be reckoned with, but the reckoning was short-lived. Unfortunately, Nash-Healey sales were never high enough to justify production, even after a modified steel body and a closed coupe were put into the lineup. After Nash picked up Hudson to form American Motors, the Nash-Healey was dropped in the company-wide rationalization scheme, and AMC went on to greater things with its Ramblers.

In the meantime, Kaiser-Frazer's compact Henry J chassis became the base of two very different machines that furthered the evolution of the postwar American sports car—the Kaiser-Darrin DKF-161 and the Excalibur J. Though each was unique, the concept behind them was the same, prefiguring the method used by the designers of the Corvette: Combine the company's production-line parts with a beautiful two-seat body and the best engine available at the time. In Kaiser-Frazer's case, as would be Chevrolet's, the best engine was not very impressive.

The Kaiser-Darrin was a fiberglass two-seater with novel sliding doors that looked a lot better on paper than they ever worked in practice. The car was conceived by Dutch Darrin, who had created the outstanding 1951 Kaiser. After a hard sell to Henry J. Kaiser, Darrin saw his sports car go into production, but only for a short run. Just 435 production Darrins—all for the 1954 model year—were built. Some have questioned just how much of a sports car the Darrin was. It did race, so the car was capable of passing technical inspection. The most successful Darrin driver was none other than Mrs. Laura Cunningham (wife of Briggs), who scored a few fair performances in West Coast Region events of the Sports Car Club of America (SCCA).

Brooks Stevens' Excalibur J was more pure sports car than the Darrin, constructed around the Henry J chassis and given the overhead valve Willys engine. Whereas the Darrin started at $3668, Stevens hoped that the trim little Excalibur could retail for $2000 or so. Several prototypes were built for SCCA racing, and on occasion an Excalibur would lead a group of Jaguar XK-120s down the straights at Elkhart

Briggs S. Cunningham conceived his original C-1 sports car (*top*) in 1951 with racing in mind. The C-4R (*above*) finished fourth at Le Mans in 1952. The dramatic sliding-door Kaiser-Darrin (*top right*) featured a Willys F-head engine, fiberglass body, and Henry J chassis. Only 394 copies of the ill-fated 1951-54 Muntz Jet (*right*) were built.

Lake…and an occasional Ferrari to boot.

Unfortunately for both the Darrin and the Excalibur, Kaiser-Frazer's epic financial problems prevented either car from achieving any sort of mass production. What they did do was to prove that plug-ordinary passenger car componentry would work in the sports car mold. "Barney Roos, chief engineer of Willys, told us we'd put a piston through the hood if we turned that engine any further than 5500 rpm," Brooks Stevens recalled later. "We consistently turned them at 6500 rpm, and never blew so much as a freeze plug." Further, the Kaiser-Darrin offered another technological breakthrough that would be crucial to the Corvette's development—production bodywork of glass-reinforced plastic (GRP).

Thoughts of plastic bodies had occupied the mind of Henry Kaiser long before the Darrin. In 1942, he had conceived of a tiny economy car made entirely of GRP, selling for $400 new. Darrin himself had come up with a full-size convertible built of GRP in 1946. And another engineer sometimes associated with Kaiser-Frazer—

Bill Stout—used an Owens-Corning GRP body for one of his Scarab experimental cars. The material obviously worked. GRP lent itself easily to low-production bodies and thus appealed to builders of one-off or limited-production specials. Manufacturers knew that interest in sports cars was high. At least dealer interest for "line leaders" was running rampant. Inevitably, many custom GRP bodies would be offered for everyday chassis. The most successful supplier of such bodies was Glasspar, founded by Bill Tritt in 1950.

Bill Tritt used GRP on boats, as well as on cars. GRP was really developed first for the water. But by the early Fifties, Glasspar was making sporty bodies for everything from Ford Tudors to Crosley Hot Shots. Vast expansion occurred when Tritt convinced the U. S. Rubber Company in Naugatuck, Connecticut, of his idea's wisdom. In early 1952, the two firms undertook the joint manufacture of GRP bodies for 100-inch-wheelbase cars at a retail price of only $650. The bodies were sporty two-seaters, with provision for folding fabric or vinyl tops.

One Willys dealer—Woody Woodill of California—offered a Glasspar sports body for the Aero-Willys chassis, calling it the "Wildfire." Since finished Wildfires could be bought right off Woody's show room floor, this Willys-based two-seater had the honor of being the first production sports car with a GRP body. It beat the Corvette and the Darrin by one year, and its production continued into 1956.

All of these diverse influences culminated in the early Fifties to spark the creation of the Corvette: the reborn interest in genuine sports cars, at least among a handful of enthusiasts; the dealer demands for show room traffic builders, which reached a crescendo after the initial postwar seller's market was satiated; and the practical development of GRP bodywork for automobiles.

One day, representatives of U. S. Rubber received an invitation to visit Chevrolet Division of General Motors. Interest was being expressed by Chevy engineers in the mass-volume applications of glass-reinforced plastic.

The birth of the Corvette was now at hand.

The second-generation 1952-54 Nash-Healeys
were styled by Pininfarina, powered
by Nash, and built in England.

CHAPTER TWO

Leading Off for the General: Harley Earl and Ed Cole

If the efforts of small firms like Nash and Kaiser had been credible, they didn't make much of an impression at Ford or Chrysler. Ford was quite busy rescuing itself from the malaise of the elder Henry's last years of command. It had sunk all of its resources into the redesigned Ford, Lincoln, and Mercury for 1949, and it was slowly recovering number two spot in the industry from Chrysler. And Chrysler had its hands full staving off Ford, and although MoPar stylist Virgil Exner turned out a number of interesting one-off sports cars in the early Fifties, the company was in no position to put any of them into production.

Things were different at General Motors Corporation. The mighty colossus had emerged from the war mightier than ever, thanks to fat government contracts. Though temporarily eclipsed by Studebaker and its all-new 1947 models, GM reclaimed its position as industry styling leader with the tailfinned Cadillacs and Oldsmobile 98s of 1948. The next year saw the birth of the modern, efficient, high-compression ohv V-8 and of the hardtop-convertible body style, inaugurated at Buick, Cadillac, and Olds. These met with overwhelming acceptance. As the Fifties opened, sales seemed headed only one way—straight up. If anybody was going to make a serious attempt at building a homegrown sports car, it would be GM.

A key figure in GM's high success during these years was Harley J. Earl, founder and head of the firm's Art and Colour Section—the industry's first in-house styling department. Earl not only loved cars, but also was very imaginative. He had the good sense to surround himself with equally talented assistants, for whom he provided the most stimulating and creative work environment possible. Earl had almost single-handedly "invented" the dream car with his prophetic Buick Y-Job—a long, low, two-seat convertible first displayed in 1938. The Y-Job not only set the design themes for the company's styling in the immediate prewar and postwar years, but it proved the value of giving the public a "sneak preview" of things to come. This, in turn, led to the Motoramas, those exciting extravaganzas of chrome and choreographed chorus girls that thrilled visitors in cities and towns all over the country between 1949 and 1961.

Earl was eager to return to experimental projects after World War II. And once the corporation's new 1949-50 models had been wrapped up, he did. Significantly, his first postwar dream cars were two-seaters—the aircraft-inspired LeSabre of 1951 and the Buick XP-300 shown a year later. Both featured ideas advanced for their day, like wraparound windshields, folding tops hidden just aft of the cockpit under metal covers, sculptured rear decks with prominent tailfins, and a low, ground-hugging stance.

But Harley had something else on his mind. As writer Karl Ludvigsen tells it: "As an antidote to post-LeSabre creative depression, Earl began thinking seriously about a low-priced sporty car during the late fall of 1951. He'd do this in his office on the 11th floor of the anonymous-looking brick structure on the south side of Milwaukee Avenue, opposite the imposing GM Building. Then he'd wander...down to the ninth floor. There, in a small enclosure adjacent to the main Body Development Studio, Earl could work privately with a personal crew on projects—like this one—that he wanted to shield from premature exposure. Earl was well aware of the perishable quality of a new idea." That new idea was the genesis of the Corvette.

The first sketches and scale models for Earl's pet project were, as Ludvigsen describes, "most like an amalgam of the classic British sports cars and the [Willys] Jeepster, for Earl had in mind a very simple car, one that could be priced at only $1850—about as much as a Ford, Chevy, or Studebaker sedan in 1952. Such a moderate price meant that the design had to be based on a more or less stock chassis, and that's the way the first tentative studies went." New inspiration came from a car displayed for a time in GM's Styling auditorium. Called "Alembic I," it was essentially the original Bill Tritt design for U. S. Rubber Company, which had purchased it and

loaned it to GM. Earl now stepped up the pace, and work proceeded as "Project Opel." Perhaps this name was chosen to confuse outsiders, because Chevy frequently did advanced studies for GM's German subsidiary at the time. The project was all very hush-hush, with access to it limited only to those with a "need to know." If an employee wasn't directly involved with the Opel program, chances are that he never would have heard about it.

At this time, Edward N. Cole was transferred from Cadillac Division to Chevrolet, where he took over as chief engineer. Cole would be another key figure in Corvette history, but his list of credits was already impressive. He had begun working at Cadillac in 1933 after taking part in a work-study program at the GM Institute. His first assignments involved designing military vehicles such as light tanks for the Army. After the war, he worked on rear-engine prototypes for both Cadillac and Chevrolet, then concentrated on engines, helping Cadillac's John Gordon to develop that division's short-stroke ohv V-8 for 1949. Cole then managed Cadillac's Cleveland plant for 30 months before taking over his new job at Chevy. Once installed, he tripled the engineering staff (from 850 to 2900 people), then turned to designing a new engine for Chevy. It would be the legendary small-block 265-cubic-inch unit introduced for 1955.

Meanwhile, Earl had tapped a young sports car enthusiast with degrees from Cal Tech in both engineering and industrial design to come up with a basic layout for Project Opel. Although told that the method couldn't work, Robert F. McLean started from the back of the car, not the front as was usual practice. With the rear axle as a reference point, he placed the passenger and engine compartments as close to it as possible. The goal was the balanced 50/50 weight distribution desirable in a sports car for optimum handling. Ultimately, he achieved a 53/47 distribution. The wheelbase, cribbed directly from the Jaguar XK-120 (one of Harley Earl's favorites), was set at 102 inches. Track dimensions would be 57 inches front and 59 inches rear. Track was wider than the Jaguar's, but not as wide proportionally as the track of the funny-looking little rear-engine Porsches, which were as much an ana-

Opposite page: Harley J. Earl (*top*) practically invented the "dream car" with the prophetic 1938 Buick Y-Job (*center*). His 1950 LeSabre (*bottom*) indicated that sporty styling was on his mind. Earl was already thinking about a low-priced sports car when the 1952 Buick XP-300 (*above*) debuted.

thema to GM Design then as we dare say they are today.

By mid-1952, Harley Earl's staff at GM Art and Colour was coordinating its efforts with the engineers, leaning perhaps too heavily on the styling of the famous LeSabre and XP-300 show cars. A panoramic windshield, toothy oval grille, "definition" at the rear fenders, and shadow-box rear license plate frame were evidence of the show cars' presence in designers' minds. But Earl was also a practical man, and he told his colleagues that he expected this Chevy sports car to drive out the foreign invaders quickly. That chant would become a familiar one. Earl figured that he could undersell the foreign sports cars, offering far more car for the money with the added benefit of local dealer sales and service.

The way to undersell them was to use GRP bodywork.

A major question concerning GRP remained unanswered, however: Just how strong was the new body material? It was answered inadvertently, when a proving grounds driver unexpectedly rolled over a GRP-bodied prototype at high speed, escaping uninjured. All of the body's major components were intact following the crash, including the doors, hood, and deck lid.

McLean and Chevrolet engineers doubled their efforts to find chassis/drivetrain components that were already in production to go along with the plastic body. Since time was short, off-the-shelf hardware was of crucial importance. Of course, Chevrolet had quite a bit of hardware available.

Nevertheless, the chassis had to be designed from scratch, owing to McLean's unusual engine location. The layout of the rear end was also unique to the Corvette. For the first time in Chevrolet history, an open or Hotchkiss drive was used instead of the traditional torque-tube drive. Conventional leaf springs located the rear axle, but, unlike former Chevy design, they were outboard of the main frame rails for added stability—a feature picked up later in the 1955 Chevrolet passenger cars.

The engine? Only one unit was on the shelf—the tried and true 235.5-cid ohv six, which produced 105 brake horsepower in standard tune. That wasn't nearly enough, of course, for a sports car, so modifications were abundant, including a high-lift, long-

duration camshaft, similar to that of the 261-cid Chevy truck engine; solid instead of hydraulic valve lifters; and dual valve springs to cope with the higher engine speed. Since aluminum pistons were new to the Chevy engines hooked up to Powerglide transmissions in 1953, conventional pistons were used so that the Corvette could avoid unforseen problems. The head casting, however, was modified to produce an 8.0:1 compression ratio instead of the 7.5:1 ratio in the top-line Chevy passenger cars. The water pump flow capacity was increased, and the pump was lowered at the front of the block so that the large, four-blade fan could clear the anticipated low hood line. The induction system received the most serious modifications. Triple Carter "YH" sidedraft carburetors were mounted on a special aluminum intake manifold on the left side of the engine. All three functioned at the same time, the opposite of progressive linkages. Each carb fed two cylinders and had a separate choke. Initially, automatic chokes were used, but tests revealed their impracticality. The three chokes could not be synchronized because they did not warm up at the same rate. Thus only the Motorama Corvette carried automatic chokes, while production models had a manual setup. Contrary to popular belief, the carburetors were not created by Carter for the Corvette, but were ordinary production items. A dual setup had already been used in the Nash-Healey; it operated fine with automatic chokes, but, of course, it only needed two. Another unique but

simple change on the Corvette engine was its redesigned rocker arm cover, though it looked similar to the one used on the passenger car. The passenger car cover would not clear the low hood of the sports car. The Corvette cover was lowered at the front, and the "hat sections" for two through-bolts were turned inside out. The oil filler location was moved to the rear, eliminating the last hood obstruction. A minor but effective change was the special dual exhaust system that resulted in lower restriction and better sound. All the various engine changes produced significant increases in output. The free-breathing Corvette six ultimately produced 150 bhp at 4500 rpm, and it could rev higher than that.

The transmission used on the first Motorama show Corvette proved to be one of its more controversial features. Engineering did not believe that it had a manual gearbox suitable for the high-powered engine, and it had no time to tool one. The Powerglide two-speed automatic was selected, not for the sake of pansy Yankee drivers, as is often supposed, but because Chevrolet didn't have anything available that was better. Powerglide was simple, rugged, and reliable, and it was installed essentially unchanged from its passenger car specifications. One alteration was in the transmission's shift-point curve, which was changed to meet the new engine's torque characteristics. Tests showed that the conventional oil cooler wasn't necessary because of the sprightly acceleration possible with the lighter car, so all oil lines normally running for-

ward to the cooler were plugged. The shift control was floor-mounted for both practical and aesthetic reasons.

A rumor persists that the Corvette front suspension was identical to that of the conventional passenger cars. While the suspension design was the same as that found on the 1949-54 Chevrolets, the spring rates, shock settings, and ride stabilizer were all recalibrated for Corvette application. The steering gear was also the conventional Saginaw recirculating ball type, but its ratio was quickened to 16:1. Also, the Corvette steering wheel was one inch smaller in diameter than the passenger car wheels.

While the engineers labored with the production drivetrain, Harley Earl and company were busy finalizing a show car for the GM Motorama. By

Opposite page: Work on GM's sports car began under the
code name "Project Opel." The drawing (*top*)
shows the layout of what ultimately became the Corvette.
Edward N. Cole (*bottom*) served as chief engineer.
The 1953 Corvette Motorama show car (*above*) was a hit.

mid-year 1952, the basic outlines of the car, along with its inner components, had been well established. The Motorama show car was nearing completion. By virtue of his new position, Cole was one of the first people within Chevrolet Division to see Harley's masterpiece. Karl Ludvigsen has recorded that Cole "literally jumped up and down," promising to support Earl in his efforts to win approval all the way to the top.

To the top they duly went, to give their sales pitch to GM president Harlow Curtice. A few weeks after Cole had seen the full-size plaster model, Earl had it set up in the Styling auditorium for a presentation to Curtice and Chevrolet Division general manager Thomas H. Keating. The curtain flew up with a flourish. Then,

Earl led Curtice and Keating around the car, explaining enthusiastically that here was not only a profitable new product, but a car that would add much-needed sparkle to the Chevrolet line. His persuasiveness worked. It was agreed that the car would be shown at the first Motorama of 1953, scheduled for the grand ballroom of New York's Waldorf-Astoria hotel in January. Meanwhile, engineering work with a view to eventual production would proceed as Project EX-122, with the final go/no-go decision based largely on show-goers' reactions.

The gleaming Polo White show car, with its bright Sportsman Red interior, was a hands-down success at the 1953 Motorama. Chevrolet was soon being pressured by inquiries from all over the country: When

would it be produced, and how much would it cost? It was apparent from drawings and production dates that Harley Earl and Ed Cole never doubted that Chevrolet would produce the Corvette. Chevy would start building the car as a 1953 model.

With the exception of cowl-mounted fresh air scoops (that eventually appeared in non-functional form for 1956-57), the Motorama Corvette was one of the few show cars to go into production with its styling virtually intact. That Earl's pure original was retained, unsullied by committee modifications, enhances the early Corvettes' appeal among collectors and enthusiasts today. The styling has aged well, and the car still turns as many heads as it did 35 years ago.

CHAPTER THREE

1953-1955:
Brave New Sports Car or Fiberglass Folly?

Perhaps the Corvette's reception at the 1953 General Motors Motorama has been overemphasized as a factor in deciding its production. Corvette production had already been decided after Curtice and Keating gave their blessing to Harley Earl's mockup. No doubt a poor reception would have caused management to rethink the project, but in those sports-car-conscious days, imagining a poor reception would be difficult. An estimated four million people saw the Motorama Corvette, and their response was overwhelmingly positive. Production would commence as soon as possible, and the new sports car would be available from neighborhood Chevrolet dealers at a suggested retail price of $3513.

As for the critics who questioned whether any car worthy of the name *sports car* could have a "slushbox," GM engineer Maurice Olley replied: "The answer is that the typical sports car enthusiast, like the 'average man' or the square root of minus one, is an imaginary quantity. Also, as the sports car appeals to a wider and wider section of the public, the center of gravity of this theoretical individual is shifting from the austerity of the pioneer towards the luxury of modern ideas.... There is no need to apologize for the performance of this car with its automatic transmission."

Olley's use of the word *luxury* is significant. *Automobile Quarterly* pointed out in a 1969 retrospective that "during 1952 the Corvette evolved entirely away from the simple roadster originally visualized by Earl...[and] by January 1953...had become a 'luxury'

machine." Such a place in the market plus the rigid time and cost targets imposed on the development program go a long way toward explaining why the first Corvette emerged as a curious combination of the crude and the civilized. For example, Powerglide readily pleased Chevy's marketing people as much as it saved time and money for the engineers. Earl's body design, though clean and appealing, was still too gimmicky for some tastes, especially the rocket-like rear fenders with their tiny fins, the dazzling vertical grille teeth, and the sunken headlights covered by mesh stone guards. The top was neatly concealed under a flush-fitting metal cover and could be raised or lowered fairly easily by one person. But the clip-in side curtains, perhaps favored over roll-down windows as a cost-cutting measure, were

every bit as anachronistic as they were on British roadsters of the period. The license plate was housed in a modern-looking recess covered by plastic—which tended to turn cloudy. In the transition to production, the show car's exterior door pushbuttons were eliminated—which meant that the only way to open the door from the outside was to reach inside for the release. The first Corvette was a mixed bag indeed.

Though most 'Vette fans tend to assume otherwise, the decision to go with fiberglass body construction was made quite late in the game. GRP was expeditious for getting the Motorama show car ready on time, but Chevy seriously considered steel throughout most of the Corvette's harried gestation. Said engineer Ellis J. Premo at a meeting of the Society of Automotive Engineers: "At the time of the Waldorf show, we were actually concentrating on a steel body utilizing Kirksite tooling for the projected production of 10,000 units for the 1954 model year." Though a die made of Kirksite is faster and cheaper to create than a conventional die, its life is limited, and it would have been unsuitable had the volume been achieved. The Kirksite dies were thus never cast.

The GRP used for the Motorama show car body was 2/10-inch thick and was hand-laid into a mold taken directly from the preproduction plaster styling model in Harley Earl's studio. GRP molding techniques were still not fully developed, and more experimentation would be needed before actual production could begin. Ultimately, improvements in process chemistry

The Corvette was made of lightweight fiberglass
(*opposite page; this page, center left*). It
looked low-slung indeed parked next to a 1953 Chevy (*top*).
The Chevy six (*above left*) pumped out 150 horsepower.
Production shifted to Saint Louis for 1954 (*above right*).

allowed the production body to be only 1/10-inch thick with no loss in surface quality or structural strength. Chevy would have to build several interim bodies as a trial, however, before it was convinced that fiberglass was feasible.

After months of frantic activity, Corvette production got underway in a small building adjacent to the Chevy plant in Flint, Michigan, on the last day of June 1953. According to a press release issued much later, on that day the "division made automotive history. Amid shouted instructions and with flashbulbs popping to record the

event, Tony Kleiber, a body assembler, drove a car off a Chevrolet assembly line." It was a grand accomplishment. Corvette had made the transition from dream car to road car with remarkably few alterations and in an amazingly short time. Said general manager Keating at the event: "This occasion is historic in the industry. The Corvette has been brought into production on schedule in less than 12 months from designer's dream to a reality tested on road and track.... The engineers want to keep on testing these first cars for a few thousand

more miles. It may be important to Chevrolet's future plans to learn the amazing flexibility that is demonstrated here in working out new design ideas in plastics." Had he wanted to be more specific, Keating could have mentioned that the 1953 models were essentially handmade cars, and photographs of early models indicate much improvisation.

All '53s were finished in Polo White, with Sportsman Red and White interiors and black tops. All were equipped with 6.70 × 15 whitewall four-ply tires, Delco signal-seeking

Opposite page: Among the many sporting touches on the
Corvette was the inclusion of stone shields
over the headlights (*top*). Power came from the old
Chevy stovebolt six. Renamed the "Blue Flame Special,"
it sported triple carbs for more oomph (*bottom*).
This page: Although the Corvette
created quite a stir back in 1953 with its wraparound
windshield and true roadster configuration,
it did not sell well initially.

1953 Corvettes:
Nonconformity and Forgeries

1953 models vary in a number of areas. The National Corvette Restorers Club notes, for example, that early cars were not equipped with Guide Y-50 outside rearview mirrors, which became standard on later '53s and would remain part of the package through 1962. About the first 25 cars used snap-on full wheel covers from stock Chevrolet Bel Airs. Only after these were run off did Corvette switch to Motorama-like (but not identical) wheel covers with dummy knock-offs. On the other hand, all 1953 models had signal-seeking Delco radios and recirculating hot-water heaters, as well as a 5000-rpm tachometer that contained a counter of total

engine revolutions. The counter was retained through 1959.

Because the 1953 Corvette is rare and the first of the marque, its values lead the 1954 model by a considerable margin. In turn, the situation has resulted in a number of forgeries—1954 models converted to be 1953s. A number of components are usually overlooked by the forgers, however:

1. Chevrolet always placed a number corresponding to the body number plate on the frame. On 1953 models, the number appears twice and can be found with a flashlight and a small mirror without removing the body from the frame.

2. The fuel line on the '53s exited from the bottom of the fuel tank outside the righthand main frame rail—not so for the '54s.

3. Some early '53s carried wheel cover knock-off style hubs mounted at 90 degrees from the standard location.

4. All '53s had two inside hood releases at the lower outside corners of the dashboard. However, some early '54s were made the same way, so this is not a hard and fast clue.

5. The first 175 model-year 1953 Corvettes had foot-activated windshield washers. Beginning with serial number 001176, a dashboard-controlled vacuum system was substituted.

6. Although some cars lack the standard stainless-steel headlamp stoneguards or the clear Plexiglas cover over the rear license plate nacelle, their absence is not proof of a forgery since certain states required their removal for compliance with motor vehicle laws.

Compared to the stodgy design
of Chevy's passenger cars, the Corvette
sported swoopy styling (*left*) with built-in exhaust
outlets, twin-finned rear fenders, recessed license
plate holder, and fake knock-off wheel covers.
Bumper protection was minimal. The interior (*above*)
featured bucket seats and full instrumentation
and—unlike the typical British sports car—
a good heater.

radios, and recirculating hot-water heaters. The heaters were considerable improvements over the standard heaters found on imported British sports cars. Corvette owners also received a complete needle-instrument dashboard, including a 5000-rpm tachometer with a counter for total engine revolutions.

Of course, the new car had its detractors—purists raised in the MG and Jaguar traditions condemned the Corvette as nonfunctional and faddish. To them, the presence of a fake knock-off wheel cover meant that the rest of the car was no good at all. Such an analysis was superficial. More thorough inspection proved that, on the whole, the Corvette was quite a good sports car, definitely worthy of being raced as

well as used for daily transport. Even with Powerglide and the six-cylinder engine, a well-tuned Corvette would do 0-60 mph in 11 seconds and notch up 105 mph for top speed.

Most road testers found the combination of ride and handling to be excellent. Said Walt Woron, dean of them all, in *Motor Trend:* "Chevrolet has produced a bucket-seat roadster that will hold its own with Europe's best, short of actual competition and a few imports that cost three times as much."

Road & Track, more critical, asked if it was really a sports car. But the editors went on to say that it made "a favorable impression immediately on the score of clean lines with a minimum of chrome trim. It looks like a sports car, a very modern one at that.... The out-

standing characteristic [is probably its] deceptive performance. Sports car enthusiasts who have ridden in or driven the car without benefit of stopwatch seem to have been unimpressed with the performance. This is an injustice, as the figures shown in our data panel prove.

"The second most outstanding characteristic of the Corvette is its really good combination of riding and handling qualities. The ride is so good that few American car owners would notice much difference from their own cars. Yet there is a feeling of firmness about the car, and none of the easy slow-motion effect of our large, heavy sedans. The biggest surprise is the low roll angle—actually less than two of the most popular imported sports cars.

Visual Differences—Motorama Vs. 1953 Production Corvette

Motorama Car	Production Car
Chromeplated engine parts	Many plated parts now painted
Shrouded fan	No shroud
Nameplate front and rear	No nameplate front and rear
Hydraulic door and hood opening	Manual door and hood opening
Exterior door pushbuttons	No exterior door controls
Small front fender chrome molding	Full-length chrome fender molding
Chrome inside door knob	White plastic inside door knob
Two extra dash knobs, right side	No knobs
No windshield end seals	Windshield end seals
No drip moldings and seals	Drip moldings and seals
Upper front fender scoops	No front fender scoops
Narrow headlamp bezels	Wide headlamp bezels
Oversize wheel spinners	Smaller spinners
Upper dash edge painted	Upper dash edge vinyl-covered
Automatic choke	Manual choke

The Corvette corners flat like a genuine sports car should...Chevrolet may have committed some errors in presenting and merchandising a sports car [but] frankly, we like the Corvette very much."

About the merchandising, Keating was quite serious when he expressed hesitation to produce any kind of volume until the engineers were satisfied with the product. Chevy stuck to its projected 300 units for 1953, and it hand-picked most of the owners. The first few went to the engineers, although production cars 001001 and 001002 are believed to have been destroyed. The balance went to GM managers or VIPs—film stars, sports personalities, and industry moguls. Chevrolet didn't begin addressing the backlog of orders until the new plant in St. Louis, Missouri, was geared up for

the 1954 models. However, the initial 14 or 15 Corvettes for 1954 were built in Flint, as were all of the engines for that year.

Few significant changes were made for 1954, but running changes took place throughout the model year. The black tops and top irons were replaced by tan ones, and gas and brake lines were relocated inboard of the right-hand main frame rail. The storage bag for carrying the side curtains in the trunk was mildly reshaped and color-keyed to the interior. For the first time, more than one color was available. Pennant Blue accounted for about 16 percent of production and came with a tan interior. Sportsman Red, selling at about four percent, and Polo White, at about 80 percent, were teamed with red interiors. A very small number of cars—as few as six—were painted

In addition to the roadster (*left*),
several other Corvette variations were built,
such as the fastback Corvair (*top right*),
a 1954 Motorama show car, and the 1954/55 Nomad
(*above*), which reappeared as a full-size Chevy.
The '54 Corvette even looked good with this
proposed removable hardtop (*center*).

The 1954 Corvette received a new camshaft that
boosted horsepower to 155. White was still
the favorite color (*above*). *Opposite page:*
An early-day Corvette cavalcade negotiates Chicago's
infamous Lake Shore Drive S-curve (*top*). Nine '54
Corvettes parade around a race track (*bottom*).

black and also carried a red interior.
Some '54 'Vette owners claim to have
original factory paint in colors other
than these four, though they are not
listed officially. However, paint bulletins are known to have listed a
Metallic Green and a Metallic Bronze.

The 1953 model had carried two
short stainless-steel exhaust extensions that protruded from the body in-

board of the rear fenders. However, air
turbulence tended to suck exhaust
fumes back against the car, soiling the
lacquer. An attempted correction was
to lengthen the extensions and route
them below the body, but the change
didn't solve the problem entirely. It
would persist until the 1956 redesign,
when Corvette chief engineer Zora
Arkus-Duntov relocated the tips to

the rear fender extremities.

Some of the Corvette's initial incon-
veniences were remedied for the 1954
model year. For example, the original
two-handle exterior hood latch was replaced by a more manageable single-
handle mechanism after the first 300
or so '54s. The choke control was relocated from the right to the left of the
steering column, swapping places with

the wiper switch. The move eliminated the problem of having to reach across or through the steering wheel to operate the choke with the left hand while turning the ignition key with the right. In the back, moisture in the rear license plate recess tended to cause its plastic cover to fog up, so Chevy threw in two little bags of a desiccant material to keep the area dry.

Under the hood, a new camshaft boosted the engine's rated power output by 5 brake horsepower—to 155 bhp—though the increase wasn't announced until the following year. Other changes: The engine carried a newly styled rocker arm cover (about 20 percent had a chrome finish—serial numbers 1363 through 4381); the wiring harness was made tidier; and more

plastic-insulated wire replaced the fabric type. The three bullet-shaped air cleaners were replaced by a two-pot type after the first 1900 cars and through the balance of the model run. Engines were suffixed F54YG.

Another niggling problem concerned the top mechanism. On the early cars, the main top irons had to poke through slots in the chrome moldings behind the seats and were capped with spring-loaded flippers. Beginning with serial number 3600, the top irons were redesigned with a dogleg shape that allowed them to slip between the body and the seat back. Unhappily, the redesign led to another annoyance—the top irons rubbed the upholstery. Because the preferred top-folding procedure was not that obvious, the factory began sticking explanatory decals on the underside of the top cover.

The Corvette's price had been a sore point with critics and would-be customers. In a ploy to make the car appear more competitive, Chevy dropped the advertised base figure from $3498 to $2774 for 1954. The catch was that the Powerglide automatic was now an option. Since a

Production of the 1953 Corvette totaled a disappointing 300 units. While the '54 model looked the same, colors other than white became available. Chevy built 3640 units for 1954, a vast improvement, but many remained unsold at year's end.

manual gearbox was not yet available (and since nobody wanted a transmissionless car), a safe assumption would be that all 1954 models had the $178.35 "mandatory option." Even when the prices for all the legitimate options (directional signals, heater, radio, whitewalls, parking brake alarm, courtesy lights, and windshield washer) were added together, the sticker was still about the same as before—precisely $3254.10. Unfortunately, this marketing sleight of hand did nothing to spark sales.

The early Corvette may have had its faults, but reliability wasn't one of them. It was not a temperamental machine prone to breaking down like a Jaguar, nor did it demand the constant attention required by a Ferrari. Corvettes did have a few quirks, of course. The main ones were water leaks and synchronization of the triple carburetors for smooth idle and throttle response. The leaks were found mostly around the top and side curtains, though the leading edges of the door openings were suspect on some units. But these problems were hardly major, and Chevy issued service bulletins to cover them. The engine and running gear were just as boringly reliable in the Corvette as they were in Chevy's everyday passenger models—though expected, this aspect of the car was pleasant nonetheless.

By the end of 1954, a watershed in Corvette history was reached: General Motors was now giving serious consideration to dropping the car, opting out of the sports car business. Looking at the situation in retrospect, such a move would seem almost ludicrous. But the Corvette had in fact laid a considerable sales egg, and everybody at GM knew it. Despite the initial huzzahs of the Motorama crowd, the complimentary press reaction (even from the purists at Road & Track), and steady improvement of the product through the 1954 model year, the Corvette was not selling well. "We needed and expected 20,000 sales a year," said one manager active at the time. "When we got 3600—well, what more could be said."

Were the slow sales due to the Corvette's failure as a pure sports car, or to the minuscule size of the sports car market? No one has ever been able to focus on the exact cause of the problem. Certainly in comparison with

1954 Six-Cylinder Sports Cars

	Corvette	Kaiser-Darrin	Nash-Healey
Price (NADA list):	$3523	$3668	$4721
Production units:	3640	435	90
Dimensions and Capacities			
Wheelbase (in.):	102	100	108
Length (in.):	167	184	180
Weight (lbs):	2705	2175	2990
Engine and Drivetrain			
Type:	Ohv 6	L-head 6	Ohv 6
Displacement (ci):	235.5	161	252.5
Brake horsepower @ rpm:	150 @ 4200	90 @ 4200	140 @ 4000
Transmission:	Powerglide auto	3-speed manual with overdrive	3-speed manual with overdrive
Axle ratio:	3.55:1	4.55:1	4.10:1
Performance*			
0-60 mph (sec):	11	15	10
Top speed (mph):	106	98	105

* Performance figures are based on the following references: For Corvette, Karl Ludvigsen's *Corvette* (1972). For Darrin, the average of *Motor Age* and *Motorsport* road tests. For Nash, the only available figures are from *Motor Trend*, September 1951, though car weight and horsepower were approximately the same in 1954.

Comments: Despite the Darrin's very low weight and high axle ratio, the Corvette easily had the better of both it and the Nash-Healey, although the latter weighed considerably more. The Nash-Healey was the roomiest of the three with its 108-inch wheelbase, though the Corvette was almost equally roomy and best in terms of utilizing space and having the least overhang. Where the Nash product suffered was in price—well over $1000 more than either the Corvette or the Darrin—and in styling, since people didn't like the inboard headlamps of the 1952-55 models. Also, the Nash had certain bizarre features, like an accelerator located between the brake and clutch pedals and a horn ring operating the overdrive. The Corvette was clearly the most competitive of the three, besides its advantage of being sold by Chevrolet dealers. Powerglide notwithstanding, it was a relatively hot performer, a good looker, the least expensive of the three, and the only one produced by a Big Three manufacturer. That meant continued parts availability, good trade-in value, wide distribution, and, usually, a choice of show rooms. Demand for the Corvette was initially brisk, and volume handily out-paced that of the other two 1954 sports cars.

rival sports cars, the 'Vette had its weaknesses. It was a cross between a boulevard tourer (like the Kaiser-Darrin and the up-coming Ford Thunderbird) and an out-and-out sports/racing roadster (like the Triumph TR2 and the Jaguar XK-120). Sporting types objected to the Powerglide transmission and non-functional add-ons like the dummy knock-off wheel covers, while comfort-lovers hated the clapped-on side curtains and the manual folding top. Some complained that the recirculating heater didn't allow any fresh air into the car. There were a few service problems, with water leaks being the main one. But perhaps none of these things were the real difficulty.

Most importantly, though, the

sports car market was still incredibly small. It was adequate enough for an import like Jaguar or even Triumph, but ridiculous by Detroit standards. And the traditional thinking in Detroit didn't help—the attitude that nothing was a success unless hundreds of thousands were sold every year. Dealers reported some 1500 Corvettes unsold as the 1955s debuted—almost half the 1954 production run. That seems almost impossible today. And on the surface, the '55s looked to be just a repeat of the '54 model. Art and Colour had proposed a mild facelift involving a wider grille in egg-crate pattern that closely related to the division's passenger car. Planned were a functional air scoop, dummy louvers in the side panels, and a redesigned rear

Although the 1955 Corvette (*below*) looked like the
1953-54 models, Chevy's 265-cubic-inch V-8
was now available. It was rated at 195 horsepower and
and quickly built an enviable reputation. The
"twin-cowl" dash (*top right*) was continued,
as were the fussy twin-fin rear fenders
(*bottom right*).

deck with the exhaust tips moved outward. But persisting questions over the car's future prevented any of the changes.

But one difference that was not immediately visible transformed the Corvette for 1955 and proved to be part of its salvation. In all but six of the '55 models, the six-cylinder engine was replaced by Ed Cole's potent new 265-cubic-inch V-8. "I had worked on V-8 engines all my professional life," Cole said in a 1974 interview with *Special-Interest Autos*. "You just *know* you want five main bearings—there's no decision to make. We knew that a certain bore/stroke relationship was the most compact. We knew we'd like a displacement of 265 cubic inches, and that automatically established the bore and stroke. And we never changed any of this. We released our engine for tooling direct from the drawing boards—that's how crazy and confident we were."

One of the outstanding features that made the 265 such a pivotal development was the lack of a common rocker shaft. Each rocker arm was entirely independent of the others, so that the deflection of one had no effect on the rest. Each was assembled over a valve stem and pushrod, retained by a

The Corvette (*above*) saw production of only 674 units for 1955, but the arrival of the new V-8 (*bottom right*) heralded the make's salvation. Free revving and more powerful, it actually weighed 30-40 pounds less than the trusty old six. A big "V" in the Chevrolet side script (*top right*) announced to the world that this Corvette could "Go!"

fulcrum ball and lock nut. Regardless of whether mechanical or hydraulic lifters were used, the valves were lashed by turning the lock nut. In addition, the arrangement reduced reciprocating weight, which allowed higher rpm and cut down on raw materials. The intake manifold provided a common water outlet to both heads. The heads were die cast with integral valve guides, and they were completely interchangeable. A short stroke meant short connecting rods. Pressed-in pis-

ton pins eliminated the splitting of the rod and the required locking bolt. Five main bearings of equal diameter carried maximum loads in their lower halves. Weight was saved by circulating the oil through hollow pushrods, providing splash lubrication to the rocker arms and valve stems, thus eliminating the need for separate and costly oil feeder lines. Further engine details included "autothermic" pistons with three rings, slipper-type aluminum units with a circumferential ex-

pander for the single oil ring providing axial and radial force to control oil burning. Instead of being made of iron, the crankshaft was made of pressed forged steel because of its higher specific gravity and modulus of elasticity. Because the new V-8 had better heat rejection properties than the six, a smaller radiator could be used, reducing weight and frontal area. The new engine actually weighed 30 to 40 pounds less than the six.

The new engine was Chevy's second

Gypsy Red replaced Sportsman Red on the 1955 Corvette
(*above*). The fiberglass bodies were smoother
and slightly thinner in section, and boasted
improved workmanship. A three-speed manual
transmission was made available late in the model
run. The stick control was a short chrome stalk
rising vertically from the side of the
transmission tunnel (*opposite page*).

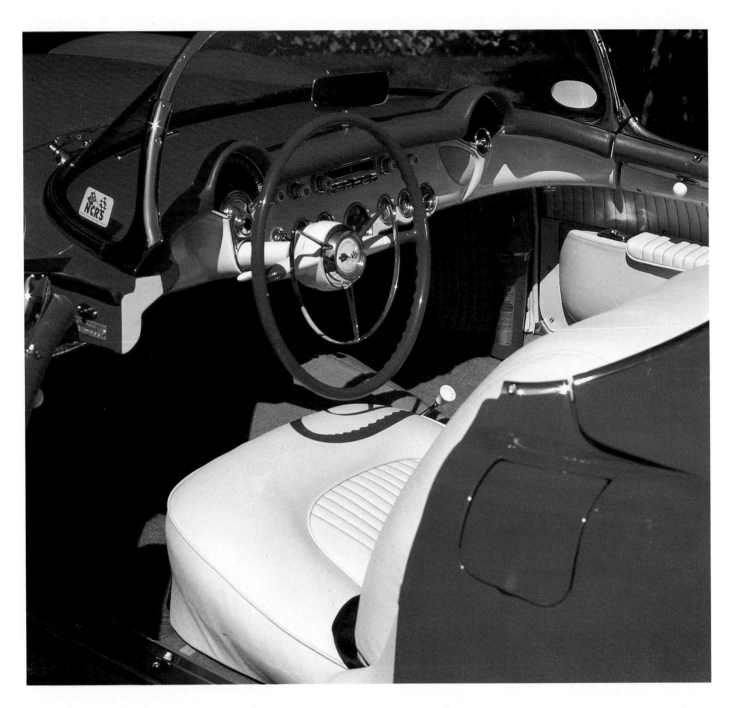

V-8. The first was the disastrous 1917 design. But the new one was nearly perfect, and it has gone down in automotive history as a classic. Some 43 percent of all 1955 Chevys were equipped with it, putting Chevrolet into the performance field with Ford, where it had never been before. It also did wonders for the languishing Corvette.

In the Corvette application, the V-8 produced 195 bhp at 5000 rpm—33 bhp more than in standard Chevrolet passenger car tune. The effect on Cor-vette performance was stunning: The crucial 0-60-mph sprint could now be done in 8.5 seconds and the standing quarter-mile in just 16.5 seconds. The light roadster's top speed was close to 120 mph. Yet, despite the manifold improvements in performance over the six, gas mileage actually increased—*Road & Track,* for example, recorded between 18 and 22.5 mpg, some two to three mpg better than the average for the six. *Road & Track* editors also commented favorably on the V-8's smoothness and refinement, rated the brakes "more than adequate for ordinary usage" (if not for racing), termed riding qualities excellent, and called stability at high speeds near-perfect.

Shortly after the start of 1955 production, the Pennant Blue color option was replaced by Harvest Gold, with contrasting green trim and dark green top—a popular combination. Metallic Copper was also made available, while Gypsy Red replaced 1954's Sportsman Red. The latter came with white vinyl interior, red saddle stitching, and tan carpet and top. These items greatly im-

proved the dazzle of the 1955 model. Besides the color changes, the only exterior modification was a gold letter *V* placed over the *V* in the *Chevrolet* side script to identify the models with V-8 power.

Generally, 1955 bodies were smoother and slightly thinner in section than the 1953-54 bodies, while workmanship improved commensurately. Early '55s still displayed holes in the frame rails for mounting the six-cylinder engines. The X-brace on the underside of the hood was replaced by a lateral brace to clear the V-8's air cleaner.

Automatic chokes were carried for the first time since the Motorama Corvette. Since the V-8 revved higher, the tachometer was extended to 6000 rpm in 500-rpm increments. The electrical system was 12 volt, like most '55 GM cars, although the six-cylinder '55 Corvettes retained the six-volt system. The V-8s also featured an electric rather than vacuum-operated wiper motor, and a foot-operated windshield squirter returned.

The transmission, unfortunately, remained Powerglide, although the vacuum modulator feature was dropped in keeping with all production in 1955. The kickdown was governed solely by speed and throttle position. Late in the model run, a small quantity of cars were finally built with a new close-ratio, three-speed manual gearbox—too late to effect the road-test monthlies, but a harbinger of the future. The stick control was a short chrome stalk rising vertically from the side of the transmission tunnel and

A hinged lid hid the Corvette's soft top when not in use (*left*). By 1955, Chevy could boast truthfully that it built the only "true" sports car in America (*below*).

culminating in a small white ball. The boot around the lever was clamped to the floor with a bright metal ring that was marked by the gear symbols, and the stick shift axle ratio was lowered to 3.7:1 from the Powerglide ratio of 3.55:1.

On balance, the 1955 Corvette was a quantum leap forward—if not in styling, certainly in engineering. Unfortunately, the V-8 engine wasn't enough to bail out Chevy's sports car, and even though the automotive press couldn't put its finger on the reason, it still quibbled about the overall package. Said *Road & Track,* "The Corvette comes so close to being a really interesting, worthwhile, and genuine sports car—yet misses the mark almost entirely." Apparently some people were simply embarrassed about liking a Detroit product. Worse than

that, the '55 didn't sell any better than the '54. Indeed, sales were down. Production closed with only 700 units for the model year, marking the end of the Motorama-based production cars and what looked like the end of the Corvette. Quality of workmanship and performance had been improved mightily, the option list had been broadened, and more appealing color and trim had been added, but the market remained dubious and elusive.

What, then—if not the V-8—saved the Corvette? Ford did. For direct tes-

Serial Spans, Production, and Base Prices

Year	Serial Prefix	Serial Span	Prod. Units	Price
1953	E53F	001001-001300	300	$3513
1954	E54S	001001-004640	3640	$3523
1955	E55S*	001001-001700	6	$2799
1955	VE55S**	001001-001700	668	$2934

* 6-cylinder
** V-8

By sports car standards, the Corvette's trunk
provided more-than-adequate luggage space
for two for long-distance touring.

timony to this novel Dearborn bail-out, we refer to Zora Arkus-Duntov, then in his mid-40s—a German-born racing driver, designer, and engineer who had joined GM Research and Development Staff in 1953. Duntov was to become a key figure in the future of the Corvette. Even on the 1953-55 series his efforts had vastly improved the product. ("The front end oversteered; the rear end understeered. I put two degrees of positive caster in the front suspension and relocated the rear spring bushing. Then it was fine—very neutral.") Duntov described what happened at Chevrolet when the Ford Thunderbird appeared: "There were conversations...about the Corvette being dropped. Then the Thunderbird came out and all of a sudden GM was keeping the Corvette. I think that Ford brought out the competitive spirit in Ed Cole." If not that, Ford embarrassed Chevy, because the 1955 Thunderbird racked up 16,155 sales—23 T-Birds for every 'Vette.

Another booster, crucial at this stage, was design chief Harley Earl. So many of his proposals had received negative reaction that he deserved something positive. Stuck with the tremendous tooling cost of the 1955 model passenger line, Chevy had denied Earl a planned facelift for the Corvette. The division had also refused to allow production of a neat lift-off hardtop that Earl had proposed in the form of a show car for the 1954 Motorama, as well as a Corvette fastback coupe called the Corvair. Harley Earl argued that the presence of the Thunderbird made the continuation of the Corvette essential—for Chevrolet's performance image, if not for a production-line "advanced study vehicle." Earl pointed to how Corvette's basic body styling had influenced the 1954 Motorama Nomad wagon, which evolved into the production Chevy Nomad. Besides, Earl said, Art and Colour had an entirely new body ready for 1956 and beyond, and the tooling costs using fiberglass weren't that formidable.

Evidence proves the Thunderbird directly responsible for the Corvette's survival. The V-8 was secondary. But the Corvette's survival and eventual evolution to become America's only true sports car was now in the hands of four people—Harley Earl, Ed Cole, Bill Mitchell, and Zora Arkus-Duntov.

Major Specifications 1953-55 Corvette

Chassis and Body
Frame: Box section steel, X-braced
Body: Glass-reinforced plastic, 2-seat roadster
Front suspension: Independent, wishbones, coil springs, anti-roll bar, tubular hydraulic shock absorbers
Rear suspension: Longitudinal leaf springs, hydraulic tubular shock absorbers
Wheels: 15" bolt-on steel
Tires: 6.70 × 15 4-ply whitewalls

Dimensions
Wheelbase (in.): 102.0
Length (in.): 167.0
Height (in.): 51.3
Width (in.): 72.2
Track front/rear (in.): 57.0/59.0
Ground clearance (in.): 6.0
Weight (lbs): 2850

Engine
Type: Ohv inline 6-cylinder, water-cooled, cast-iron block (Ohv V-8)
Main bearings: 4 (5)
Bore × stroke: 3.56 × 3.95 (3.75 × 3.00)
Displacement (ci): 235.5 (265)
Compression ratio: 8.0:1 (8.0:1)
Induction system: 3 Carter sidedraft carburetors (1 4-barrel Carter carb)
Exhaust system: Split cast-iron manifolds, dual exhaust (dual exhaust)
Brake horsepower @ rpm: 150 @ 4200 (195 @ 5000)
Lbs/ft torque @ rpm: 223 @ 2400 (260 @ 3000)
Electrical system: 6-volt, Delco-Remy ignition (12-volt)

Drivetrain
Transmission: 2-speed Powerglide torque converter automatic (3-speed manual)
Gear ratios: First—3.82:1
            Second—1:1
            Reverse—3.82:1
Rear axle type: Hotchkiss drive, semifloating
Rear axle ratio: 3.55:1
Steering: Saginaw worm-and-sector
Ratio: 16:1
Turns lock-to-lock: 3.7
Turning circle (ft): 37.0
Brakes: 4-wheel hydraulic, internal expanding drums, 11" diameter
Brake lining area (sq. in.): 154.5

Performance*
0-30 mph (sec): 3.7
0-40 mph (sec): 5.3
0-50 mph (sec): 7.7
0-60 mph (sec): 11.0 (8.5)
0-80 mph (sec): 19.5
Standing-start quarter-mile (sec): 17.9 (16.5)
Top speed (mph): 107 (120)
Average fuel consumption (mpg): 14-18 (18-22.5)

* *Road & Track* road test, June 1954

Profile:
Harley J. Earl

Corvette enthusiasts generally agree that the impetus for the first Corvette came from Harley Earl, pioneering automotive stylist and founder of GM's Art and Colour Section. Therefore, some consider him to be more the "father" of the Corvette than engineer Zora Arkus-Duntov. Regardless, the fiberglass-bodied two-seater could not have progressed from Motorama dream car to production reality without Earl's backing. He fought for the Corvette from the very first, against some fairly stiff odds, and for a reason: It was just his sort of car. Of course, Earl carried considerable clout with GM management, the kind that comes from a swift, sure rise to fame and a winning track record.

Harley Earl was almost born to be a stylist. His father had designed horse-drawn carriages in Los Angeles, and by the time young Harley had graduated from Stanford, he was a genuine car buff. In the early Twenties, he secured a post designing dashing custom bodywork for Don Lee, a coachbuilder who catered to the Hollywood elite. While at the Lee studios, Earl was discovered by Lawrence P. Fisher, then general manager of Cadillac, who hired the 32-year-old as a consultant. One of Earl's first assignments was body design for the 1927 LaSalle, the first edition of Cadillac's companion make. It would be the first mass-produced car to be styled in the modern sense. Its lines were gracefully handsome and reminiscent of the contemporary Hispano-Suiza—not much of a surprise, since Earl was quite familiar with European design trends of the day.

The first LaSalle proved to be an instant hit, and many attributed its success to its styling. The connection wasn't lost on GM's astute managers, and Earl was soon invited by president Alfred P. Sloan, Jr., to work for the company full time, with the specific task of setting up an in-house styling department. It was duly organized as the Art and Colour Section; the English spelling for the word color was Earl's way of denoting prestige. The department was an industry first, and after 1927 the professional hand of the stylist would be increasingly evident in American automotive design.

Earl's approach to his work was impressive. He pioneered the use of modeling clay to evolve the forms of various body components, and in those days clay was considered a highly unusual material for the purpose. Earl also

created complete automobiles—the main body, hood, fenders, lights, and other parts were conceived in relation to each other so as to blend into a harmonious whole. The method contrasted with most custom body builders, who usually worked from the cowl back, leaving a car's stock hood, radiator, and headlights intact.

Earl realized that one person couldn't hope to carry the styling work load at GM single-handedly, so he surrounded himself with talent. Many of the designers would owe him their careers. For example, Virgil Exner, who would later win fame with the "Forward Look" at Chrysler in the mid-Fifties, trained under Earl and headed the Pontiac studio in the Thirties. Other luminaries like Frank Hershey, Art Ross, Ned Nickles, and William L. Mitchell learned their craft from Earl, making their marks at Cadillac and Buick. Clare MacKichan, who would later create the classic 1955 Chevy, was yet another Earl pupil. Mitchell, of course, went on to become Earl's successor.

Earl's impact on the shape of GM cars was enormous. In fact, for most of his 31 years with the company, the GM design philosophy and Earl's philosophy were one and the same. He was an exuberant artist, unexpectedly playful and often elfish.

His elfishness contrasted sharply with Earl's physical stature. He was a large man, standing over six feet tall. Because this gave him a visual perspective most of his designers lacked, they would often do their modeling while standing on wooden boxes to view their efforts the way he would see them—though they never did so in his presence. Earl's height

explains the distinctive ribbed or fluted roof of the 1955-57 Chevrolet Nomad, as well as the use of brushed aluminum—one of Earl's favorite materials—on the roof of the 1957-58 Cadillac Eldorado Brougham and, before that, on a variety of show cars.

Earl liked nothing better than to work on flashy show cars. He personally designed many of the Motorama experimentals, including the original Corvette. Often in his sketches, he would picture himself at the wheel, with a grin on his face. His very first dream car may well have been his most significant. The Buick Y-Job of 1938 literally defined the shape of Detroit cars for the next two decades, with its dramatically low body, absence of the traditional running boards, strong horizontal lines, and long boattail rear deck. Though it may not look so modern now, the Y-Job boasted features that are becoming common practice only today—like hidden headlights.

Harley Earl's other show models were equally striking. The experimental Oldsmobile F-88 from 1954 had seven nerf bars nestled in between twin tail pieces instead of a rear bumper. The Oldsmobile Cutlass shown that same year was marked by a fastback roofline severely tapered in plain view, plus twin chrome-accented tail fins and a louvered backlight that predicted today's popular accessory rear window slats by almost 20 years. The two-seat LaSalle II featured abbreviated rear fenders, as on an early-1900s runabout, along with exhaust pipes routed through the sills to exit immediately ahead of the rear wheels. Earl's last show car—the Cadillac Cyclone of 1959—was a wild-looking concoction, more like a fighter plane than a car.

Aircraft design practice can be found in much of Eurl's work. For example, the trend-setting tail fins that first appeared in production on the 1948 Cadillac were inspired by the twin-tail Lockheed P-38 Lightning, a World War II pursuit plane powered by GM-built Allison engines. During the war years, Earl took his designers to see the plane, then under development at the Lockheed plant in California. They then returned to their studios, where Earl had them adapt a number of the aircraft's design elements for GM's first postwar cars. According to Irwin W. Rybicki, who succeeded Bill Mitchell as head of GM Design Staff in 1977, Earl favored rounded, massive forms like the P-38's, and these showed up in the pontoon fenders, fastback roofs, and heavy chrome accents that came to characterize GM's postwar look. Even the first Corvette sported rocket-like vestigial fins.

In essence, Harley Earl liked to do things

his way, and usually had the wherewithal to accomplish them. He never lost his enthusiasm for cars during his long career with GM. Of course, his long and hard fight for the production Corvette came toward the end of that career, and he kept on fighting for it during its difficult infancy. Right up to his retirement in 1958, he continued looking for new ways to keep his cars exciting, yet always within the bounds of public acceptance. As the chief designer for the world's largest automaker, Earl put his personal stamp on more different cars than any other single individual up to that time. History has already recorded the Corvette as one of his best efforts.

Harley Earl on Harley Earl: The following quotations include excerpts from a 1954 interview conducted by Arthur W. Baum:

On GM Art and Colour
"When I refer to myself I am merely using a short cut to talk about my team. There are 650 of us, and collectively we are known as the Styling Section. I happen to be the founder of the section and the responsible head, but we all contribute to the future appearance of GM automobiles, and it hasn't been too long ago that we settled what your 1957 car will look like."

On Work Standards
"We work informally and, of course, secretly. Since our job is to generate and present design ideas, we have methods of keeping new ideas popping and stirring. To help keep us young, we introduce a freshman squad every year, mostly from two design schools on the East and West coasts. We have contests and idea races."

On Inspiring Designers
"I often act merely as prompter. If a particular group appears to be bogging down over a new fender or grille or interior trim, I sometimes wander into their quarters, make some irrelevant or even zany observation, and then leave. It is surprising what effect a bit of peculiar behavior will have. First-class minds will seize on anything out of the ordinary."

On His Office
"It is a hidden room with no telephone. The windows are blacked out and a misleading name is on the door... In it is a scale model of the first sedan I ever designed for the company, a 1927 LaSalle. I have a great affection for the old crock, but I must admit it is slab-sided, top-heavy, and stiff-shouldered. [But] there is something on it that explains what I have been trying to do in the last 28 years. On the line we now call the beltline, running around the body, there is a decorative strip like half a figure eight fastened to the body. This strip was placed there to eat up the overpowering vertical expanse of that tall car. It was an effort to make the car look longer and lower."

Opposite page: Harley J. Earl. *Below:* Harley Earl, then vice president in charge of Styling, took time to pose with GM's Fiftieth Anniversary 1958 passenger car line-up. He supervised the design of over 35 million cars during his career with GM.

Earl designed the 1954 turbine-powered Firebird I as an earthbound version of the Douglas Skyray, a U.S. Air Force jet fighter.

On Longer-Lower-Wider

"My primary purpose for 28 years has been to lengthen and lower the American automobile, at times in reality and always at least in appearance. Why? Because my sense of proportion tells me that oblongs are more attractive than squares, just as a ranch house is more attractive than a square, three-story, flat-roofed house or a greyhound is more graceful than a bulldog."

On Dictating to the Public

"There are always some indignant critics. The most amusing brickbats I get accuse me of being a shrimp and wanting to squash passengers down to the ground to suit my own anatomy... I am six feet four inches tall and weigh over 200."

On Government Regulation

"Highway regulatory bodies keep us fenced in. If we wanted a single headlight on a car, the states would prohibit it, since many of them control the number, brightness, position, and height of headlights. They exercise similar control over tail and stop lights."

On Other Limits on Designers

"The engineers quite properly will not let us interfere with the efficiency and soundness of their powerplants. If we wanted to try our hands on a three-wheeled car, I am sure the engineers wouldn't encourage us. They think three-wheel cars are inherently dangerous. They won't give us a rear engine, either, until problems like weight distribution are solved, and only then if there is a compelling advantage to the owner."

On Chrome

"I am not particularly committed to chrome... But when chrome arrived as a decorative trim for the industry, it was imperative that I find out how people felt about it... I dispatched my staff to key cities to pose as reporters. They asked hundreds of questions about customer response to or rejection of chrome trim. The conclusions were in favor of chrome, more so on used-car lots."

On Vehicle Attitude

"American cars have always had a comfortably blunt, leonine front look. This is good, as long as the car as a whole is poised right. There was a time when automobiles tilted down in front as if they intended to dig for woodchucks. Subsequently, they went tail-heavy and appeared to be sitting up and begging. Now I think we have them in exactly the right attitude of level alertness, like an airplane at take-off."

On the Motoramas

"A Motorama is more than a good show with good promotion. Frankly, it makes my styling job easier, as visitors express themselves vividly, and by the time hundreds of thousands of these critics have examined your show and commented on your exhibits, you have a firm idea of their likes and dislikes. And it is hardly necessary for me to say that it is vital for us to keep in tune with American thinking about automobiles."

On Color

"The public's greater tolerance has already been expressed in color—have you recently looked down from a tall building onto a large parking lot? People are also making up their minds that all American cars are good, so why shop for anything more than attractive, pleasant lines and an established worth in the trade-in market? I can't quite go along with that, considering my preference for GM cars and since one color on the road today strikes me as something that belongs on the underside of a railroad bridge."

Summing Up

"Most of our thousands of hours of work every year are small refinements and revisions to improve the comfort, utility, and appearance of our automobiles. But we also need explosive bursts of spanking-new themes, and somehow we get them. I have enjoyed every minute of both kinds of this labor for 28 years... I hope designing is always like that."

CHAPTER FOUR

1956-1957: No More Mister Nice Guy

On the surface, the influence of a low-volume product like the Ford Thunderbird on the decision to continue the production of the expensive, special-edition Corvette seems preposterous. The situation can be better understood by recollecting the state of the Ford-Chevy rivalry in those days. The Thunderbird, by happy coincidence, arrived at the historic pinnacle in the traditional sales battle between the top two makes.

For 18 months after mid-1953, Ford had engaged in production warfare against Chevrolet in a determined bid to be ranked first in sales, a standing that Ford had not held since the early Thirties. Ford dealers were sent thousands of cars, whether or not they had been ordered. The dealers were expected to get rid of them by whatever means possible. General Motors naturally responded in kind, and the production blitz was on. Both Ford and Chevrolet took to the media at the end of 1955, each claiming to have built the most cars. Whoever was first depended on which set of statistics a person read. The ultimate result of the 1953-55 sales blitz was the damage done to neither Ford nor GM, but to Chrysler and the independents. Shortly thereafter, Kaiser-Willys, Hudson, Nash, and Packard came to the end of their product lines, and Chrysler was critically wounded. The Ford competition did harden attitudes at Chevrolet, and the unwritten goal was now to stop Ford—in every segment of the market, including the sports car portion.

That the Thunderbird could outsell Chevy's two-seater by a 23:1 ratio was more than a slap in the face to USA-1.

It was a direct challenge to Chevy's supremacy. Electing not only to continue Corvette production but to make it a superior performer in every way to the Thunderbird was just a symbolic way of taking up Ford's challenge. Besides, everybody at Chevy Division knew that the pre-1956 Corvette had somehow lost sight of the original objective. It was neither a small, fun-to-drive runabout that everyone could afford, nor a serious performance sports car. It was something else—a puffy, well-equipped showboat priced at close to $3500, $1500 more than one of the Low-Priced Three.

The irony was that just as Chevrolet was planning a future of ever-more-powerful and potent Corvette two-seat sports cars, Ford was making the decision to produce puffy, well-equipped showboat Thunderbirds—with four seats now, in order to grab more sales. The fact was that 16,000 units a year was not Ford's idea of success, any more than 700 a year was for Chevrolet. But Chevy would be happy to sell 16,000 Corvettes a year—for the time being.

In 1955, Chevy's small-block V-8 had been greeted with high enthusiasm, and its performance gain was as welcome in the Corvette as it was in the standard Chevrolets. Even so, the buff magazines weren't all that enthusiastic about the 1955 Corvette. *Road & Track* snidely suggested that the car might fill the need "for an open roadster the lady of the house can use as smart personal transport"—not exactly the macho image the Corvette would later embody. *R&T* did concede that the V-8 cars had benefited from

the engine's power, but it brought up the nagging complaints about creature comforts, especially the pesky side curtains. Clearly, what America's sports car needed was a more up-to-date body to match its hearty new small-block soul.

Harley Earl had been taking Corvette criticisms to heart, and had been working on those very things. He did, no doubt, still consider it *his* car. On February 1, 1955, just as Ford's Thunderbird was beginning to be seen in serious numbers, Earl had all but finalized a new Corvette body design in a full-scale clay model. With some minor trim changes, it was shown to GM management in mid-April and approved on the spot. The 1956 Corvette and the near-identical '57 model are considered by many today as the epitome of Corvette styling, at least before the 1963 model.

The roots of the second-generation design were in three 1955 Motorama show cars—the Biscayne and two exercises dubbed LaSalle II. The Biscayne was a compact four-door hardtop painted light green, with a color-keyed interior. Appearance features included headlamps mounted inboard, parking lights placed in the fenders, and a grille made up of a series of vertical bars. Air scoops were positioned under the windshield on the cowl, and the passenger compartment floor was level with the bottom of the frame. The LaSalle II name appeared on a hardtop sedan and a roadster. Also carefully color-keyed, both had prominent vertical bar grilles and displayed a styling feature the '56 Corvette would inherit: a concave section on the body sides. It swept back from the front wheel wells, imitating the LeBaron sweep of the classic period. New for the 1956 'Vette was a lift-off hardtop, which used the greenhouse directly from the show car prototype displayed at the 1954 Motorama. The 1956 Corvette was among the last GM production cars designed in Detroit before the design department was moved to the new Technical Center in Warren, Michigan.

The new Corvette styling looked very fresh in 1956. It was, in essence, only an evolution of the original concept, but with all the bad elements removed and the good ones emphasized. Perhaps the most appealing aspect of the first-generation Corvette had

been its definite "face," and the second generation would improve on that theme. The eyes that had been covered by wire screens had the effect of being veiled—not appropriate for a "man's" car. So the headlamps were moved forward out of their recesses and the mesh stoneguards were discarded. The nose-like, large, round Corvette emblem was given more prominence. The original mouth with its magnificent teeth was left alone.

The rear was just as tastefully revised. The jet-pod taillamps and the fin-like extended fenders were trimmed, and new taillights were artfully frenched into the remaining sheet metal. The license plate, which had occupied an indentation in the

trunk lid, was moved down between decorative bumperettes. The change left a smooth, gently curved deck, with the matching fenders protruding slightly—but only slightly—from either side. Thankfully, Earl's staff resisted an impulse to have the dual exhausts exit through the sides of the rear fenders, routing them instead through the rear bumper guards.

The body-side "coves," as they were nicknamed, gave the '56 Corvette a styling personality all its own. They also helped to relieve the slab-sided look that had led some people to refer to the first generation as the "plastic bathtub." Even surrounded by a narrow band of chrome—one of the few last-minute trim changes made to the

The 1956 Corvette sported "coves" on the sides and
a smoother rear end (*above*), while the front
received squarer fenders (*below*).

The Corvette adopted wind-up windows (powered at
extra cost) for 1956 along with revised interior
door panels (*above*). The rear end was shorn of
its jet-pod taillights and mini twin fins
in favor of new taillights that were artfully frenched
into the newly curved rear fenders (*above right*).
A more integrated, tighter-looking top
was also part of the package.

production prototype—the sculptured body sides were still extremely clean and attractive. The only gimmicky pieces on the entire '56 design were the small dummy scoops perched on the tops of the front fenders near the windshield. They were supposed to be functional—for cowl ventilation—but cost considerations ruled that out. The redesign also extended to a more integrated convertible top, tighter-looking and with a rounded curve at the rear

that echoed the car's rear quarters. The new factory hardtop also had rounded contours, and its rear side windows afforded much better visibility than the soft top's. The new-for-'56 wheel covers tried to simulate genuine knock-off hubs. They, too, looked a bit contrived, but they remained standard issue until 1963 and have become some of the best-known wheel covers in history.

Even more than 30 years later the

design looks fresh, despite bearing a few typically Fifties clichés. And it passes the real test—it still draws admiring glances. It is one of those rare automobiles that looks good from any angle.

Like many other cars that have had enduring designs, the '56 Corvette didn't just look better than its predecessor, it worked better, too. The fussy side curtains were gone forever, replaced by proper roll-up door glass.

This page: The 265-cid V-8 returned for 1956 rated at 210 horsepower (*top*), but could be brought up to 225-240 bhp with dual carbs. The Corvette emblem (*above left*) was given more prominence, while the exhaust exited through the rear bumper guards (*above right*). Corvette styling (*opposite page*) looked very fresh in 1956.

Power window lifts were available at extra cost! Genuine outside door handles ended once and for all the hassle of reaching in through the side curtains on a rainy day. The interior was much as before, except for revised door panels to go with the wind-up windows. A waffle-pattern vinyl was used over a delicately sculptured arm rest that blended into the door shape. A transistorized signal-seeking radio was another new feature, though it was not yet engraved with the words "Wonder Bar."

Under the hood was more good news. The small-block V-8 returned not as an option but as standard equipment. It had even more muscle: 210 brake horsepower at 5200 rpm with a single four-barrel carburetor and higher 9.25:1 compression. That was 15 bhp more than the '55 unit, and a big improvement over the 155-bhp six of just two years earlier. Special camshafts, a cast-aluminum intake manifold, and dual four-barrel carburetors were available to increase output to 225-240 bhp. Premium fuel was mandatory, of course. The special cam, developed by Zora Arkus-Duntov, helped raise torque on the 225-bhp powerplant to an impressive 270 lbs/ft peaking at 3600 rpm.

Running gear was beefed up to handle the new Corvette's extra power. The standard gearbox was now the three-speed manual, and its clutch was strengthened with 12 heat-treated coil springs to replace the former diaphragm-type spring. Final drive with the manual transmission was still 3.55:1, but a 3.27:1 cog was offered. The Powerglide automatic became a true option, and it listed for $189.

The Corvette ceased being considered an also-ran. It was now a genuine screamer with svelte styling and all the amenities that any sporting motorist could desire. Where the '54 car had made the 0-60-mile-per-hour sprint in about 12 seconds with an automatic gearbox, the '56 could do it in 7.5 seconds with the manual transmission and standard rear axle ratio. It could run the standing-start quarter-mile in 16 seconds at 90-plus mph. It was capable of nearly 120 mph right off the show room floor. Some questions still were raised about handling and stopping, however. Brakes—cast-iron drums with a total of 158 square

inches lining area—were a weak point. They "faded into oblivion," as one tester said after a hard application. Handling was good, but understeer was ever-present. The steering, however, was quick—just 3.5 turns lock-to-lock. Weight distribution was nearly perfect for a sports machine at 52/48

percent front/rear. In all, road behavior was greatly improved on the '56, compared to earlier Corvettes. America's sports car had come of age.

Duntov believed that a race-winning image was vital to the Corvette's sales, and he would be proven correct. As Carroll Shelby, the man whose cars

would become the Corvette's arch enemies in the Sixties, said later, "Racing was the thing that actually saved the Corvette." Duntov's high-lift cam had been developed specifically with an eye to competition. If the 'Vette could set a few speed records and win some races, Chevy advertising would do the rest.

Accordingly, the Duntov cam was slipped into a modified '56 Corvette

specially prepared at GM's Arizona proving grounds. The car was then shipped to Florida, where Betty Skelton and John Fitch would drive it at the Daytona Speed Weeks trials in January. The goal was to reach 150 mph. Although beach conditions weren't favorable, the car managed an impressive two-way run of 150.583 mph with Duntov at the wheel.

Development work continued, and

the addition of a new, high-compression head raised power output on the 265-cubic-inch V-8 to a claimed 255 bhp—nearly the magic level of one horsepower per cubic inch. In the Speed Weeks trials, the 'Vette was beaten in the production standing-mile contest by a Thunderbird prepared by ex-racer Pete DePaolo and driven by Chuck Daigh. However, in the modified class, a 'Vette was the

By 1957 Chevy was pushing performance like never before. The engine was enlarged to 283 cubic inches and horsepower increased to as high as 283—one bhp per cubic inch!—with the newly available fuel injection. A four-speed manual was offered in mid-year. What better place to showcase Corvette's get-up-and-go than in the SR-2, a racing show car from 1957?

The Corvette SR-2's most prominent styling features were the aerodynamic-looking fin behind the driver, which doubled as a headrest, and the low-cut dual racing-style windshields (*right*). Needless to say, the engine (*below*) featured fuel injection. The instrument panel (*bottom*) was much modified from stock, with a large speedometer and 8000-rpm tachometer directly in front of the driver and better placement of the gauges.

fastest car. John Fitch won with a two-pass average of 145.543 mph. By September, ads touting this feat appeared in the buff books, boasting that "the 1956 Corvette is proving—in open competition—that it is America's only genuine production sports car"—a swipe at the *boulevardier* Thunderbird. Another ad proclaimed, "Bring on the hay bales!" Said the copy: "The new Corvette, piloted by Betty Skelton, has established a new record for American sports cars at Daytona Beach. But that's only the start. Corvette owners

may enter other big racing tests in the months ahead—tests that may carry America's blue-and-white colors into several of the most important European competitions." And indeed they did. One modified Corvette made a decent showing at Sebring in 1956, finishing ninth in the grueling 12-hour run. And at Pebble Beach, a Corvette finished a strong second behind a Mercedes-Benz 300SL.

Road & Track, which generally had been favorable to the Corvette since its inception, described the '56 as "good to excellent compared to other dual-purpose sports cars." At long last, the critics seemed willing to admit that the Corvette qualified as dual-purpose. The new V-8 had made all the difference. One person who agreed was Dr. Richard Thompson, a dentist from Washington, D.C. In the spring of 1956, he began campaigning a Corvette in the Sports Car Club of America's C-Production class. With the help of Duntov and others, Thompson won the C-Production championship that year. It was another boost to the "competition-proven" image that Duntov and Chevy managers were after, and the ads were quick to capitalize on it.

Corvette production rose to one-fifth the Thunderbird level for the 1956 model year. That disappointed the bean counters, but heartened those car nuts at Chevrolet who had been campaigning for the 'Vette's retention. After all, they said, 3467 units were better than one for every other dealer, and the cars had added greatly to floor traffic while building up a performance reputation that Chevrolet

never had before. Besides, the now widely accepted American sports car would sell even better in 1957, the supporters said. And it did—by about twice as many.

Nevertheless, the production volume was still a long way from a profitable enterprise, and Chevrolet Division had become rather used to operating in the black on all of its products. Performance imagery, free publicity, spiffy cars for big dealers and division brass were fair enough. But in the long run, any Chevrolet, no matter how esoteric, had to be profitable or it

would be dropped from the line.

As 1957 dawned, a change in attitude concerning the Corvette was apparent at GM. Chevrolet's management was willing to sustain the effort. Despite the modest sales, no more talk about dropping the Corvette had been heard since 1955. Besides, things were looking up for the '57 model year. The V-8 was larger, and, at mid-year, the four-speed gearbox that had been called for by purists became available.

The 283-cid V-8 was destined to become one of Chevy's legendary engines—the immortal small block, en-

shrined by a generation of car enthusiasts and all the collectors who would follow. The engine was the 265-cid V-8, of course, with a one-eighth inch bore increase. In Chevrolet passenger cars, it produced 185 bhp in base form, but the standard Corvette version had a four-barrel carburetor and developed 220 bhp at 4800 rpm. Dual four-barrels took the V-8 to 245 and 270 bhp, and with new Ramjet fuel injection the 283 delivered 250 or 283 bhp—once again, one horsepower per cubic inch.

Fuel injection was a concept alien to

This 1957 (*top row*) Corvette sports the removable
hardtop that first became available in 1956.
It is also one of only 240 cars out of 6339 built
for '57 that were equipped with Ramjet fuel injection
(*bottom right*). Lest anyone fail to notice,
"Fuel Injection" is spelled out on all four sides
of the car. Off-the-line go was electrifying,
with 0-60 mph coming up in 6.5 seconds. The
Corvette could handle, too; by 1957, it was becoming
respected as a car that could run with the best.

This page: A 1957 Corvette is being put through its paces (*top*). Upholstery that year featured a waffle-pattern vinyl (*center*). This photo (*above*) shows off the fake knock-off wheel covers and fuel injection badging. From whatever angle (*opposite page*) there was no mistaking a Corvette.

major American automakers in the Fifties. The story of how Chevrolet's system came about began in 1955, when Chevy had struck a marketing and performance blow with its small-block 265-cid V-8. But Ford had the experience of two generations of V-8 engines already behind it. By 1957, the 265 was old hat; Ford and Plymouth had fresh, new '57 models ready. Chevrolet and the rest of General Motors were relying on a facelift of a two-year-old body shell. With the memory of the Ford blitz and the hot Dearborn rivalry of 1955 still fresh in mind, GM management worried that the '57 Chevys would be overshadowed by the competition. However, speed had already helped Chevy's sales once. It could certainly do so again.

The obvious key to higher horsepower was to first enlarge the V-8 and then give it more carburetors, both of which were duly done. The engineers then considered supercharging, something attempted by Studebaker and Kaiser contemporaries. But the high heat and extra internal stress of a blower were considered undesirable for a make that had built its reputation on reliability. So the engineers took a page from the European performance book and settled on fuel injection.

Zora Arkus-Duntov had been working on injection since early 1956, and under unusual circumstances. In April he had taken a Corvette hardtop around the GM proving grounds for tests. The car had no seatbelts and was running with experimental disc brakes. At a good rate of speed, Duntov lost control, left the track, and hit a drainage ditch. He was thrown up into the roof, and the impact broke a vertebra in his back. For six months, he worked standing up, confined by a body cast. But he continued pushing because the fuelie program had top priority. With almost superhuman speed the engineers put together a system that appeared to be relatively inexpensive to manufacture while still promising significant power gains. Unfortunately, reliability problems would surface, and the higher cost of fuelies made them fairly unpopular among Corvette customers.

Despite injection's problems, it did give Chevrolet the performance magic that was needed. Ironically, in view of all the hubbub concerning one bhp per

The fuel-injected Corvette engine of 1957 (*below*) carried the code designation EL. Reportedly, it actually delivered about 290 horsepower—more than advertised! Unfortunately, reliability problems and high cost limited FI's appeal, but the badges (*left*) added snob appeal.

cubic inch, the top fuelie actually delivered about 290 bhp—more than advertised. The engine, which carried the code designation EL, should not be confused with the racing EN version, which was sold as a package complete with column-mounted tachometer and a cold-air induction system. Chevy warned potential purchasers that the EN option was not for the street, and actually refused to supply EN Corvettes with heaters.

In the long run, though, the four-speed manual gearbox that arrived in May of 1957 was more important to the marque than fuel injection. Priced at only $188, the RPO (Regular Production Option) 685 four-speed was essentially the three-speed Borg-Warner unit with reverse moved into the tailshaft housing to make room for a fourth forward speed. The ratios were close. Positraction limited-slip differential was available with four different final drive ratios, to help the customer get the most out of the new

engines and gearbox in each particular driving or competition situation.

The experts still complained about handling and braking deficiencies, which Chevrolet solved with RPO 684. This was a $725 "heavy-duty racing suspension" package comprising heavy-duty springs, front anti-sway bar, Positraction, large-piston shock absorbers with firmer valving, a faster steering ratio that reduced turns lock-to-lock from 3.7 to 2.9, and ceramic-metallic brake linings with finned ventilated drums. Together with the RPO 579E 283-cid V-8, it produced a race-ready car that could be bought directly from a dealer. And race it did. Two production examples finished 12th and 15th at Sebring in 1957, and they were the first GT-class cars across the line. The 12th-place car, driven by Dick Thompson and Gaston Audrey, ended up some 20 laps ahead of the nearest Mercedes-Benz 300SL. The larger engine bumped the 'Vette into SCCA's B-Production category, but that wasn't

important. Dr. Thompson promptly took the championship.

In almost any form, the 1957 Corvette had absolutely staggering performance. Walt Woron of *Motor Trend* tested the 250-bhp fuel-injected version and whizzed through the 0-60-mph sprint in just 7.2 seconds. The 283-bhp cars were even more incredible. *Road & Track's* four-speed example with 4.11:1 final drive clocked 5.7 seconds in the same test, breezed through the quarter-mile in 14.3 seconds at better than 90 mph, and sailed on to a top end of 132 mph. Another *MT* car with the 283-bhp engine, dual exhausts, special cam, and solid lifters reached 134 mph, and Woron wasn't convinced that it was fully extended at that. *Sports Car Illustrated* found its Corvette "the fastest accelerating genuine production car [this magazine] has ever tested." *Road & Track* headlined its test report, "Add fuel injection and get out of the way."

Corvette advertising continued to push the performance image, with headlines such as "Lesson from Lombard Street" and "FI = 1 H.P. per CU. IN. × 283." The first ad showed a 'Vette winding down San Francisco's serpentine Lombard Street hill and stressed the car's handling abilities. The second ad's cryptic headline referred to "the formula ... for the most significant advance yet recorded in American sports cars. It means: The 1957 Corvette V-8 with fuel injection turns out one horsepower per cubic inch of displacement—and there are 283 cubic inches on tap! To anyone who knows cars," the ad continued, taking direct aim at sports car enthusiasts, "that fact alone is a warranty of significant engineering. But the driver who has whipped the Corvette through a series of S-turns really knows the facts of life: This sleek powerhouse handles! Matter of fact, you can forget the price tag and the proud names—no production sports car in Corvette's class can find a shorter way around the bends!"

Undoubtedly, 1957 marked the Corvette's arrival as a sports car respected as much by the cognoscenti as the kids on the street. One European writer said, "Before Sebring, where we actually saw it for ourselves, the Corvette was regarded as a plastic toy. After Sebring, even the most biased

Serial Spans, Production, and Base Prices

Year	Serial Prefix	Serial Span	Prod. Units	Price
1956	E56S	001001-004467	3388	$3149
1957	E57S	100001-106339	6246	$3465

With (*opposite page*) or without (*above*) the
hardtop, the design of the '57 Corvette was remarkably
clean and free of excess chrome and trickery.
One exception, perhaps, was the fake vents on the top
of the fenders ahead of the windshield.
Unfortunately, they were kept functionless
because of cost considerations.

The 1956-57 Corvette became more civilized with the adoption of exterior door handles and wind-up windows (*below*). Ford's Thunderbird, of course, had them from the very beginning. One had to know how to operate the convertible top (*bottom left*).

Chevrolet Press Release

CORVETTE AT SEBRING 1956

Sebring, Florida—5.2 miles of slick straightaways and treacherous curves—is one of the world's toughest road courses, calling for the utmost in every phase of automobile performance. The ruggedness of the course and the demands it makes on the machines are shown by the fact that of the 60 cars entered (including such famous European marques as Ferrari, Jaguar, and Maserati) only 24 finished. Three

of the finishers were Corvettes—a magnificent tribute to the cars' overall competitive performance.

Particularly significant was the completion of the 12-hour endurance race by a stock Corvette, entered by a private individual with a team of two amateur drivers. This Corvette, the owner's personal car, received no special preparation for the race and ran with such unracing-like equipment as a radio, heater, and power-operated top. The car was still in the race—and running well—long after many of the spe-

cially built, expensive European race cars had dropped out.

Of the other two Corvettes entered, one won its class in the Production sports car division and a modified Corvette won the title for its class.

Also significant was the fact that the Corvette was the only American production sports car entered in the race. The Corvette proudly carried American colors into international competition at Sebring, and proved conclusively that it is America's hottest sports car.

were forced to admit that the Americans had one of the world's finest sports cars—as capable on the track as it was on the road. Those who drove and understood the Corvette could not help but reach that conclusion."

All of the progress that the Corvette had made in 1957—mechanical and social—was reflected in the production figures: 6339 for the model year, which was a record number almost double that of 1956, and certain to be broken quickly in 1958. Yet only 240 of the total were fuelies. Generally, though, the division was pleased with the 'Vette's increasing popularity, and it predicted a 10,000-car year in 1958. And despite one of the most dismal years for Detroit in postwar history, that goal was almost reached.

However, one cloud was on the horizon, and it had to do with racing—just when the Corvette was beginning to show its mettle. In June 1957, the

Automobile Manufacturers Association responded to critics of the horsepower wars and the emphasis on performance by Detroit. They voted to adopt a two-point resolution that called on its members to cease immediately all sponsorship of and assistance for racing cars and drivers. GM president Harlow Curtice solemnly voted for the resolution along with the rest of the automakers. It effectively banned all factory-sponsored racing activities. The AMA declared that racing "oversells speed and power and undersells safety." The National Safety Council, which had been advocating just such an edict, hailed it as a "big step toward a safer America." Evidence suggests that Detroit went along with the anti-racing movement out of sheer self-interest. One unnamed executive said that competition was costing the companies millions and "the whole thing got to be a monkey on everybody's back."

Whatever the whys and wherefores, the AMA decision threatened to axe the Corvette's blossoming competition effort. Duntov called it "a tremendous shock," but he had never paid

To many eyes, the 1956 and 1957 Corvettes
are the most beautiful ever built. Apparently,
many customers agreed, as sales picked up
from a lowly 300 units in 1953 to 6246 for 1957.
The Thunderbird was still ahead by more than three-to-
one, but Corvette was closing the gap. Prices
started at $3465 for 1957.

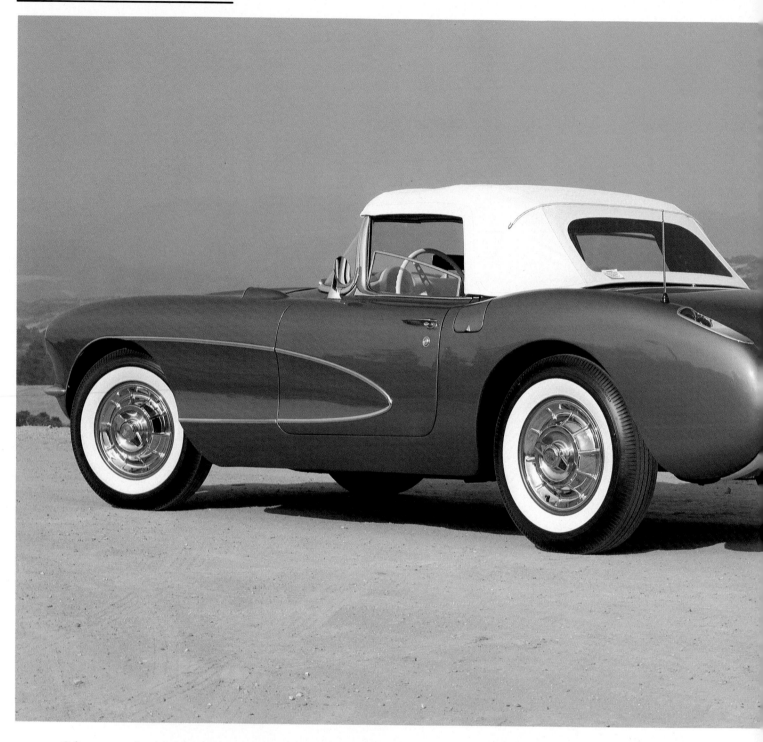

Often overlooked because of the massive horsepower increase given the '57 Corvette was its handling prowess. Not that Chevy didn't advertise it—one of their ads proclaimed that, "...the driver who has whipped the Corvette through a series of S-turns really knows the facts of life: This sleek powerhouse handles! Matter of fact...no production sports car in Corvette's class can find a shorter way around the bends!"

much mind to such executive decisions at General Motors. The AMA ban was soon being circumvented as easily as thirsty drinkers had handled prohibition. Immediately after the resolution, not much change could be seen at Chevrolet. Many employees continued working directly with the competition people. Duntov himself saw to it that anyone who wanted a racing Corvette could have one by checking the right options, and he began work-

Major Specifications
1957 Corvette

Chassis and Body
Frame: Box section, X-braced
Body: Glass-reinforced plastic, two-seat roadster
Front suspension: Independent, unequal-length A-arms, coil springs, double acting tubular shock absorbers, anti-roll bar
Rear suspension: Live axle, semielliptic leaf springs, anti-roll bar, tubular shock absorbers, optional heavy-duty settings
Wheels: 15" slotted steel, bolt-on
Tires: 6.70 × 15 4-ply

Dimensions
Wheelbase (in.): 102.0
Length (in.): 168.0
Height (in.): 51.9
Width (in.): 70.5
Track front/rear (in.): 57.0/59.0
Ground clearance (in.): 6.0
Weight (lbs): 2850

Engine
Type: Ohv 90-degree V-8, water-cooled, cast-iron block
Main bearings: 5
Bore × stroke: 3.875 × 3.00
Displacement (ci): 283
Compression ratio: 10.5:1
Induction system: Rochester Ramjet continuous-flow fuel injection
Exhaust system: Dual
Brake horsepower @ rpm: 283 @ 6200
Lbs/ft torque @ rpm: 290 @ 4400
Electrical system: 12-volt, Delco-Remy ignition

Drivetrain
Transmission: 4-speed manual
Gear ratios: First—2.20:1
            Second—1.66:1
            Third—1.31:1
            Fourth—1:1
Rear axle type: Hypoid semifloating
Rear axle ratio: 3.70:1 (4.56, 4.11, and 3.55 optional)
Steering: Worm-and-ball semireversible
Ratio: 16:1
Turning circle (ft): 37
Brakes: 4-wheel hydraulic, internal expanding drums, 11" diameter
Brake lining area (sq. in.): 157 (121 optional sintered metallic)

Performance
0-50 mph (sec): 4.8
0-60 mph (sec): 5.9
Standing-start quarter-mile (sec): 14.5 @ 95 mph
Top speed (mph): 135
Average fuel consumption (mpg): 10-15

ing on more of them. Despite the ban, Duntov continued to appear "casually" at numerous races. Other GM executives also could be spotted in or near the pits at many events.

While the factory did downplay competition in the years immediately following the AMA edict, Duntov's enthusiasm for the Corvette never waned, nor did his desire to make the Corvette a winner—not only in America but in international competition.

Nor did the ban disconnect Duntov's busy telephone, over which he reportedly dispensed priceless technical advice and occasional "back-door" parts to promising racers.

The last major race in which an American production car participated as an official factory entry was the Grand Prix of Endurance at Sebring on March 23, 1957. Two Corvette Super Sport test cars were in the race, which was won by a 4.5-liter Maserati. "The Corvettes were the latest creation of Chevrolet Division of General Motors," reported *The New York Times*. "They were described as the first real threat to European sports car supremacy."

One BHP Per Cubic Inch— 1957 Fuelie

The great small-block Chevy V-8 reached its second plateau in 1957, when it was enlarged to 283 cubic inches by punching out the bore to 3.88 inches. In its mildest form it produced 185 brake horsepower at 4600 rpm. A four-barrel carburetor brought this up to 220 bhp. Twin fours gave 245 or 270 bhp. Chevy's new Ramjet fuel injection system boosted horsepower to no less than 250 or 283 bhp. The last was the ultimate, achieving the magic goal of one horsepower per cubic inch displacement—a feat not previously achieved by large V-8 engines. The "Fuelie" 283 was offered only with the close-ratio

three-speed manual transmission.

The engine was designed to provide good reliability. Mechanical valve lifters were substituted for hydraulics when injection was specified. Longer-reach spark plugs with metal deflection shields were used to protect wiring and plug caps from manifold heat. The top of the block was a thicker casting to prevent cylinder wall distortion through over-tight hold-down bolts. Fuel passages were tapered in cross-sectional area toward the inlet ports and in the "ram's horn" exhaust manifold to provide better scavenging and increased volumetric efficiency. The engine had a new distributor, with breaker points directly above the shaft bearing to help reduce fluctuations in the gap setting. And the front and intermediate

Opposite page: Several views of the 1957 Corvette highlight the styling that helped it achieve better acceptance in the Fifties and endears it to collectors today. *Below*: While the fuel-injected V-8 got most of the publicity, the 283 with dual four-barrel carbs was almost as powerful—and far more reliable.

main bearings were 0.063-inch thicker.

Though made by GM's Rochester Carburetor Division, the Ramjet unit was designed almost entirely by GM Engineering Staff, simplified for production by Harry Barr and Zora Arkus-Duntov. It consisted of three main components—fuel meter, manifold assembly, and air meter—that replaced the intake manifold and carburetor of a conventional engine. The unit took in air first, then injected fuel directly into each intake port for mixing. The amount of fuel used was very precisely controlled, again for better volumetric efficiency and mileage. Cold-weather starting and warm-up were improved, and the unit by itself boosted output by about five bhp compared to the twin four-barrel carburetor engine. Chevrolet claimed that fuel injection eliminated manifold icing and reduced the tendency to stall when cornering hard.

A special two-piece aluminum manifold casting was used on 283-cid V-8s equipped with fuel injection. The upper casting contained air passages and air/fuel metering system bases, while the lower casting made up ram tubes and covered the top center of the engine.

A major engineering development is never simple, nor is it easy. Although the introduction of Ramjet injection was a milestone in Chevrolet history, bugs were inevitable. At the Daytona Speed Weeks, for example, the fuelie's characteristic fuel cut-off during acceleration was eliminated since it created a flat spot in response. Fuel nozzles, too, required attention: They were extended further into the air stream to prevent them from absorbing too much heat and causing rough idling.

While no formal published tests of the fuel-injected 283 V-8 in a standard Chevrolet seem to have been done, plenty exist of the engine in Corvettes. The 0-60-mph times of the most potent versions consistently averaged just over six seconds, and top speeds were very close to 140 mph. Driving a 250-bhp version, Walt Woron of **Motor Trend** whizzed through the 0-60-mph sprint in just 7.2 seconds. With a special 283 sporting 10.5:1 compression, dual exhausts, special cam, and solid lifters, the car did 134 mph—and Woron felt that it was not up to full potential!

Profile:
Zora Arkus-Duntov

In the automotive world, the years since the Forties have been typified as an age of automobile companies being run by anonymous people in grey flannel suits and carrying brief cases. No longer have great cars been designed by gifted individuals working alone. To a large extent, this overview of the industry is accurate. After World War II, automobiles became too complicated for successful one- or two-person efforts as had been exemplified in the past by Bugatti, Bentley, and the brothers Duesenberg. All in all, the development of the Corvette has not been an exception. From the beginning, it was very much a "committee car." Its success has been due to the facts that the committee itself was almost always composed of talented individuals and that they worked well with each other.

With all of that said, Zora Arkus-Duntov still emerges as "Mr. Corvette." Certainly, no one like him had ever been employed by Chevrolet Division, nor is anyone like him ever going to be there again. No Corvette story is complete without broad reference to Duntov—the one man above all others who insured that the Corvette would become a respected sports car—not only at home, but abroad.

Duntov was not present at the beginning. Nor was his background such to indicate that he had a place at Chevrolet Division—a company that had built comfortable, reliable, workaday transportation for three generations. Duntov was a European—Belgium-born—who had worked for "the Blacksmith" Sydney Allard. Zora Duntov had developed the appropriately named Ardun cylinder head conversion used to soup up the Ford V-8.

Zora Arkus-Duntov came to the attention of Chevrolet shortly after Ed Cole became its chief engineer, when Duntov sent a paper on high-performance engines to Cole for review. Was there a place for Duntov on the new, tech-oriented Chevy engineering team? There was, but not until Zora had dickered long and hard over salary and benefits. Chevrolet had not been in the habit of employing expensive European high-performance engineers. But Ed Cole had carte blanche from Tom Keating and Harlow Curtice for a massive upgrade and enlargement of Chevrolet Engineering. Duntov came aboard.

Duntov's initial review of the 1953 Corvette reminds one of the way that Ken Richardson viewed the prototype 1953 Triumph TR2: "I think that it's the most bloody awful car I've ever driven." In inter-

views, Duntov has been kinder than that toward the 'Vette. But GM retirees tend to have kind thoughts about their old company. In fact, the handling of the '53 was abominable, and Duntov immediately set about doing something about it—unofficially, at first. He was hired to work on the full line of Chevrolets, among which the Corvette was a very peripheral product. But before long he was engaged nearly full time on the sports car.

Duntov was not only a superb engineer, but a capable racing driver. In 1956, for example, he and Betty Skelton drove modified Corvettes at better than 150 miles per hour at the Daytona Speed Weeks. The event marked the birth of the famous Duntov cam, which transformed the performance of the new small-block V-8 for the hot rodders of the mid-Fifties. In 1957, Duntov became involved with track-testing the futuristic Corvette SS racer at Sebring, although his car retired after only 23 laps owing to an over-tight suspension bushing.

When the Automobile Manufacturer's Association agreed that its members should cease all racing activities and performance advertising in the spring of 1957, Duntov advocated violating the rule in secrecy. He was soon involved with GM's "closet" NASCAR program and other under-the-table competition efforts, which ultimately broke down the impractical and ill-conceived AMA ban in the mid-Sixties.

Zora Arkus-Duntov retired in 1974, after almost 20 years as chief Corvette engineer. But he remains very close to the company and to the car. His energy is that of a much younger man.

Duntov's accomplishments in terms of product are too numerous to recount, but here are a few: He created the prototype mid-engine Corvette Q-model, and he still regrets that it was never produced. He designed the 1963 Sting Ray chassis, which remained in production essentially unchanged for 20 years. Most recently, Zora developed the Duntov-Corvette, a conversion that turns the stock post-1975 coupe into a rip-snorting powerhouse with full roadster bodywork.

Following is the result of several interviews with Zora Arkus-Duntov over the years. The authors, editors, and Mr. Duntov covered all aspects of the Corvette—a vivid experience, reflecting his remarkable drive and personality.

Editor: Why did you leave Allard and join General Motors?

Zora Arkus-Duntov: I wished to return to America. I had talked to an American general who was stationed in England, and he told me to write to Ed Cole at Chevrolet. I did, but it was not promising. I found a position with Fairchild Aviation, and after I had been in the States for some time, I sent to Ed Cole a copy of a research report on high-performance engines which I had written. We discussed salary and benefits for some time before I accepted. I came to GM in May, 1953.

Ed: What did you think of the new Corvette at that time?

ZAD: That it was the most beautiful car I had ever seen. The engine was a letdown, but the proportions and aesthetics were right. I borrowed one in May, when I first joined GM. The handling was not good. I took it upon myself to give this car better handling. This was not part of my normal assignment; just fiddling on the side.

Ed: When, then, did you formalize the Corvette relationship?

ZAD: On the '55, when I was assigned to investigate exhaust staining on the rear of the fenders, which was connected with fumes in the passenger compartment. I attached streamers to a test car and took motion pictures of the air flow. If you opened the vent pane, the exhaust was carried from the rear to the front and into the passenger compartment. Moving the exhaust tips to the very rear of the fenders on the 1956 model corrected both problems.

Ed: Tell us about the Duntov cam.

ZAD: I wished to start building a racing image, and to exceed 150 mph at the Daytona Speed Weeks. I calculated that I needed an additional 30 horsepower from the 265 V-8 in high-performance trim. I changed the camshaft design to hold the valves open longer, but not to lift them higher. This provided a fuller valve-opening curve. Engine speed rose to 6500 rpm and I had the horsepower I needed. But the Corvette was still too heavy for racing, and we were not ready yet.

Ed: So you kept testing and had that terrible accident?

ZAD: Yes, in April 1956. It was my own fault. I arrived at the proving grounds to make carburetor tests, and found that this car had no seat belts. It had experimental disc brakes. There were many things wrong with this car. Still, I drove it. Sure, like hell. I got sideways and went off the track. I was in a cast for six months. I couldn't bend. I had strings to lift my dress in the rest room. I was quite a sight.

Ed: *But you kept working, especially on fuel injection.*

ZAD: *The fuel injection project had top priority, because we needed it on both the 1957 Corvette and Chevrolet passenger cars.*

Ed: *Why didn't the fuel injection work out?*

ZAD: *It was too expensive. In 1965, when it was dropped, the option cost almost $500 extra. For only $150, we could offer the big block with more power and torque at lower speeds. The fuel injection engine had to be wound up first—the big engine was superior. It was not the bugs that killed fuel injection—they could have been worked out.*

Ed: *How did the Sebring Corvette SS come about?*

ZAD: *Harley Earl had a D-Type Jaguar and wanted us to fit it with a Corvette V-8. This was absurd, and I said that if Chevrolet wanted to go racing, we should build an entire car. The SS was the result—a combined project between Styling and Engineering.*

Ed: *Did Styling influence aerodynamics?*

ZAD: *No. I had them build a full-size model for aerodynamic testing, so that I could have some input on this body. I had them use considerable tuck-under to achieve maximum air velocity under the car. They did not want to do this at first. I could see that they would not have the car ready in time for testing, so I put the test body on a spare chassis.*

Ed: *And that was the famous "mule"?*

ZAD: *Yes. It was not a beautiful car, but Juan Fangio and Stirling Moss beat the Sebring track record with it.*

Ed: *But Fangio did not drive it in the actual race.*

ZAD: *As the race got closer and Styling failed to complete the car, Fangio feared that it would not be ready and asked to be released from his contract. Carroll Shelby was also signed and released. Finally, the drivers were John Fitch and Piero Taruffi, but that overtight bushing failed after 23 laps.*

Ed: *Were there long-range plans for the SS?*

ZAD: *Yes, I was preparing four SS cars to compete at Le Mans, under a fictitious name. But it really was a terrible lifter. Right away I lost interest in this car. It's beautiful all right, but [it has] the profile of a wing. I drove the*

Zora Arkus-Duntov, the retired Chevrolet engineer widely regarded as Corvette's "father," looks over a 1957 Corvette with "Uncle" Tom McCahill (right), one of America's top roadsters in the Fifties.

Corvette SS racer at the proving grounds at 183 mph and I ran about 155 mph at the opening of the Daytona track in 1959. But the AMA ruling in 1957 was a tremendous shock. Until 1961 I promoted racing in secrecy.

Ed: Why did the AMA ban finally come apart at GM?

ZAD: Bunkie Knudsen replaced Ed Cole as general manager of Chevrolet in 1961. Both wanted to see Corvettes winning races. Knudsen approved a plan for another pure-racing Corvette. I wanted to build at least 100 specials that would weigh only 2000 pounds and which would have powerful new engines. That was the start of the Corvette Grand Sport.

Ed: What happened to the Grand Sport program? Why was it cut?

ZAD: Higher management.

Ed: Didn't Carroll Shelby approach Chevrolet with the Cobra idea before he went to Ford?

ZAD: Yes. He got two chassis from us and had them bodied in Italy, but nothing ever came of that project. He settled with Ford instead.

Ed: When did work begin on the first Sting Ray?

ZAD: Both chassis and engine work began in 1959. I had by then been named director of high-performance vehicles. I took pride in the small-block Chevrolet engine.

Ed: What do you recall about designing the Sting Ray chassis?

ZAD: Mainly that everything worked as designed—it lasted up to the 1982 model. In 1962 we produced the Grand Sport with the disc brakes, vented in front, solid at the rear. In '64 we had Girling Brake Co. throw their hands in the air and say they couldn't make discs because Corvettes have too much weight for their performance. I worked with Kelsey-Hayes, and they succeeded in providing excellent brakes for the Corvette.

Ed: But the brakes were by Delco, weren't they?

ZAD: Kelsey-Hayes did not get the contract because Delco Division [of GM] used their leverage. Delco produced a brake identical to Kelsey-Hayes'. For '65 we produced four-wheel disc brakes, and they were so good they stayed until 1982. With the mid-engine Corvette we used a Bendix brake identical to the Delco brake—four pads per caliper.

Ed: Did you like Mitchell's styling?

ZAD: Overall, we were on the same wavelength. I only remember one disagreement—the split window on the '63 Sting Ray [coupe]. We took it out [of the '64 model].

Ed: Overall, how did you view the '63 Sting Ray?

ZAD: The ergonomics were very good. It was quite adequate as an envelope, with such things as a shift lever location that would fall into the hand readily, good legibility of the gauges, and performance that was nonpareil overall.

Ed: What was your opinion of the 1968 Corvette styling?

ZAD: As a whole, design-wise, it was a very good car. Something got lost in the ergonomics, though. You had to move to operate the gearshift. At that time Bill Mitchell was impressed by supersonic jets. The first thing I did was to provide more shoulder room. It was so pinched you couldn't drive it without leaning. To gain a half-inch per side, I spent $120,000 retooling door inners. This half an inch was very significant. Another consideration: The '63-'67 car was a terrible "lifter" aerodynamically. The subsequent design was also a lifter, but not to that extent.

Ed: How important was racing?

ZAD: At that time, very important. I considered that it was necessary. To establish the sports car, you have to race it. After a car gets established, like the mid-Seventies, the racing is second place. We had all the optional items to enable people to race. CERV 1 [an experimental open-wheel single-seat racer] was the progenitor of the Sting Ray suspension-wise.

Ed: Did you like GM's experimental rotary engine?

ZAD: Not at all. But as things began to shape up in '71, I had either a mid-engine car and a rotary engine or not at all. Therefore, I had to accept the rotary engine. [GM president] Ed Cole was enamored with the rotary engine. Therefore, I showed him the two- and four-rotor Corvettes. The four-rotor engine was interchangeable with a reciprocating engine; it could easily be replaced with the small-block V-8. When GM got off the Wankel kick, they went back to a reciprocating engine. The Aerovette [the four-rotor design] got a 400-cid small-block engine. It also had the space to accept four-wheel drive. I told them... four-wheel drive [would be important in the future]. First with rear-wheel drive and, two years later, four-wheel drive. If you look at the Aerovette, you see a big tunnel to fit four-

wheel drive. But it was just a styling exercise. The mid-engine Corvette minus energy-absorbent bumpers was under 3000 pounds with the 400 or 350 small block. Torsional stiffness was in the area of 6000 pounds-feet per degree. It was a very good car; it had good luggage space. When I think about it, it's a pity it did not come about.

Ed: Who killed the mid-engine design?

ZAD: In '74, I had a conversation with the chairman of the board [Thomas A. Murphy]. He said, "Let's wait. Right now we cannot build enough cars to satisfy the demand. When we see the demand will slacken, we'll bring the mid-engine car out." I disagreed with him. I thought Chevrolet should be at the forefront, but he had the last word.

Ed: What do you think of the newest generation Corvette and what would you have done differently with it?

ZAD: Very good. I tried to promulgate the mid-engine car. If I was not forced to retire [the new model] would probably be a mid-engine car. The mid-engine design in '69 and '73-'74 was in the picture on and off. I think I would have won the fight given time, but, unfortunately, I was forced to retire. Styling-wise, aerodynamic-wise, [the current model] is excellent. It is ergonomically well thought out. The chassis is not as good as I wish it were. But second guessing is unfair... Digital gauges I don't care for at all. They're good for slow-moving processes, like fuel gauge, clock, or oil level. But the speedometer and tach should have round faces to show where you have been and where you are going. Instantaneous readouts have no place in a sports car.

Ed: Can they race the car?

ZAD: They're not man enough. That's a break in tradition with Corvette.

Ed: What do you think the next Corvette will be like?

ZAD: By the time they get the money I will be already dead and buried... Chassis-wise, the previous Corvette [Duntov's own design] lived from 1963 to 1982. The amortization of the tooling happened in one year. In subsequent years, it was gravy. The [current] Corvette will live maybe 20 years—I don't know. As for product costs, the '63 Corvette [came in] less than the '62 Corvette. It sounds incongruous with independent rear suspension and everything, but with the front suspension, I made up the cost of the independent [rear] suspension. Using suspension pieces of earlier cars was very cost-effective.

CHAPTER FIVE

1958-1962: Beginning the Golden Age

Perhaps the selection of a classic era for an automobile that has seen only 35 years of production is a bit premature. But in the Corvette's case, the late Fifties and early to mid-Sixties are a fairly safe bet. They were years of vast transition: From Harley Earl's styling to Bill Mitchell's. From the second-generation two-seater to the Sting Ray, Corvette's first grand touring model. From the small-block 265 and 283 engines to the mighty Mark IVs. Within this rapid-fire evolution of the marque lay the most exciting years in the Corvette story.

Perhaps the present Corvette generation—introduced for the 1984 model year—is on balance the best Corvette ever. Perhaps the 1953 model is a prize collectible. Perhaps 1957 is the quintessential year for the fuelie. Nevertheless, taken as a whole, the transition years of 1958-67 will stand in history as Corvette's Golden Age.

The '58s didn't indicate what effect the new generation would have right away. To many people, including not a few Corvette enthusiasts, the 1958 model was a large step backward—much as the 1958 Chevrolet passenger cars seemed to be a backward step from the 1957s. The '58 design was, of course, a facelift, and as facelifts go, it was not very successful. Chevy stylists designed the car around 1955—still under the heavy influence of Harley Earl, who might be said to have been going through his rotund period. The car seemed to take some cues from the SR-2 prototype racing car, but it was more glitzy than any others that had carried the Corvette name. Its basically clean, rounded, smooth lines from

1956-57 were still there, but decorated with simulated hood louvers, dummy air scoops on either side of the grille and in the side coves, and twin chrome bars running down the trunk lid. The car now had quad headlights—quite the fad in 1958—surrounded by wide chrome bezels that met bright strips on top of the fenders. Stylists considered replacing the distinctive grille teeth that had originated with the first Corvette in 1953, but everyone universally rejected the mesh insert that was proposed. Still, the grille had

fewer teeth—nine instead of 13. The new bumpers were more positive. Where they had been attached to the body previously, they now were secured to the frame by long brackets, providing significantly greater protection. Another exterior change was the switch from enamel to acrylic lacquer paint.

The car was just as heavily revised inside, but here the revisions were far more successful. Stung by criticism of the original instrument panel layout, the interior designers made sure that every dial save the clock was placed right in front of the driver. Dominating the new dashboard was a large, semicircular, 160-mph speedometer, and perched in front of it on the steer-

ing column was a round, 6000-rpm tachometer. The customary four minor gauges were strung in a row on either side of the tach. A vertical console dropped down from the dash center and housed the heater controls, clock, and the Wonder Bar signal-seeking radio. A grab bar in front of a semicircular cutout made up the passenger's side of the dash. A locking glove compartment was installed between the seats just below the release button for the integral convertible top tonneau. The door panels were restyled, with reflectors added at arm rest level for safety when opening the doors at night, and a "pebble-grain" upholstery fabric was used.

The newest generation also put on some weight. It tipped the scales at over 3000 pounds for the first time— about 200 pounds heavier curb weight than the '57 model, thanks to some 9.5 inches of extra length and two inches of added width.

Far greater changes than these had been contemplated for the 1958 model year. The most ambitious proposal had been a new closed grand touring model, heavily influenced by the Mercedes-Benz 300SL gullwing coupe that had drawn so many rave reviews from the motoring press. Even more interesting than the coupe was the idea of making it a unit body/chassis instead of the traditional separate body and frame. Styling highlights included pontoon-like fenders—traditionally one of Earl's favorite attention-getters—along with quad headlamps and a fastback roofline. Although gullwing-type lift-up doors were not contemplated, hinged roof sections were.

The 1958 Corvette (*above and right*) seemed to take some cues from the SR-2 prototype racing car, shown here with Bill Mitchell (*top*). Designed around 1955, it was more glitzy than any others that had previously carried the Corvette name.

They flipped upward when a door was opened, harking back to several earlier Motorama cars. The front end featured two large air inlets. Corvette enthusiasts will recognize here certain features that did appear in time—on the 1963 Sting Ray coupe. The coupe body style had cut-in roof sections (though not hinged) and large air inlets in the front.

One facet of the coupe proposal that

never did materialize was the plan to build the car's skin out of aluminum instead of fiberglass, with the unibody construction providing the necessary rigidity. The benefit, Chevrolet thought, would be the ability to produce them in higher volume, something the Corvette desperately needed in order to make a return on its investment. "At one time, we thought it was possible to produce fiberglass for just

10,000 cars," Zora Arkus-Duntov recollected. That wasn't a high enough number with which to make any serious money. But in due course, Chevrolet learned how to produce more fiberglass—much more. In the end, other projects such as a whole new body for the 1958 passenger cars precluded anything in the way of completely redesigning the Corvette for 1958. Chevrolet had been whipped by

Ford in the 1957 production race and was itching to get even. The result for the Corvette was its almost gaudy facelift.

And yet the 1958 Corvette wasn't all that bad. In fact, it pointed the way to greater 'Vettes in the years ahead. For one thing, the 1958 model was quick. The most potent engine in the line was still the high-compression, Duntov-cammed fuelie with 290 brake horse-power at 6200 rpm. A similar arrangement with twin carbs returned 270 bhp, still on 9.5:1 compression. The car didn't take a back seat in a drag race. Of course, the average buyer did not opt for the mighty small-block engines. Nearly half of the '58s were equipped with the base 230-bhp 283-cubic-inch V-8, and only 1500 cars had fuel injection—1000 with the 290-bhp setup, 500 with the 250-bhp version.

Speed freaks could still order a near race-ready Corvette straight from their local Chevrolet dealers. Certainly, the prices were right. The hottest engine setup ($484.20), Positraction ($48.45), heavy-duty brakes and sus-pension ($425.05), four-speed trans-mission ($188.30), and metallic brake linings ($26.90) added about $1200 to the reasonable $3631 base price. For less then $5000, the 'Vette was more than a match for Jaguars, Porsches, and other machines for supremacy in sports car performance, and even exotics like Ferraris were not out of reach.

The car magazines were mostly positive about the '58's mechanical changes. Stephen F. Wilder, writing for *Sports Cars Illustrated,* said, "We were able, in a very short time, to discover how the 1958 Corvette behaves in nearly every conceivable road situation. It may be summed up as 'very well indeed.'" The optional four-speed gearbox got special praise: "It is at least the equal of any box we've ever tried, not only with respect to the suitability of ratios to the engine performance, but the smoothness of the synchromesh brings to mind the old metaphor about a hot knife and butter." With the 250-bhp injected engine, *SCI* reported a 0-60-mph time of 7.6 seconds and top speed of around 125 mph.

Midget and Indy car veteran Sam Hanks, writing for *Motor Trend,* tested four versions of the '58 model and came up with some interesting comparative statistics. It would appear that for economy as well as speed, fuel injection was the way to go. Not many buyers chose the fuel-injected engines for their fuel efficiency, though they did better in both categories. That Hanks liked the 'Vettes was no secret: "Any way you look at it, I think the Chevrolet designers ought to be proud of the style of the Corvette and their engineers should be proud of a fine sports car. It's real great to have an American-built production car that's available to the public as a combination cross-country, city traffic, competition sports car. I'm impressed."

Despite the somewhat overblown styling, the '58 impressed the buying public, too. For the first time in its brief life, the Corvette turned a profit for Chevrolet. Model year production was well up above 1957 levels, totaling precisely 9168 units and making the 'Vette one of the few domestic models to score a sales gain in that recession-ridden season—a fact usually ignored by automotive historians. The only other '58 models registering gains instead of losses were the Rambler American, Lincoln, and Ford's new four-seat Thunderbird.

Critics have tended to scoff at the '58 Corvette, feeling that Chevy was beginning to move away from the

Although the clean lines of the 1956-57 Corvette were still there, the '58 (*below*) was decorated with dummy air scoops on either side of the grille and in the side coves and twin chrome bars running down the trunk lid. Wide chrome bezels that met bright strips on top of the fenders surrounded the quad headlights. The instrument panel (*right*) was new (with all important gauges in front of the driver) as were the simulated hood louvers (*far right*).

race-and-ride concept as quickly as it had embraced it with the 1956-57 design. Yet the styling changes and the added bulk were appropriate for the late Fifties, and, although they detracted some from the car's agility,

they didn't do irreparable damage. As noted, the heavy-duty handling package was still available, and the 'Vette remained one of the quickest volume-production cars in the world.

Thanks to the efforts of Jim Jeffords

and his "Purple People Eater," Corvette again won the SCCA's B-Production crown in 1958. Jim Rathmann and Dick Doane took the GT class at Sebring that year, and veteran Ak Miller won the sports car class at the

Fuel injection remained an option on the 283-cid V-8 (*top*), churning out 290 horsepower at 6200 rpm in its most potent form. The $484.20 option was duly noted on the front fenders (*above*). Prices started at $3631 for the '58 Corvette (*right*), but speed freaks added about $1200 in options to make it really perform.

Pikes Peak Hill Climb with a time of 15 minutes, 23.7 seconds.

None of the racing triumphs were mentioned in Corvette advertising. Chevy soft-pedaled performance in the wake of the AMA's "anti-racing" edict, with the emphasis on such things as the "silken cyclone of a V-8," the "beautifully compact body," and "a chassis that clings to the road like a stalking panther." Headlines asked, "What's as effortless as a Corvette?" and "What happened to gravity?" The latter led to a spiel about the car's handling virtues. A somewhat nationalistic tone was sounded in one ad titled, "Corvette Does America Proud," in which a two-tone roadster

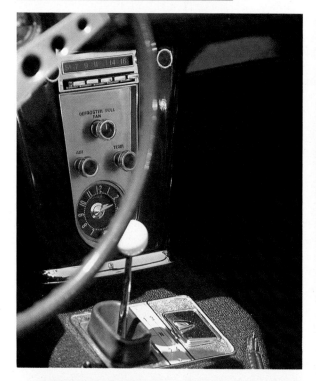

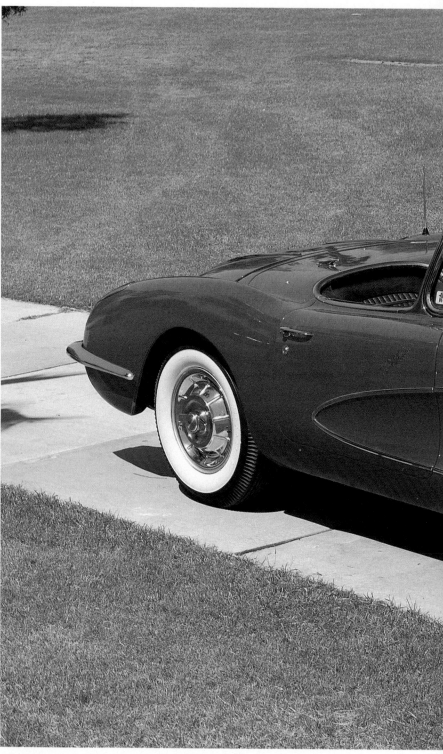

was shown at the famous Pebble Beach, California, Concours d'Elegance surrounded by an impressive array of vintage automobiles. Another pictured a roadster running at speed as a sailplane floated overhead, making the obvious comparisons with florid phrases like this: "...acceleration as easy as a giant's stride, a liquid grace in motion, steering as sharp and precise as a scalpel. In plain truth, a Corvette travels in a way no other American car can equal." Apparently, it was all right to talk about performance as long as the word wasn't used or race results weren't published.

The Corvette's chrome period would prove to be mercifully brief. In fact, to Chevrolet's credit, it began cleaning up the otherwise mostly unchanged follow-up model. As *Road & Track* noted: "The appearance of the 1959 Corvette has been improved by the simple expedient of removing the phony hood louvers and the two useless chrome bars from the decklid." But the editors also observed that "trim on

Corvette's four-speed T10 transmission became a $188.30
option in May 1957. The shift pattern was clearly
noted for those not used to so many forward gears
(*top left*). The fake vents in the fender "coves"
were not appreciated by purists (*bottom left*).
The grille on the '58 Corvette (*above*) had
nine teeth, compared to 13 in 1957.

A 160-mph speedometer and a 6000-rpm tachometer greeted the driver of a 1958 Corvette (*above*). Three carbureted versions of the 283-cid V-8 (*below*) were offered for 1958 with horsepower ratings of 230, 245, or 270. Although still offered only as a roadster (*right*), the Corvette was beginning to catch on with the buying public—a record 9168 were built for the 1958 model year.

Corvettes, like all GM cars, is extremely well executed whether it is functional or mere decoration." Interior alterations were equally minor, but just as welcome. They included repositioned armrests and door handles, reshaped seats providing better lateral location in cornering, and the addition of a shelf under the passenger grab bar for extra small-item stowage space. For the first time, sunvisors were available as an option. Instruments were given concave rather than flat lenses to cut down on reflections, and a T-handle lockout was added to the manual transmission shifter to prevent accidental engagement of reverse.

A minor mechanical change for 1959—the only one—was the addition of trailing radius rods from the frame to the rear axle. They helped to counteract rear axle windup brought on by the extra torque of the more powerful

engines. Powertrain choices remained the same.

Despite its carryover design, the 1959 Corvette was a very desirable car. The cleaner body and strong powerplants combined to make a package that was strong, indeed. Many examples could shoot through the quarter-mile in less than 15 seconds, and 0-60-mph times of less than eight seconds were typical. By now, *fast car* and *Corvette* had become synonymous.

Auto writer Ray Brock used nothing but superlatives in his 1959 test report: "Handling and brakes are plenty good in stock trim. There is absolutely no need for any of the heavy-duty racing extras unless the car is intended for sports car racing." *Road & Track's* reaction was only slightly less exuberant: "Taking everything into consideration, the Corvette is a pretty good car. It probably has more performance per dollar than anything you could buy,

and parts are obtainable without sending to Italy, Germany, or England." The 290-bhp fuel-injected powerplant got the most praise from *R&T.* The magazine reported 6.6 seconds in the 0-60-mph dash, with the quarter-mile coming up in 14.5 seconds at 96 mph. Top speed was listed at 128 mph with 4.11:1 final drive.

In its April 1959 issue, *Motor Trend* compared a Porsche 356 convertible D to a '59 'Vette, and it arrived at 0-60 figures of 7.8 seconds for the American machine and 15.2 seconds for the German one. The Corvette also beat the Porsche in the quarter-mile—by more than four seconds—and was a big winner in the handling contest. The Porsche was superior only in fuel economy, getting 24.5 mpg compared to the Corvette's 14.3 mpg. Of course, the match up had something of an "apples and oranges" quality about it, as *MT's* report concluded: "If getting

Chevy cleaned up the '59 Corvette, shown here in
Snowcrest White and Inca Silver, by eliminating the
chrome bars on the decklid and the simulated louvers
on the hood (*above*). Interior alterations included
repositioned armrests and door handles, reshaped seats
for more lateral support, and extra small-item storage
under the passenger grab bar (*top right*). The 230-bhp
283 (*bottom right*) was the most popular engine choice.

performance from a precision-built, small-displacement engine is intriguing, then Porsche is the answer. If you like the idea of having one of the world's fastest accelerating sports cars, then pick the Corvette.... The truth is that both are excellent buys. They're sturdy, reliable, comfortable, and, above all, fun to drive. What more can you ask of a sports car?"

The *R&T* test concluded with a broad hint that big changes were in store for the Corvette: "The changes ... in the last six model years are not so great as we think will come about in 1960. We predict that this will be the year of the big changes for Corvette, and most of them for the better."

R&T was both right and wrong. Chevy had indeed been working on a new and far more radical concept for America's sports car—the so-called Q-model. It was a much smaller and lighter two-seater with very streamlined styling and an independent rear suspension likely derived from the transaxle being prepared for the rear-engine Corvair. How close the Q-car came to production is known, but the hype about it could have been nothing more than a smokescreen to divert attention from the Corvair project. The Corvair arrived on cue for 1960, but a new Corvette did not accompany it. However, the first real break with the Corvette's original offerings were developing, having begun in 1959.

Sales for 1959 were better than they had been in 1958, but not by much. The cleaner styling probably had little to do with the improvement. For 1959, sales of almost anything had to be better than they had been in 1958, when only Corvette and three other marques—Thunderbird, Lincoln, and Rambler—had outsold their '57 levels. Corvette sales were steadily increasing—but not fast enough. At 9670 and 10,261 units for the 1959 and '60 model years, the car still wasn't making enough money.

The 1960 model was virtually indistinguishable from the '59. The high-compression 283 fuelie still stood atop the engine chart, but an even tighter 11.0:1 compression squeeze and solid lifters had now boosted power to 315 bhp at 6200 rpm. A second version with hydraulic lifters for easier maintenance produced 275 bhp at 5200

continued on page 94

The cleaner styling of the 1959 Corvette, along with its growing reputation as a true sports car, sent production to another record: 9,670. Even in stock form, there was no need for heavy-duty racing extras unless the car was intended for sports car racing.

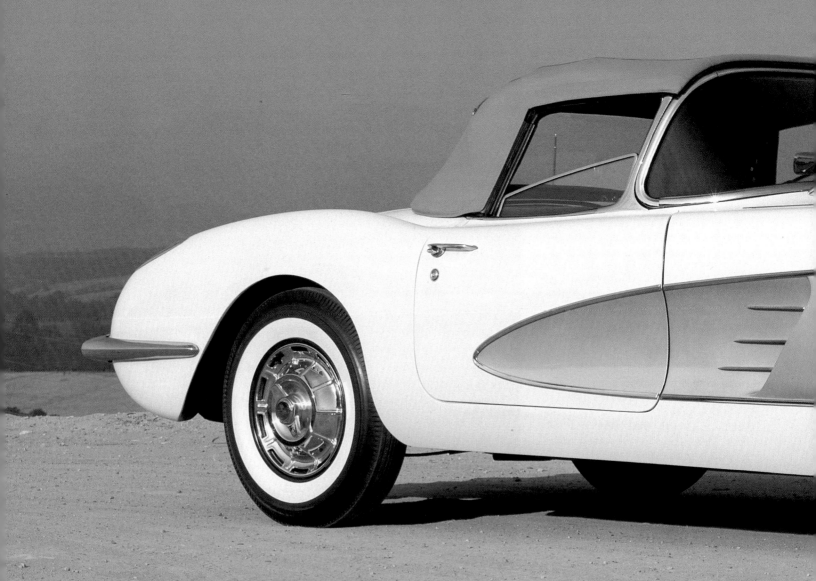

The Q-Model

Although the Corvette has always been a bona fide sports car and a unique entity in the Chevy line, it has always shared some parts with the division's high-volume models—a practice that has enabled the Corvette to be one of the real values in its field. The proposed Q-model would have been no different, had it gone into production. The difference would have been in the parts borrowed by the Q-car.

In the late Fifties, when planning got under way for the 1961-62 models, Chevrolet contemplated a radical departure from its traditional design philosophy. The company considered a separate line of cars featuring a rear-mounted transaxle and all-independent suspension. The transaxle, an unusual piece of hardware in itself, sported integral inboard brakes. With it, engineer Zora Arkus-Duntov could at last realize his dream of a Corvette with fully independent rear suspension. Not only that, but the transaxle was slated to be made in both manual and automatic versions, some with an integral starter motor. Before anyone could say the word exoticar, Chevrolet engineers and stylists were drawing up Corvette proposals around this Q transaxle. One of the cleanest looked like a slimmed-down version of what would eventually become the 1963 Sting Ray. It too was a split-window coupe, but the split was in front. Two pieces of glass wrapped around from the sides to join at the car's longitudinal centerline, thus forming both windshield and side windows. Other design aspects were just as radical: dry-sump lubrication, unit body/chassis construction, and pop-up hidden headlights. The Q-model was quite light and, with its all-independent suspension, at least promised good handling.

But even as the "European-inspired" Corvette was being developed, car sales as a whole remained in the doldrums, brought about by the 1958 recession. With the market showing few signs of strong recovery—and with the compact rear-engine Corvair already a top priority—Chevy abruptly halted work on the Q-model.

A similar transaxle setup with swing-arm rear suspension did appear in production for the 1961 Pontiac Tempest. It proved to be one of the most wicked-handling cars that Detroit ever built. In retrospect, then, perhaps Corvette lovers can breathe a sigh of relief that the Q-model never materialized, innovative though it would have been.

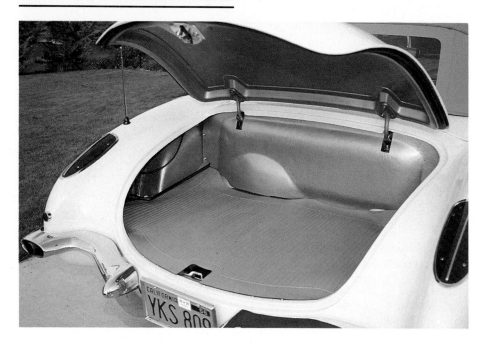

A flat, unobstructed cargo area made the Corvette a "practical" sports car (*above*). The Corvette emblem (*below*) was becoming more familiar to Americans. Note the gas filler location near the driver's door and the way the side window retracted into the door (*right*).

continued from page 91

rpm. Because of these gains, Powerglide was no longer offered with fuel-injected engines. The automatic transmission simply couldn't stand the extra torque. The carbureted engines remained much as before. The tamest was the 230-bhp V-8 with single four-barrel carburetor, followed by the dual-quad 245-bhp hydraulic-lifter unit and the solid-lifter 270-bhp engine with twin four-barrel carbs.

Mechanical refinements for 1960 included new aluminum clutch housings on all cars with manual transmissions (saving 18 pounds) and aluminum radiators for cars with the Duntov cam. A power-saving thermostatically controlled cooling fan was a new option, as was a long-range 24-gallon fuel tank for extended cruising. One victim of the AMA competition ruling was the Corvette heavy-duty suspension RPO 684, which was chopped from the option list. Compensation was at hand, however, with a large-diameter front anti-roll bar and a new rear bar as standard equipment. These, plus an extra inch of rear wheel rebound travel, gave the 1960 model a smoother ride and more neutral handling characteristics.

Despite the shift in marketing emphasis toward smooth, no-fuss touring, plenty of performance goodies were still available. The 315-bhp engine cost $484.20, with Positraction available at $43.05. The four-speed gearbox continued on at $188.30, ceramic-metallic brake linings (RPO 687) were a steal at just $26.90 (sintered-iron linings were also offered, as RPO 686), and 6.70 × 15 nylon tires cost only $15.75 (5.5 × 15s were standard).

Road & Track reported that the 1960 "high-performance engines (intended primarily for racing) are given very special treatment. In addition to customary inspection, many critical parts are now routed through a special department for a very painstaking examination of dimensions, flaws, finish, and quality of materials. Included in this group were valves, rocker arms, pushrods, pistons, connecting rods, and crankshafts. Just a few years ago, Chevrolet would have laughed at such a suggestion. This certainly shows how serious they are about the sportscar side of the business."

Another indication came in an interesting "experiment" that never quite got going. Early in the model year, Chevy offered cylinder heads cast from a high-silicon aluminum alloy as an option for the two fuel-injected engines. Based on the design first tried with the Corvette SS race car from Sebring 1957, they had the stock 11.0:1 compression, but featured improved intake and exhaust breathing. The high silicon content of the heads prefigured the block construction of the four-cylinder Vega engine of a decade later, which proved just as troublesome. The aluminum heads were fine in theory, but tended to warp if the engine overheated, and Chevy had quality control problems with the castings. The option was quickly withdrawn, but Duntov was far from finished with aluminum-head engines.

By now, the Corvette's abilities on the highway and race track were acknowledged by everyone, with the possible exception of *Road & Track*. Competition had not gone under-

ground in the wake of the AMA ban. In 1960, Briggs Cunningham enjoyed a fine success with a three-car Corvette team at the classic Le Mans 24-Hours. A Cunningham Corvette driven by Bob Grossman and John Fitch finished eighth overall in a field of very hairy sport-racing machinery.

Corvette fans, perhaps more than

any other group of one-marque enthusiasts, always have been interested in the future. Around 1960, rumors began circulating about an entirely new Corvette. Lending credence to the rumors was the track appearance of a dramatic special called the Stingray. It was campaigned "privately" by GM chief of design Bill Mitchell. The

The 1960 Corvette (*above*) was virtually indistinguishable
from the '59, but detail improvements underneath gave
it a smoother ride and more neutral handling
characteristics. Detail shots (*below*) show the
door panels, the fender cove with simulated air
extractor, 230-horsepower 283 V-8, and front end styling.

Corvette celebrated the 1960 model year by building slightly over 10,000 cars, a first. By then, it was also making a modest profit for Chevy, listing at $3872 without options. Its weight had snuck up slightly to 2840 pounds.

fact that Mitchell had just succeeded to that position to replace the retiring Harley Earl convinced many 'Vette watchers that the Stingray was the shape of things to come. In many ways, it was.

Meanwhile, Mitchell was moving to put new life into the current body, which had been around since 1956. His studios had no shortage of ideas for new and different Corvettes. In the

end, though, few changes were made between 1956 and 1962. Even the 1953-55 models can be seen to relate closely to their successors in plain view. Of course, many changes were proposed and rejected—the most interesting being the Q-model.

But Chevrolet had other priorities— the Corvair for one. Clearly, Ed Cole's technically fascinating compact had been the most interesting of the Big

Three small cars when it debuted, but it was beset with service problems—oil leaks, thrown fan belts, and premature tuning problems, for instance. And it did not outsell the conventional Ford Falcon. Money was being set aside for a more conventional Falcon-beater, ultimately known as the Chevy II. The Corvette would have to get by as it was for a few more years.

In doing so, the 1961-62 models established themselves as the best Corvettes since the "classic" 1957. Bill Mitchell made it happen, giving the cars fresh, new styling with a mild, clean-lined facelift—a vast relief from the chrome-laden 1958-60 period. The facelift was accompanied by numerous mechanical modifications aimed at improved efficiency and higher performance. The result was a back-to-back pair of superb vintage cars—'Vettes that were so refined that they almost qualified as being all new.

Externally, the most pronounced change for 1961 was a completely new rear end design. It had been lifted virtually intact from Mitchell's Stingray racing car, having been seen on his XP-700 show car, too. The XP had a certifiably insane front end, with a huge loop-style bumper/grille protruding

well forward of the quad headlights set above it, and it was rightly forgotten. But the rear portion was unique and wholly satisfying—a simple flowing shape that just happened to mate well with Harley Earl's production 1958

front end design. A bonus of the new aft section was that it increased luggage space by perhaps 20 percent. It was quickly dubbed the "ducktail." Highlighting the ducktail were twin taillights on either side of the central license plate recess and a modest longitudinal creaseline running down the trunk lid through a large, round Corvette medallion. Simple chrome bumperettes bracketed the license plate frame, and for the first time the Corvette's dual exhausts exited below the body, rather than through it or the bumper as it had previously. Up front, the basic four-lamp nose was retained, but considerably cleaned. The chrome headlight bezels were now body color, and the trademark vertical teeth were jettisoned in favor of a fine, horizontal-mesh insert that had been under consideration for several years. The round medallion that had traditionally announced the 'Vette was replaced by a crossed-flags symbol and separate letters spelling out the car's name. The 1961 Corvette was also the last of the breed available with a contrasting color for the body-side cove indentations and, for just $16.15, most buyers ordered it.

Other options for the '61 included a heater, outrageously priced at $102.25 over the suggested $3934 base figure. Air conditioning, power steering, and power brakes weren't available, but

The serious driver could order a 1960 Corvette tailor-made for performance (*both pages*) by starting with the 315-bhp fuel-injected engine (*bottom and center left*), close-ratio four speed, Positraction, wide wheels, and the like—and then doing without a radio, heater, courtesy light, sun visors, and hardtop (*top left*).

Externally, the most pronounced change for the '61
Corvette (*above*) was a completely new rear end
design. It had been lifted virtually intact
from Bill Mitchell's Stingray racing car, and
had also been seen on his XP-700 show car (*top
right*). It was a simple flowing shape that just
happened to mate well with the 1958 front end design.

you could order a Wonder Bar signal-seeking AM radio, whitewall tires, Positraction limited-slip differential, and the all-important four-speed manual transmission. More than 7000 lusty souls—nearly three-fourths of all Corvette customers for the year—paid the $188.30 asking price for the four-speed. Electric windows and an overly complex power top were of-fered, and the standard equipment list was bolstered by windshield washers, sunvisors, a temperature-controlled radiator fan, and a parking brake warning light.

Mechanically, the 1961 Corvette retained the basic running gear used the year before, but with a few significant changes. One of the most important was the substitution of an aluminum radiator for the previous copper-core unit on all cars. The new radiator not only offered 10 percent more cooling capacity, but also weighed half as much as the 1960 assembly. Side-mount expansion tanks were added as a running change during the year.

Engine choices were basically carry-overs. Chevy's renowned 283-cid small-block V-8 was offered in five

versions—230, 245, 270, 275 and 315 bhp. The last two were fuel injected. Again, the standard gearbox was the familiar manual three-speed, now available with a wider choice of axle ratios. Powerglide automatic and the four-speed manual returned as extras. Powerglide was not listed with the three hottest engine choices and, as mentioned, most buyers opted for the four-speed over the base manual—a good choice, because the four-speed came encased in aluminum for the first

Up front, the '61 'Vette (*right*) sported a fine horizontal-mesh grille and painted headlight bezels. The standard engine (*top left*) was still the 230-bhp, 283-cid V-8 with a four-barrel carb. The interior (*above*) featured a narrower transmission tunnel.

time, effecting a weight saving of 15 pounds.

Inside, the '61 had no major changes, except for a narrower transmission tunnel, which added more needed room in the two-passenger cockpit. Four interior color schemes were available: black, red, fawn, and blue.

Even with the mildest 283 and Powerglide, the 1961 Corvette was a fast little car by any standard. Buff magazine testers recorded 0-60-mph acceleration of just 7.7 seconds for the

Evolution of the 283-Cubic-Inch Small-Block V-8

Bhp @ rpm	Years Offered	Induction	Compression Ratio
230 @ 4800	1958-61	1 4-barrel	9.5:1
245 @ 5000	1958-61	1 4-barrel	9.5:1
250 @ 5000	1958-59	fuel injection	9.5:1
270 @ 6000	1958-61	2 4-barrels	9.5:1
275 @ 5200	1960-61	fuel injection	11.0:1
290 @ 6200	1958-59	fuel injection	10.5:1
315 @ 6200	1960-61	fuel injection	11.0:1

Corvette began using the 327-cid V-8 exclusively in 1962.

powertrain. A fuel-injected/four-speed car knocked another two seconds off that time, making it one of the fastest cars in the history of street racing. Top speed with Powerglide was listed at 109 mph, limited mainly by transmission gearing. The close-ratio four-speed car lacked the long-legged overdrive ratio of most modern five-speed manuals but, even so, many of the fuel-injected and double-four-barrel-carbureted models could see the far side of 130 mph.

Though Corvettes still lacked independent rear suspensions like those of some more expensive European rivals, that didn't seem much of a factor on either street or track. Testers for the major car magazines sang the praises of the 1961 model's handling virtues, and almost no one found any particular vices. For the first time, the Corvette was one of the most roadable cars built anywhere in the world—by contemporary standards, at least. Proof could be found in the running of the grueling Sebring 12 Hours of Endurance for 1961, where a near-stock Corvette finished 11th overall against much more expensive and exotic prototype machinery.

If the 1961 Corvette was good—and it was—the 1962 edition was even better. It offered both more power and a more sophisticated appearance, making it the most desirable of the 1958-62 cars. The biggest news was under the hood. The 283 small block got the traditional hot rod treatment—a bore-and-stroke job that increased cylinder dimensions to 4.00 × 3.25 inches for a

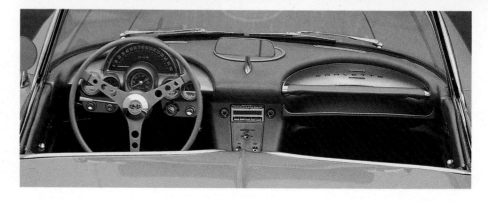

Serial Spans, Production, and Base Prices				
Year	Serial Prefix	Serial Span	Prod. Units	Price
1958	J58S	100001-109168	9168	$3631
1959	J59S	100001-109670	9670	$3875
1960	00867S	100001-110261	10,261	$3872
1961	10867S	100001-110939	10,939	$3934
1962	20867S	100001-114531	14,531	$4038

The four-speed shifter (*top left*) included a lockout to prevent accidental shifts into reverse. Among the instruments, only the clock was in a hard-to-read location. The dash and interior of the '61 Corvette continued virtually unchanged (*left*). The restyled rear end (*above*) apparently found favor with buyers as Corvette production for 1961 set yet another record: 10,939 units built.

Major Specifications 1958 Corvette

Chassis and Body
Frame: Box section steel with five crossmembers
Body: Glass-reinforced plastic, two-seat roadster
Front suspension: Independent, unequal-length wishbones, coil springs, hydraulic shock absorbers, anti-roll bar
Rear suspension: Live axle, longitudinal leaf springs, hydraulic shock absorbers
Wheels: 15″ steel bolt-on
Tires: 6.70 × 15 4-ply

Dimensions
Wheelbase (in.): 102.0
Length (in.): 177.0
Height (in.): 51.0
Width (in.): 73.0
Track front/rear (in.): 57.0/59.0
Ground clearance (in.): 6.0
Weight (lbs): 2912

Engine
Type: Ohv V-8, water-cooled, cast-iron block
Main bearings: 5
Bore × stroke: 3.88 × 3.00
Displacement (ci): 283
Compression ratio: 9.5:1 (10.5:1 with Duntov cam)
Induction system: Ramjet fuel injection
Exhaust system: Split cast-iron manifolds, dual exhaust
Brake horsepower @ rpm: 250 @ 5000
Lbs/ft torque @ rpm: 305 @ 3800
Electrical system: 12-volt Delco-Remy

Drivetrain
Transmission: 4-speed manual (Powerglide optional)
Gear ratios: First—2.2:1
Second—1.66:1
Third—1.3:1
Fourth—1:1
Rear axle type: Hypoid semifloating (positive lock differential optional)
Rear axle ratio: 3.70:1 (4.11:1, 4.56:1, 3.55:1 with Powerglide optional)
Steering: Recirculating ball
Ratio: 17:1
Turns lock-to-lock: 3.7
Turning circle (ft): 38.5
Brakes: 11″ 4-wheel hydraulic, internal expanding drums
Brake lining area (sq. in.): 157

Performance*
0-30 mph (sec): 3.3
0-40 mph (sec): 4.5
0-50 mph (sec): 5.8
0-60 mph (sec): 7.6
0-80 mph (sec): 12.2
Standing-start quarter-mile (sec): 15.7 @ 90 mph
Top speed (mph): Est. 125
Average fuel consumption (mpg): 15-18

* *Sports Cars Illustrated,* December 1957

total displacement of 327 cubic inches. It would form the basis for Corvette muscle through 1965. The emphasis was definitely on power, because even in its most docile form the 327 pumped out a claimed 250 bhp. For true acceleration fanatics, a Rochester fuel injection system took the engine to 360 bhp on the dynamometer—more than enough power to nail you and your passenger to the seats in a banzai run.

What was the secret of the new-found power? In addition to greater bore and stroke and heavier-duty bearings, the top three engines received larger ports and a longer-duration camshaft. The injected 327 used the Duntov solid-lifter cam, as did the top carbureted engine, rated at 340 bhp. The compression ratio for these engines was 11.25:1, while the two lower-output mills had a 10.5:1 ratio. Perhaps the best choices for all-around use were the standard 250-bhp and step-up 300-bhp versions. Both had more than enough power while benefiting from the simplicity and easy maintenance of hydraulic cams and a single four-barrel carburetor. In fact, after 1961, the super-trick but troublesome twin-four-barrel carburetion went out the window altogether, and it was replaced by a single four-barrel Carter. In the 340- and 360-bhp engines, peak power speed was a screaming 6000 rpm, quite high for a pushrod mill, while in the 250- and 300-bhp versions it was 4400 and 5000 rpm respectively. Powerglide automatic was available only with the latter two, and it was treated to a significantly lighter aluminum housing.

The added power made better stopping abilities a virtual necessity. Accordingly, the sintered metallic brake linings that appeared on the Corvette option list brought a notable improvement in fade resistance.

Despite the other aspects of the '62 models that were new, the styling wasn't. The quad-headlight body had been around since 1958 and was beginning to look a bit dated, even though Chevy stylists had by now removed most of the original design's worst excesses. In fact, quite a bit of brightwork disappeared on this final version of the body style, making it the cleanest yet. One obvious alteration was the removal of the chrome outline around the body-side coves. The reverse front fender air scoops lost their triple chrome accent spears in favor of more conservative ribbed aluminum appliqués. And to emphasize the more cohesive look, contrasting color inserts for the coves vanished from the options sheet, so no factory two-tone '62s were made. Other styling elements were similarly updated. The chrome mesh grille introduced the previous year was painted black, as were the backgrounds of the trunk lid medallions. The optional whitewalls were now significantly slimmer than previous ones. The only place where decoration was added was the rocker panels, now adorned with ribbed ano-

Corvette Performance Comparisons 1958-62

Year	Disp.	Bhp	Axle	Seconds: 0-30	0-50	0-60	0-100	Speed: 1/4-mi.	1/4-mi.	Top
1958	283	230	4.11	—	—	9.2	—	17.4	83	103
1958	283	250	3.70	3.3	5.8	7.6	21.4	15.7	90	120
1959	283	250	3.70	—	—	7.8	—	15.7	90	120
1959	283	290*	4.11	3.1	5.1	6.8	15.5	14.9	96	124
1960	283	270	—	—	—	8.4	—	16.1	89	—
1961	283	230	3.70	3.8	—	8.3	—	—	—	—
1961	283	316*	3.70	2.6	4.6	6.0	14.2	15.5	106	Est. 140
1962	327	360*	3.70	2.5	4.5	5.9	13.5	14.5	104	Est. 150

* fuel injection

Though little changed, the design of the Corvette for 1962 was the cleanest yet. Contrasting color inserts for the side coves vanished from the options sheet, so no factory two-tone '62s were built. The big news for '62, however, was under the hood, where the faithful 283 had been bored and stroked to 4.00 × 3.25 inches for a displacement of 327 cid. Horsepower ratings started at 250, but with Rochester fuel injection jumped up to 360.

dized-aluminum moldings.

Whatever the '62 Vette may or may not have been for its styling, it was a star on pavement. The new power and torque of the larger 327 V-8 resulted in ferocious 0-60-mph and quarter-mile acceleration times. In fact, the car magazines routinely reeled off quarters in 15 seconds or less at trap speeds of 100 mph or more. Equipped with the stiffer competition springs, the car was an excellent production-class racer. The Sports Car Club of America's A-Production champion in 1962 was Dr. Dick Thompson, who would go on to greater glories with later versions of the plastic-bodied car. Even with only minor modifications, the Corvette was a serious competitor. Don Yenko took SCCA's B-Production title that same year.

The '62 Corvette marked the end of an era for America's sports car, a changing of the guard. Its design was finalized long before the car actually appeared because Chevy stylists and engineers were already hard at work on the completely reengineered body and suspension ordained for '63. Yet the '62 did introduce the first of the new engines—the versatile 327—and thus bridged the gap between the old and the new. The fiberglass body panels and the X-braced frame both

The 1962 Corvette (*above*) looked almost somber without two-tone paint. Note the narrower whitewalls and the ribbed anodized-aluminum rocker panel moldings. The interior remained the same (*top left*); the engine was enlarged to 327 cid, here in base 250-bhp form (*far left*). The coves (*left*) not only lost their two-toning, but they also lost their chrome outline, and the reverse air scoops were toned down. The grille's chrome mesh (*below*) was painted black for '62.

harked back to the first '53s, yet thanks to Duntov, the car had long since shed its pedestrian origins. The '62 Corvette was faster, handled better, looked neater, and was significantly more modern than any of the earlier models, yet somehow it managed to retain much of the charm of the original roadster concept. As an example of its transitional character, the '62 was the first Corvette with a heater fitted as standard equipment and at last available with factory air conditioning or power brakes as options. It was also the last Corvette to have an external opening trunk lid.

Far more important to its future than the many evolutionary improvements made during 1961-62 was the Corvette's final coming of age as a serious profit-maker. Its maturation happened in 1962, when Chevrolet Division sold 14,531 units for the model year—an increase of about 40 percent over 1961. Chevy had been making a profit on the Corvette since 1958, but only barely. In 1962, the only surviving American sports car was showing a return on investment that even its staunchest proponents had not counted on a few years before. The improving financial condition of the Corvette came as a sizable relief to people like Duntov, Cole, and Mitchell, who had kept the faith in the darkest days and had used all their influence to keep the Corvette in production.

GM's Corvette supporters had reason to be satisfied: The Chevy sports car was obviously enjoying golden years—and better things were just around the corner.

In many ways, the 1962 Corvette was a transitional car that blended the old with the soon-to-be-introduced Sting Ray. More importantly, it saw production of 14,531 units—an increase of about 40 percent and another record—turning it into a serious profit-maker for Chevrolet. Even better days were coming.

CHAPTER SIX

1963-1967: The Golden Age Arrives

The 1961-62 Corvettes had been satisfying and successful conclusions to the styling generation that had begun in 1956—or maybe even 1953. Finally, its time had passed, and the long-rumored, all-new Corvette was on its way. Bill Mitchell had just the name for it, split into two words, but lifted otherwise intact from his svelte racer—*Sting Ray.*

The Sting Ray hit the American sports car market like a thunderclap, reminiscent of the knock-'em-dead debut of the Jaguar E-Type two years previously; comparisons were not slow to materialize. For the first time in its history, the Corvette was a sell-out success—so much so that the St. Louis factory had to hire a second shift, and it still couldn't begin to supply cars rapidly enough. Its inventory, which dealers like to see around 40 days in a good year, went down to a couple of weeks, and customers were waiting up to two months for their orders to be filled—at the full retail invoice price.

The excitement was not merely over an arrestingly styled traditional roadster. For the first time, the roadster had a linemate—a magnificent looking new *gran turismo* with distinctive styling to match its speed and agility. It had come off the Mitchell drawing boards with all the flair that typified his Art and Colour Studio during that time. To say that the Sting Ray was revolutionary would be an overstatement—many components were carried over. But to say that it was an instant hit would be to minimize the record. Within St. Louis' scale of automobile production, it was a block-

buster. Model year production at 21,513 was 50 percent better than for the record-setting year 1962.

Nor was the success to be a passing fad. The whole Sting Ray generation—from 1963 to 1967—has since become modern classics. Within five years after the last one was built, their values had turned around and started increasing on the used car lots. They were among the first postwar collector models to surpass their original list price on the old-car market. They have since become the most desirable Corvettes in the history of the marque—the 1963 split-window coupe, in particular.

The Sting Ray was very much Bill Mitchell's car, and the first one to absolutely rewrite the prevailing Harley Earl design dictums. Mitchell himself considered the car his private preserve—his personal pet project. But much of the Sting Ray's styling background was wrapped up in an earlier design by young Bob McLean—the same McLean who had laid out the original Motorama car 10 years before the Sting Ray debuted. McLean had been working on a Corvette coupe since 1958. It was a purposeful-looking car with peaked fenders, a long nose, and a short, bobbed tail. While the styling had merited GM management approval, the chassis and drivetrains proposed by Zora Arkus-Duntov had been considered too expensive at the time, and the coupe project was cancelled—but not forgotten.

Another contributor to the Sting Ray's styling was the Stingray Special, privately financed by Mitchell with a little help from his friends. It was one

of the "bootleg" projects Mitchell had continued after the AMA performance ban without GM's formal approval, and Duntov helped out by developing its chassis and drivetrain. The Sebring assault of 1957 had taught Duntov much about chassis design. Mitchell had bought the SS mule from that effort, spiriting its chassis away to his Studio X special projects area at the Tech Center in Warren, Michigan. Here he designed the Stingray Special body, while Zora fiddled with its innards. Here Dr. Dick Thompson (the Flying Dentist), one of the SCCA's leading Corvette campaigners, came to behold the result—he said that he would like to drive this new machine in C-Modified competition.

Thompson's showing in the hotly competitive C-Modified class, dominated by European racing cars of noble pedigree, stunned even the loquacious Mitchell. The car walked away with the championship in 1959, and again in 1960. Unfortunately, the rules prevented the car from being revealed as a Corvette, let alone one designed and engineered at "good-citizen" General Motors. A lot of the people who saw the Stingray Special race predicted that it was the next-generation Corvette—not exactly a shot in the dark. Everybody knew of Dick Thompson's relationship with Chevrolet, and they couldn't miss Mitchell and Duntov in the pits. The Stingray's shape made a good impression on the public, and it remained strong impetus for the shape of the production Sting Rays to come.

The planning for what eventually appeared as the 1963 Corvette initially

involved four different projects—three of which were gradually eliminated: the Q-model, a Corvair base, a reskinned 1958 Corvette, and the XP-720. The Q-model was a smaller Corvette with independent rear suspension and both coupe and roadster bodies. Styling was not unlike the Mitchell racing car, and a steel prototype had actually been built before the project was shelved. Corvette's share of the Q-project was only a fraction. Originally, GM contemplated an entire line of large, rear-engine sedans for the 1960 model year.

Using certain Q-model componentry, a rear-engine Corvette was foreseen based on the Corvair power-train—including a flat-six as an alternative to the V-8. It was a technically appealing project, much liked by Duntov. But it was expensive. It, too, progressed to a full-scale model with taut, two-seat open bodywork featuring crisp body sides leading into a beveled nose and tail. The project was dropped in 1960.

Built on the "mule" chassis left over from the 1957
Sebring car, Bill Mitchell's Stingray racer (*top left*)
directly inspired 1963 production styling, particularly
the design of the humped fenders (*above*).
Chevy noted in 1963 that "Careful and final
inspection prepares the new Corvette for
its first meeting with a proud owner."

Improved passenger accommodations (*above*) were among
the goals for the 1963 Corvette. Top engine choice
that year was the fuel-injected 327-cid V-8 (*top
right*), which cranked out 360 horsepower.
Looking mean and purposeful, this '63
Sting Ray (*right*) is powered by the fuelie engine.

Some of the thinking having to do
with making the new Corvette a reskinned 1958 model resulted in the
ducktail styling of the 1961-62 Corvettes. In front, the reskinned car
would have had a low rectangular
grille, surrounded by bulging front
fenders and flanked by quad headlights recessed under jutting "eyelids."
The reskinning was the least inspired
of the unsuccessful programs.

The XP-720 was the one that became the 1963 Corvette. Begun late in
the autumn of 1959, experimental project 720 led directly to the Sting Ray.
Among its goals were improved passenger accommodations, more luggage space, superior combined ride and
handling relative to the 1958 models,
and high performance. Duntov made
sure that the performance goal received the greatest emphasis.

On the XP-720, the chassis was a
ground-up design, with the passengers located far back for optimum
weight distribution. Much of the rea-
soning behind the design was the same
that had guided McLean on the original 'Vette. The center of gravity was
kept low, both for the sake of handling
and ride quality. Ground clearance
would end up at only five inches. The
center of gravity ended up at 16.5 inches above road level, as opposed to
the previous model's 19 inches. The
passengers were located within the
frame, rather than on top of it as they
had been before. The wheelbase was
also trimmed four inches, down to 98.
With driveline components set low
and close to the center, XP-720 was actually a bit tail-heavy, having 53 percent of its weight over the rear wheels.
Compensation for the weight of the

tail would be found in the larger, heavier engines of the future.

The frame was entirely new, and not at all ordinary by Detroit standards. The X-brace was gone, and in its place was a ladder-type design with five cross members for high torsional rigidity. The rigidity was needed, not only because of the potent engines, but because Duntov's fully independent suspension would put lateral stresses on the frame that hadn't yet been considered. At one point, however, the engineers found the frame to be too stiff. It produced a harsh ride that was unacceptable to everyone, and it cost too much—also unacceptable to almost everyone. The eventual production frame was less stiff, but far stronger than it needed to be.

While the accountants had been successful in cutting the costs of the frame, they had no success with Duntov when it came to the rest of the chassis. He wanted independent rear suspension, and he would have it. Don't misjudge the people who buy the cars, Duntov argued. The Corvette needed to be more than a pretty face. It would compete, after all, against the vaunted Jaguar E-Type. Independent rear suspension, Duntov claimed, would help sell 30,000 Corvettes a year. Duntov won.

While Duntov was earnestly seeking an innovative and ultimately producible new chassis, the stylists had only to clean up and to refine the basic Stingray shape that had been around for some three years. The earliest XP-720 mockups looked like nothing more than the racer with a fastback roof. Wind tunnel testing helped to refine the shape, as did more practical matters like interior space, windshield curvatures, and tooling limitations.

Both body styles were tested extensively in production-ready form at the Cal Tech wind tunnel, and body engineers spent a great deal of effort on the inner structure. Compared to the 1962 Corvette, the Sting Ray had nearly twice as much steel support built into its central body structure. The extra

steel was balanced by a reduction in the quantity of fiberglass, so the finished product actually weighed a bit less than the older roadster. Despite the tighter wheelbase, interior room was as good as before and, thanks to the reinforcing steel girder, the cockpit was stronger and safer.

The Sting Ray was far more than just a beautiful body. Certainly the engines, transmissions, and axle ratios were carryovers from 1962, and from the door jambs back, the convertible version was quite similar in appearance to the 1961-62 models. But in nearly every other respect, the '63s were entirely new Corvettes. The most dramatic evidence was the first

While the Sting Ray coupe created quite a sensation in 1963, the convertible (*below*) looked almost as sleek; it outsold the coupe by a mere 325 units. Clay scale models (*above*) underwent aerodynamic testing in Cal Tech's wind tunnel.

production Corvette coupe—a futuristic fastback that attracted even larger crowds than the roadster. It had one distinctive styling feature—a split rear window.

McLean's original design called for a one-piece backlight, and Mitchell came up with the backbone split-window styling. The rear window configuration was not a unanimous decision. Duntov, for one, was opposed because it cluttered up the view to the rear. But purely practical arguments would not suffice for Mitchell, who insisted, "If you take that off, you might as well forget the whole thing." His goal was a flowing spine from front to rear, beginning as a rise in the center of the hood (necessary to clear the plenum chamber on engines with fuel injection) and continuing as a crease line over the roof, through the window, and down the deck. Mitchell was the boss, so he got his way, and most Corvette fans today would vote with him on aesthetics. The split-window Sting Ray coupe remains one of the most stunning automobiles of all time. It certainly met one of Mitchell's prime criteria: It wouldn't be mistaken for anything else.

But the split backlight took a beating in the press. *Road & Track* disliked "that silly bar," and *Car and Driver* agreed, saying the "central window partition ruins our rear view." Sometimes the motoring press has a difficult time seeing the styling forest for the trees, but many customers did. They loved the newest Corvette because it was a true go-fast machine that looked supersonic even just parked. Ultimately, Mitchell relented. He had his year of production, thus creating a car for future collectors. However, many split-window coupes were lost to customizers, some of whom fitted one-piece Plexiglas windows as a substitute. Shortly after the change had been made for the production '64 model, a one-piece glass backlight window be-

came available as a replacement item through Chevy dealers. Because of it, many more '63 Corvettes lost their value as collectibles.

The remainder of Mitchell's design was equally stunning. Quad headlamps were retained, but now they were hidden, mounted in pivoting sections that fit flush with and matched the front-end contours. The Corvette was the first car with hidden lights since the 1942 DeSoto. Another DeSoto-type element from the 1955-56 models was the gullwing dash styling. "The dual cockpit was widely criticized at the time," one Corvette designer remembers, "but it was a very fresh approach to two-passenger styling." Another interesting design element was an attractive dip in the beltline at the trailing upper edge of the door, and the coupe's doors were cut into the roof—a feature widely accepted at Ford. The interior received a few updates, such as cowl-top ventilation and an improved heater. Luggage space was also improved, though the Sting Ray was criticized for lack of an external trunk lid. The only access to

the storage area was through the passenger compartment. The spare tire was carried in a sealed fiberglass housing at the rear, hinged to drop to the ground when released. Styling critics chided the use of dummy vents in the hood and on the coupe's rear pillars. At one time, they had been intended to be functional, but the costs were too high. The nonfunctional vents wouldn't last long.

Besides the roadster and the coupe, Chevrolet also toyed with a four-place version of the Sting Ray design. The idea was suggested by Ed Cole, who felt that a back-seat model would give the Corvette broader market coverage, enabling it to compete directly with a number of upscale European 2+2s while appealing to those 'Vette fans who occasionally needed to carry more than one passenger. The plan got as far as a full-size mockup, photographed in the Design Staff auditorium in 1962 alongside a contemporary Ford Thunderbird—its main domestic rival. Based on the already approved split-window coupe, the proposed four-seater had some 10 extra

The 1963 coupe (*top left*) was Corvette's first, but in 1962 Chevy also contemplated a four-seater on a stretched wheelbase (*bottom left*). It was quickly axed because of its more ungainly proportions. The Sting Ray coupe's divided backlight (*above*) was controversial, but makes this a highly sought-after collectible car in today's marketplace.

inches grafted in between the wheel centers, plus a higher roofline to provide some semblance of rear seat headroom, revised rear fender contours, and a pair of fully engineered back seats with fold-down backrests. Unhappily, the resulting proportions were rather ungainly, which probably convinced some executives that the 2+2 might dilute the styling impact of the two-seat models. Chevy abandoned the idea, though it was basically a good one. As a matter of fact, Jaguar thought of the same thing, and a few years later released a stretched-wheelbase version of its slinky two-seat E-Type coupe with similarly awkward lines.

Though not as obvious as the styling, the new chassis was just as important to the Sting Ray's success. The solid rear axle of old was exchanged for the first independent rear suspension in Corvette history. It consisted of a frame-mounted differential joined to each wheel by halfshafts, with U-joints at either end. The entire assembly was considerably lighter than the old solid axle and brought about a significant reduction in unsprung weight. The differential was now mounted by rubber-cushioned struts, which helped to reduce ride harshness while improving tire adhesion, especially over rougher roads. A single transverse leaf spring was bolted to the rear of the differential case. Attached to either side of the case was a control arm extending laterally to the hub carriers and slightly forward. A pair of trailing radius rods was fitted behind. Twin coil springs had been considered at one point, but they took up too much space. The halfshafts acted like upper control arms in the design, with the lower arms controlling vertical wheel motion. The trailing rods took care of fore and aft wheel motion while transferring braking torque to the frame. The shock absorbers were the conventional twin-tube type.

Front suspension geometry was much as before, with unequal-length upper and lower arms and coil springs concentric with the tubular shocks. An anti-roll bar was standard. Steering was conventional recirculating ball with an overall ratio of 19.6:1. However, it could be changed easily to a much quicker 17.1:1 by disconnecting the tie rods and moving them to secondary mounting holes in the steering

The Sting Ray's twin-cowl cockpit was new and roomier
(*top left*). The independent rear suspension (*center
left*) featured a transverse leaf spring. The
convertible (*bottom left*) was still available with a
removable hardtop. Rear end styling resembled the '62
(*above*); front sported hidden headlights (*top*).

"ITS A 63" proclaims the license plate. And indeed it is (*bottom right*). With a four-inch-shorter wheelbase the new Corvette was more maneuverable, but by altering the weight distribution toward the rear the ride did not suffer and the steering lightened up. The 327-cid V-8 (*top right*) was offered in carbureted form with 250, 300, or 340 horsepower.

arm. Bolted to the frame rail at one end and to the relay rod at the other was a steering damper (essentially a shock absorber) that helped soak up bumps before they reached the steering wheel. Power assist was optional and came with the faster ratio.

Maneuverability of the '63 Corvette was improved by the shorter wheelbase. Although a short wheelbase would ordinarily imply a choppier ride, the altered weight distribution partly compensated. Less weight on the front wheels also meant easier steering, and power steering wasn't ordered often. The additional 80 pounds over the rear wheels also improved traction and gave the Sting Ray a noticeable rear end squat during hard acceleration.

Stopping power also improved. The four-wheel drum brakes had 11-inch-diameter drums, just as before. But the linings were wider. Sintered metallic linings, segmented for cooling, were again optional. Optional finned drums were made of aluminum rather than cast iron, improving cooling and reducing unsprung weight. With that combination, brake fade from excessive heat was reduced considerably. Power assist was available with both standard and high-performance brake packages. Availability of power assist for both brakes and steering was a first for Corvette. Also new was an alternator instead of a generator. Other such evolutionary changes included positive crankcase ventilation, a smaller flywheel, and an aluminum clutch housing.

The drivelines carried over from 1962 featured a choice of four engines, three transmissions, and six axle ratios. The 327-cid V-8 was offered in carbureted form with 250, 300, or 340 brake horsepower. The base and step-up versions used hydraulic lifters, a mild cam, a forged-steel crankshaft, 10.5:1 compression, a single-point distributor, and dual exhausts. The 300 produced its extra power with a larger

four-barrel carburetor (Carter AFB instead of the 250's Carter WCFB), larger intake valves, and a bigger exhaust manifold. By opting for fuel injection, the buyer paid $430.40 to get 360 horsepower. As base prices were $4252 for the coupe and $4037 for the convertible, injection was looking quite expensive. A three-speed manual transmission was again standard, but neither that nor the optional Powerglide automatic was very popular. The preferred setup was the Borg-Warner four-speed. A wide-ratio box was available with the base or 300-bhp engines, and close-ratio gearing was listed for the top two engines. The standard axle ratio was 3.36:1 with the three-speed or Powerglide. The four-speeds came with a 3.70:1 final drive, with 3.08, 3.55, 4.11, and 4.56:1 available. The latter was quite rare in production.

The Sting Ray's specifications were those of a well-developed, refined sports car. It had all the right stuff, and it proved a resounding success on the show room floors, on the streets, among the automotive press, and on race tracks. *Road & Track* magazine had been appreciative of past Corvettes, especially from the standpoint of cost. It stated in 1960 that the Corvette was "unmatched for performance per dollar...." But its review of the Sting Ray was nearly ecstatic. A few excerpts: "In a word, the new Sting Ray sticks [with] great gripping gobs of traction ...The S-bend was even more fun: every time through it we discovered we could have gone a little faster. We never did find the limit...As a purely sporting car, the new Corvette will know few peers on road or track...it ought to be nearly unbeatable."

Road & Track's verdict was unanimously echoed by the other magazines. In the May 1963 issue of *Motor Trend*, Jim Wright said: "It's far in advance, both in ride and handling, of anything now being built in the United

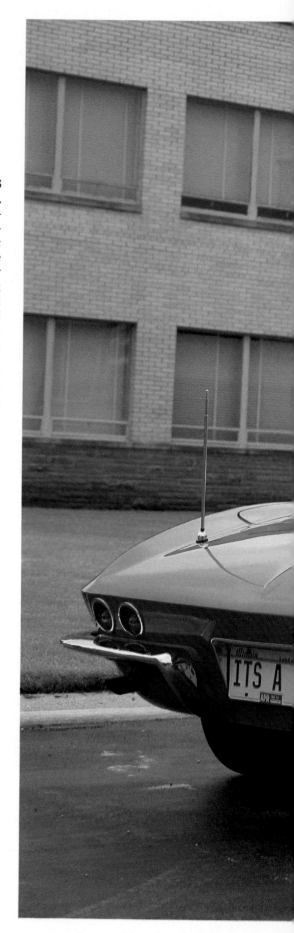

The American public loved the newest Corvette (*left*) because it was a true go-fast machine that looked supersonic even when parked. It was the first car with hidden headlights since the 1942 DeSoto. About the only points of complaint were the use of dummy vents in the hood and on the coupe's rear pillars. The gas filler cap (*below*) wore crossed racing flags, appropriate for such a fast machine.

States. It's completely comfortable without being mushy and it takes a large chuckhole to induce any degree of harshness into the ride. Sudden dips, when taken at speed, don't produce any unpleasant oscillations, and the front and rear suspension is very hard to bottom. There's very little pitch noticeable in the ride, even though the 'Vette is built on a fairly short wheelbase. At high cruising speeds—and even at maximum speeds—nothing but an all-out competition car will equal it in stability. We drove it under some pretty windy conditions and didn't notice any adverse effects from crosswind loading. We thought the old model corners darn well, but there's no comparing it to this new one. It does take a little different technique, but once the driver gets into it, it's beautiful."

Because of its 49/51 percent front/rear weight distribution, the Sting Ray handled in the classic mode—it oversteered. The same was true of the Corvette's stablemate, the Corvair—a characteristic that would eventually take GM to court. The minority who knew enough about driving to enjoy the oversteer was enthusiastic. "The ride and handling are great," said *Sports Car Graphic*. "We won't elaborate on how great: you've got to drive one to believe it." *Car and Driver* said that the Corvette was "now second to no other production sports car in roadholding and is still the most powerful."

The most consistent component of the wondrous new Corvette was its motive power—the array of 327-cubic-inch V-8s that ranged from 250 bhp to 360 bhp, just as they had been the year before. In the new Sting Ray package, though, the engines seemed transformed. While acceleration times were virtually identical, the Sting Ray wasted less wheel spin than the previous live-axle Corvette, and that gave

the '63s the edge. With his fuelie and a 3.7:1 axle ratio, Jim Wright did 0-30/45/60 mph in 2.9/4.2/5.8 seconds and the standing quarter-mile in 14.5 seconds at 102 mph. "A course longer than the Riverside Raceway backstretch would've produced something very close to the Sting Ray's theoretical top speed of 140-142 mph," Wright concluded, "because the engine was still winding when we had to back off."

Perhaps all the praise could be expected from magazines that based their income on GM advertising. The British magazine *The Motor*, perhaps harder to please but certainly not biased, stated that the Corvette wasn't as "refined" as it could be. *Autocar* noticed with apparent amazement that the 'Vette didn't use any oil during its test period.

Most American criticism concerned either the coupe's split rear window or the inaccessibility of the luggage compartment. Corvette creature comforts met with approval. The day and age of Plexiglas side curtains, handleless doors, and wheezing heaters that didn't deposit more than a warm sneeze on the inside leg had been forgotten by the contemporary sports car. Led by the Sunbeam Alpine, even the

Major Specifications
1963 Corvette Sting Ray

Chassis and Body
Frame: Box section steel, ladder-type with five cross members
Body: Glass-reinforced plastic, two-seat coupe and roadster
Front suspension: Independent, unequal-length A-arms, coil springs,
      tubular hydraulic shock absorbers, anti-sway bar
Rear suspension: Independent, fixed differential, transverse leaf spring,
      lateral struts, U-jointed axle shafts, radius rods, hydraulic
      tubular shock absorbers
Wheels: 15" steel bolt-on
Tires: 6.70 × 15 4-ply

Dimensions
Wheelbase (in.): 98.0
Length (in.): 175.3
Height (in.): 49.8
Width (in.): 69.6
Track front/rear (in.): 56.3/57.0
Ground clearance (in.): 5.0
Weight (lbs): 3150

Engine
Type: Ohv V-8, water-cooled, cast-iron block
Main bearings: 5
Bore × stroke: 4.00 × 3.25
Displacement (ci): 327
Compression ratio: 11.25:1
Induction system: Ramjet fuel injection
Exhaust system: Split cast-iron manifolds, dual exhaust
Brake horsepower @ rpm: 360 @ 6000
Lbs/ft torque @ rpm: 352 @ 4000
Electrical system: 12-volt Delco-Remy

Drivetrain
Transmission: Close-ratio 4-speed manual, floor shift
Gear ratios: First—2.2:1
        Second—1.64:1
        Third—1.3:1
        Fourth—1:1
Rear axle type: Hypoid semifloating, positive lock differential
Rear axle ratio: 3.70:1
Steering: Recirculating ball
Ratio: 17:1
Turns lock-to-lock: 3.4
Turning circle (ft): 35
Brakes: 4-wheel hydraulic drums, sintered metallic linings, self-adjusting,
      cast-iron, 11" diameter
Brake lining area (sq. in.): 135

Performance*
0-30 mph (sec): 2.9
0-45 mph (sec): 4.2
0-60 mph (sec): 5.8
Standing-start quarter-mile (sec): 14.2 @ 105 mph

* *Motor Trend*, May 1963

two-seaters from England had begun to gain roll-up windows and two-minute tops. The Corvette was a notch above even the best imported sports car standards, with contoured bucket seats, a telescoping steering wheel, functional instrumentation, and heating and ventilation systems that were up to North American conditions. True, the buckets were too low for some, but Duntov wanted them that way in pursuit of the car's low center of gravity. Also, the steering column adjustment required a little wrench work under the hood. But overall the Corvette was very good.

Competition options for the coupe were extensive, suggesting GM's intent that it become a GT-class and SCCA contender. Options included heavy-duty springs and shocks, stiffer anti-sway bar, metallic brake linings, Al-Fin aluminum brake drums, cast-aluminum knock-off wheels, dual master cylinder, and a 36.5-gallon fuel tank. Together, they made up the Z06 special performance equipment package, offered only on the coupe early in the model year. Full leather upholstery was available, too.

Four coupes equipped with the Z06 package (minus the knock-off wheels, which weren't ready yet) made their racing debut at the Los Angeles *Times* Three-Hour Invitational Race at Riverside on October 13, 1962. At their helms were Dave MacDonald, Bob Bondurant, Jerry Grant, and Doug Hooper. The Three-Hour was also the debut of Carroll Shelby's Ford-powered Cobra. Though the Cobra would go on to savage the Corvette later, the Sting Ray was well up to the challenge of the Anglo-American hybrid at the time. Three of the Corvettes failed to finish, but the fourth took the checkered flag. Hooper drove the winner, a car owned by Mickey Thompson, who was reported to say, "I don't think it's ever been done before...a new production car winning the first time out!" Sting Rays went on to other victories, but the Cobras would dominate production-class racing in the Sixties. However, the Corvette's street manners were now so good that it didn't need a racing image to promote sales. Of course, Duntov still held out hopes for the creation of a full competition version, which led to the awesome Grand Sport.

After complaints from the motoring press about the
divided rear window—*Road & Track* called it "that
silly bar"—Bill Mitchell relented and designed
in a one-piece backlight for 1964 (*top*). Three
important early Corvette racers (*above left*):
Stingray (foreground), SR-2, and the Grand Sport.
Crossed flags (*above right*) adorned the front fenders.

Fuel consumption for the '63s with their 327 engines was remarkably good considering their performance. The fuel injection units constantly corrected the gas-air mixture for humidity, altitude, and temperature. *Motor Trend* recorded better than 18 miles per gallon on the highway at legal speed limits. The rest of the time the drivers kept their accelerator feet down, but even around town they did not average less than 13.6 mpg. Overall, the test Sting Ray averaged 14.1 mpg—all that and 360 horsepower.

The base price of a 1963 split-window Sting Ray was about $4400, and with its top-of-the-line injection engine and a few other goodies, the price was about $5300. Factored for inflation, that's $14,000-15,000 in today's dollars. Another way to look at the first Sting Ray's value is to consider the cost of a prime-condition coupe today—about the same price as a brand-new Corvette.

When the last 1963 model left the St. Louis line, production totaled 21,513—split almost evenly between coupes and convertibles. More than half of the roadsters were ordered with the optional lift-off hardtop. But the coupe seemed to find its level the following year, and never again in this generation of Corvettes did it sell so well. Not until the 1969 model, when the coupe and convertible became relatively indistinguishable, did the closed car sell better than the open one.

Popular options on the 1963 cars were power brakes (15 percent) and power steering (12 percent). A mere 278 buyers specified air conditioning, which cost $421, and leather upholstery (only $81) was ordered on just 400-odd cars. The beautiful cast-aluminum knock-off wheels, manufactured for Chevy by Kelsey-Hayes, cost $323 a set. Few were sold. On the other hand, almost 18,000 Sting Rays were ordered with four-speed manual transmission—better than four out of five.

In 1963 the Corvette reached the pinnacle of its Golden Age. It would remain at that level through the passing years—the ultimate car for generations of enthusiasts, many of them not yet born when the car was new. It would be the only all-new Corvette between the original Motorama car of 1953 and the most recent generation introduced for the 1984 model year.

Chevy took pride in its "twin-cowl" dashboard (*right*), which featured full instrumentation. *Stingray* was one word on Bill Mitchell's racer, but production cars spelled it out in two words (*above*). Mildest engine for 1963-65 was the 250-bhp V-8 (*top*).

The outward styling of the Sting Ray generation would change, but the chassis would live on, thanks to the sophistication and foresight of its designers, and especially Zora Arkus-Duntov.

With Corvette sales increasing some 50 percent in a single year, logic dictated that changes for the follow-up 1964 edition would be only evolutionary in nature. As noted, Bill Mitchell gave in to pressure, and the coupe's split rear window became one piece. The two fake air intakes on the hood, although inspired by the genuine article on Mitchell's Stingray race car, were eliminated. The indentations remained. The simulated air exhaust vents on the coupe's rear pillars became functional, but only on the driver's side. The rocker panel trim lost some of its ribs, and the areas between the ribs were painted black. Wheel covers were simplified, and the fuel filler door gained concentric circles around its crossed-flags insignia. In the cockpit, the color-keyed steering wheel was replaced by one with a simulated walnut rim. Complaints about glare from the instrument bezels were acknowledged, and they were painted flat black for 1964.

An improved ride was among Duntov's original goals for the Sting Ray, and most reviewers judged him successful. But as the cars rolled on the miles, shock absorbers weakened, and owners began complaining about a deterioration in ride quality. Chevrolet attacked the problem with a few suspension refinements. The front coil springs were changed from constant-

rate to progressive or variable-rate and were wound more tightly at the top. The leaf thickness in the rear transverse spring was varied from within. The idea was that small bumps would affect only the low-rate areas of the springs, while larger bumps would affect the high-rate areas. The result was to provide a softer ride without sacrificing handling. Shock absorbers were also redesigned toward the same end. When subjected to frequent oscillations under near-full vertical wheel travel, such as on very rough roads, the standard '63 shocks tended to overheat. That caused the hydraulic fluid to cavitate, or bubble, losing effectiveness. The 1964 Corvette arrived with a new standard shock. Within the fluid reservoir was a small bag of freon gas that absorbed heat,

preventing the fluid from bubbling.

The European press had marked down the '63 model because of its relatively high interior noise. Accordingly, Chevy added more insulation and revised body and transmission mounts. It also gave the car a new shift lever boot and additional bushings to quiet the shift linkage. The result was a much more livable car for regular or long-distance transportation.

For 1964, the Sting Ray was offered with a choice of four different 327 V-8s, four different transmissions, and six axle ratios. The two least powerful engines were still rated at 250 and 300 bhp, both on 10.5:1 compression. The two high-performance mills received a few noteworthy improvements. The 340-bhp solid-lifter unit was massaged with a high-lift, long-duration cam-

shaft to produce 365 bhp. The engine used a Holley four-barrel carburetor rather than the base engine's Carter carb. The Holley could be more easily tailored to specific needs than the Carter because a large assortment of performance pieces were available for it. The 360-bhp injected unit also gained another 15 horsepower, increasing to 375 bhp. But it cost a whopping $538—a sum that fewer buyers were willing to spend. In the future, the route to 'Vette power would be through the time-honored expedient of adding more cubic inches—not injection.

If the magazine testers liked the first Sting Ray, they were thrilled with the '64. *Motor Trend's* report of September 1963 covered a fuel-injected coupe with a four-speed, 4.11:1 rear axle,

knock-off wheels, sintered metallic brakes, and Positraction. These options along with AM/FM and tinted windows pushed the $4394 base price to $6367. *MT's* test Corvette ran the quarter-mile in 14.2 seconds at 100 mph, and it notched a 0-60-mph time of just 5.6 seconds. "Acceleration in all speed ranges was, to say the least, fierce—of the 'smash-you-into-your-seat' variety. The engine proved willing, and pulled strongly right up to

6700 rpm and beyond in every gear."

Though transmission options remained ostensibly the same for '64, the two Borg-Warner T10s were replaced by four-speed units built at GM's Muncie, Indiana, transmission facility. The move was due to the wide use of the transmissions in other model lines, making their installation in the Corvette easier and less expensive. The Muncie gearbox—originally a Chevy design—featured an aluminum case

and had stronger synchronizers and wider ratios for better durability and driveability. The wide-ratio box was available only with the 250- and 300-bhp powerplants, and the gears set at 2.56, 1.91, 1.40, and 1:1. The close-ratio version for the more potent mills had spacings of 2.20, 1.64, 1.28, and 1:1. Like the Borg-Warner units, the new four-speed also had a reverse lockout trigger, but with a thicker shifter.

Changes to the 1964 Corvette Sting Ray were evolutionary
in nature and biased toward cleaning up the design a
bit. The backlight became one piece, the two fake
air intakes on the hood were eliminated, the simulated
air exhaust vents on the coupe's rear pillars became
functional (driver's side only), the rocker panel trim
lost some of its ribs, the wheel covers were simplified,
and the fuel filler door gained concentric circles.

Positraction was still a bargain option in 1964 at only $43.05, and more than 80 percent of production had it. The clutch-type differential was designed to send engine torque to the tire with greater traction, as opposed to a standard open differential that transfers power to the tire with lesser traction. The Positraction configuration worked quite well for getting good acceleration off the line and for getting out of mud or snow. But on ice or really hard-packed snow, the torque transfer from one tire to the other caused the rear end to fishtail, somewhat unnerving in such a powerful automobile. Maintaining control on slippery surfaces required a deft foot.

A much costlier option was the J56 sintered metallic brake package. Priced at $629.50, it included not only the high-performance linings but also the brakes that had been offered previously in the Z06 option. The J56 was really a competition option, and while not as easily modulated as the disc brakes yet to come, it certainly offered fade-free stopping power. The system was designed for harsh conditions, and while Duntov was busy looking at discs, he felt nothing else produced at the time was as good as J56 drums. Magazine testers agreed. *Car Life,* for example, noted: "The harder these brakes have to work, the better they are." But discs were coming into vogue at the time and, once Duntov found a set he liked, the Corvette would have them.

The Sting Ray was cleaned and muscled up for 1965. The subtle styling alterations were confined to a smoothed-out hood that eliminated the indentations, a trio of functioning vertical exhaust vents in the front fenders that replaced the sculptured horizontal speedlines, restyled rocker panel moldings, and detail interior trim shuffling.

The model year had two big mechanical surprises. One was the advent of four-wheel disc brakes as an option, accompanied by special wheel covers. The brakes were a four-piston design with two-piece calipers and cooling fins for the rotors. The dual master cylinder had one fluid reservoir serving the front brake lines and another for the rear lines. The pads were in constant contact with the rotors even when the brakes were not applied, though they caused such little

drag that fuel economy was not hurt. The light touching helped to keep the rotors clean while not adversely affecting pad life, which was, in fact, quite long. Pads were expected to last for 57,000 miles for the front brakes, which took most of the force in all-out stops, and about twice that distance for the rears. Total swept area for the new system was 461 square inches, a notable advance on the 328 square inches for the previous all-drum brakes. Road testers were amazed at the discs. Said *Sports Car Graphic* in October 1964: "After experience with the drum-sintered-lining setup—a previous HD option—we found this brake a distinct pleasure to operate, especially as the stopping potential is even greater. Repeated stops from 100 mph pro-

The 1965 Sting Ray (*top right*) sported vertical front
fender slots, revised rocker panel trim, optional four-
wheel disc brakes, and a new 396-cid, 425-bhp V-8.
Not content with that, a 427-cid Turbo Jet V-8
bowed in the 1966 Corvette (*above*), along with an
egg-crate grille, revised rocker moldings, and
the elimination of the B-pillar vents.

duced no deterioration in braking efficiency and over 20-foot decels could be made with hands off the wheel." The old drum brakes were still available for '65 as a $64.50 credit option, but only 316 of the 23,562 Corvettes built that year went without the full disc setup.

The Sting Ray hardly lacked for horsepower, but it seemed that a few customers were always craving for as much as they could get. Chevrolet obliged them at mid model year with a new optional V-8—the big-block Mark IV. The husky powerplant originated

in early 1963 with the so-called "mystery" 427 racing engine that showed up for the Daytona 500. It was notable for its "porcupine" valve-gear, an idea of engine designer Robert P. Benzinger. The Porcupine nickname referred to the way that the pushrods

Opposite page: Views of the '66 Corvette cockpit, gas filler cap, crossed-flags hood insignia, and the base 327-cid, 300-bhp V-8. The '66 Sting Ray Roadster (*below*) listed at $4084 and weighed in at 3005 pounds; 17,762 were built.

poked through little openings at the oddest angles, the result of working "backward" by starting with the ports and manifolds rather than the combustion chambers. Intake valves were set at an angle of 26 degrees to the cylinder axis, and exhaust valves were tilted 17 degrees from the same axis. That wasn't all, for both intake and exhaust valve stems were also tilted in side view, one forward and the other backward, by nine degrees. The tilting valve stems lined up with the pushrods to avoid setting up any rotation in the rocker arms. This basic cylinder-head configuration was then tested, fiddled with, honed, and polished until it provided optimal breathing—then it was frozen, and all other components were designed around it.

The 396-cid V-8 was just one of the four members of the Porcupine family, officially called Mark IV and marketed as the Turbo Jet. The four included two high-performance car engines of 396 cubic inches, a 427, and a heavy-duty marine version of the 427. The 396 was scheduled to replace the 409 in all of its applications, even though the larger engine was still young. In fact, the 409 was scrapped after only five years in production. Aside from its basic design limitations, the type W 409 had been tooled for relatively low production volume. To meet future demands, Chevy's Tonawanda, New York, plant would have to be retooled anyway. Semon E. "Bunkie" Knudsen, then division general manager, decided that only the most modern engine could justify such a major tooling reinvestment, so the Porcupine was selected. No thought was given to carrying over anything from the type W to the Mark IV. Production of the Mark IVs began in mid-1965.

An all-new block was chosen, with 4.84-inch spacing between bore centers, a bore of 4.094 inches, and a stroke of 3.75 inches. The 409 block had a deck angled at 33 degrees from horizontal to allow a wedge-shaped combustion chamber to be created with flat-faced heads. By contrast, the Mark IV block had the usual deck angle of 45 degrees to the cylinder axis. Main bearings were 2.75 inches in diameter, a quarter-inch larger than those in the type W. Main-bearing width was also increased, adding two full inches to the cap-clamping surface. The forged-steel crankshaft was cross-drilled to

The car being painted (*this page*) in the Corvette St. Louis plant in 1965 or 1966 carries the special hood used with the big-block V-8. The 396-cid Turbo Jet V-8 (*opposite page*) became available in 1965. It was part of the "Porcupine" family of engines officially titled Mark IV. With a bore of 4.094 inches and a stroke of 3.75 inches it thumped out 425 horses.

deliver oil to the rod bearings through a full 360 degrees of rotation (a feature missing in the type W) and crankpin journals were kept at a 2.20-inch diameter.

With hydraulic lifters, four-barrel carburetors, and 10.25:1 compression, the 396 Mark IV was initially offered in two states of tune—325 and 360 brake horsepower. For the Corvette, however, the big block came with 11:1 compression and belted out 425 bhp, aided by impact-extruded alloy pistons with chrome rings, solid lifters, bigger carburetors with double-snorkel air cleaner, and an oversized sump.

Though in short supply, the 425-bhp 396-cid V-8 was hardly short on performance. Geared at a moderate 3.7:1, it would produce standing-quarter-mile times of around 14 seconds, at which point the car would be hitting 102-104 mph. With enough space to allow the 'Vette to go to its limit in high gear, the same drag racer would show a top speed of nearly 140 mph. Higher or lower axle ratios would produce, respectively, greater emphasis on acceleration or top speed. A 160-mph production 396 was not inconceivable.

To handle such brute force, the Mark IV option included stiff front

Although the interior of the '66 Corvette (*above*) changed little, the badging (*top right*) announced the arrival of the new 427-cid Turbo Jet engine. It was rated at the same 425 bhp as the 396, but it cranked out an extra 50 lbs/ft of torque—365 at 3600 rpm. Note the special hood (*right*).

springs and sway bar, a special rear sway bar, a very heavy clutch, and a larger radiator and fan. To provide instant recognition on those occasions when the monster was not in motion, the car was fitted with an aggressive-looking hood bulge and (as an option) side-mounted exhaust pipes. Though the big block weighed over 650 pounds, the Sting Ray's weight distribution in this guise was a near-perfect 51/49 percent front/rear—a tribute to the foresight of its chassis planners back in the early Sixties.

General Motors management had decreed that no car line smaller than intermediate should receive an engine larger than 400 cubic inches. Since the 396 fell within the limit, it replaced the 365-bhp version of the small-block V-8 on the 1965 engine lineup. But like most rules, the engine limit one was broken by competitive impulses emanating from Ford in Dearborn. Ford had no car like the Corvette, but it did have one very impressive 427-cid V-8 engine, and a man named Carroll Shel-

by was installing it into a two-seater named Cobra. Chevrolet would need a 427, too. It duly materialized in 1966.

Chevy's 427 was the 396 bored out to 4.25 inches. It came in two states of tune for the Corvette: At 390 bhp it had a 10.25:1 compression ratio. The 425-bhp version had 11:1 compression, larger intake valves, bigger Holley four-barrel carburetor on an aluminum manifold, mechanical lifters, and four- instead of two-hole main bearing caps. Ostensibly, the 427 had no more horsepower than the 396, but it offered 50 extra lbs/ft of torque—365 at 3600 rpm. Besides, the 427's true horsepower rating is the subject of debate, but 450 bhp would not be too wild a guess. Standard with all 427s were the Muncie close-ratio four-speed manual gearbox and Positraction limited-slip differential.

Performance was incredible, whatever the choice of axle ratios. *Car and Driver* did 0-60 mph in 5.4 seconds and the standing quarter-mile in 12.8 seconds at 112 mph—with the modest

Who cares if there wasn't a decklid on the '66 Sting Ray (*right*)? After all, it's what's under that bulged hood that counts, in this case the Mark IV 427 engine. Depending on gearing, it could rocket from 0-60 mph in five seconds and top 140 mph.

3.36:1 ratio. *Sports Car Graphic* managed 0-60 in a nearly unbelievable 4.8 seconds, 0-100 mph in 11.2 seconds, and a flat-out maximum of 140 mph—with a 4.11:1 ratio.

Only one thing could touch a 427 Corvette, and stay ahead of it—Carroll Shelby's 427 Cobra. Chevrolet has never quite lived down its embarrassment over being beaten by the Ford, yet the Cobra was a near-competition car while the Chevy was a street-comfortable *gran turismo*. Who could quibble over *C/D's* summation of the 427 Sting Ray: "It's the power more than the engine that overwhelms every other sensation. There's power literally everywhere, great gobs of steam-locomotive, earth-moving torque."

In 1966, the 327s were reduced from five versions to two—the 300-bhp and 350-bhp units, still the best all-around engines. Both required premium fuel, with compression ratios well over 10:1, and both delivered impressive performance, if not the rocket-like take-offs of the 427. Either engine was available with Powerglide, a three-speed, or a four-speed gearbox with both close and wide ratios.

Appearance changes were minor for 1966. The roof-mounted extractor vents on the coupe had proven inefficient, so they were eliminated. Both models had egg-crate grille inserts instead of horizontal bars. Since the 1967 models were supposed to have been all new, the plan called for leaving

alone the current styling.

But the '67 Corvette turned out to be another one in the 1963-67 format. The brand-new car was found to have some very undesirable aero figures, and Duntov demanded more time in the wind tunnel before it went into production. The episode proved that even in the Sixties big car companies bowed to the demands of a rare few gifted individuals.

At any rate, the 1967 Corvette was refined to the limit, and it was the best of the five-year string of Sting Rays. Very possibly, it was the best Corvette, car for car, ever built. *Road & Track* expounded about styling: "...it finally looks the way we thought it should have in the first place. All the funny business—the fake vents, extraneous emblems and simulated-something-or-other wheel covers—is gone, and though some consider the basic shape overstyled, it looks more like a finished product now." Buy one quick, *R&T* might have added, before it changes. Five smaller front fender vents replaced the three on the '66. Less distracting flat-black and aluminum rocker panel moldings gave the '67 a lower, less chunky appearance. New and thus unique was a single backup light, mounted above the license plate. Slotted six-inch Rally wheels replaced the ornate, old-fashioned wheel covers, and were supplied with chrome beauty rings and lug nuts concealed behind small chrome caps. Alas, the

An option on the '66 Corvette was the side-mounted exhaust system (*below*) and, of course, the bulged hood (*above*), shown in closer detail here. The 1967 Corvette (*top and bottom right*) is considered by many to be the best—and most refined—of the five-year string of Sting Rays.

cast-aluminum wheels were no longer on the option list.

On the inside, upholstery patterns changed slightly, and the handbrake lever was moved from beneath the dash to between the seats. The convertible's optional hardtop was offered with a faddish black vinyl topping, not that many buyers wanted such a thing.

The power lineup changed hardly at all. The two small-block engines continued as before. The basic 427 big block—still rated at 390 bhp—sat under a redesigned hood scoop. But now the two upper-end 427s developed 400 and 435 bhp, each of them with triple two-barrels. They were separated by their respective compression ratios (10.25 and 11.0:1), and the 435-bhp unit had solid lifters and a transistorized electronic ignition.

An engine not sold to the general public was a special competition version designated L88—a code that would become famous among Corvette lovers. The L88 was the kind of powerplant that an engineer like Duntov might design if he had an open checkbook and a clean drawing board. It was based on a 427, of course, with aluminum cylinder heads, full-race cam, 850-cfm Holley four-barrel atop an aluminum manifold, no smog equipment, and a compression ratio of 12.5:1. Exactly 20 L88s were installed, of which three are known to exist

continued on page 149

The 1967 Corvette, although changed only in detail,
was the cleanest of the 1963-67 generation. Five smaller
fender vents replaced the three, while less distracting
flat-black and aluminum rocker panel moldings gave
the '67 a lower, less chunky look. New and thus
unique was a single backup light, mounted above the
license plate. Slotted six-inch Rally wheels replaced
the ornate, old-fashioned wheel covers, and were
supplied with chrome beauty rings and lug nuts
concealed behind small chrome caps.

Corvette Performance Comparisons 1963-67

Year	Disp.	Bhp	Axle	Seconds: 0-30	0-50	0-60	0-100	1/4-mi.	Speed: 1/4-mi.	Top
1963	327	300	3.36	2.2	4.2	6.1	14.5	14.5	100	118
1964	327	300*	3.36	3.2	6.1	8.0	20.2	15.2	85	130
1965	327	375**	3.70	2.9	5.2	6.3	14.7	14.4	99	138
1965	396	425	3.70	3.1	4.8	5.7	13.4	14.1	103	136
1966	427	425	4.11	2.5	4.2	5.6	—	13.4	105	135
1967	327	300	3.36	3.4	5.9	7.8	23.1	16.0	87	121

* automatic transmission
** fuel injection

On the inside of the '67 Sting Ray (*top left*), upholstery
patterns changed slightly and the handbrake lever was
moved from beneath the dash to between the seats.
The 427 (*bottom left*) came in three forms, the
top two—rated at 400 and 435 bhp—with triple two-
barrels. The roadster (*below*) listed at $4141 for '67
and 14,436 were built before the next generation debuted.

continued from page 145

today. One could wish for higher production numbers for an automobile
that would do 13-second quarter-miles
and deliver 560 bhp.

But times were changing. The new
1968 Corvette would be a different
breed entirely, and perhaps in deference to that fact, it would be introduced bereft of the name *Sting Ray*.
With its arrival would fall the curtain
on a wonderful age of unremitting
quests for power and performance by
the makers of America's only sports
car—unlike any time we may ever see
again.

Serial Spans, Production, and Base Prices

Year	Serial Prefix	Serial Span	Prod. Units	Price
1963	30837S	100001-121513	10,594 coupe	$4252
	30867S		10,919 roadster	$4037
1964	40837S	100001-122229	8304 coupe	$4252
	40867S		13,925 roadster	$4037
1965	194375S	100001-123562	8186 coupe	$4321
	194675S		15,376 roadster	$4106
1966	194376S	100001-127720	9958 coupe	$4295
	194676S		17,762 roadster	$4084
1967	194377S	100001-122940	8504 coupe	$4353
	194677S		14,436 roadster	$4141

The times were changing, and with the last of the '67s would fall the curtain on a wonderful age of unremitting quests for power and performance by the makers of America's only sports car—unlike any time we may ever see again. The Corvette represented the ultimate in performance and sex appeal to an entire generation of young Americans; today the 1963-67 Sting Rays are among the most prized Corvettes ever built.

Profile:
William L. Mitchell

During the Sixties and Seventies, General Motors' Bill Mitchell influenced the looks of Detroit's production automobiles more than anyone else. He had a great deal to do with the Ford Granadas, Chrysler Cordobas, and Lincoln Versailles of those days—more, perhaps, than their manufacturers were willing to admit. Each of those cars, along with many more besides, represented a response, an attempt to one-up General Motors Styling in a come-from-behind, late edition of the gospel according to Bill Mitchell. Some succeeded; others did not. The gap that they needed to overcome was significantly large. As Theodore MacManus said in his immortal Cadillac ad "The Penalty of Leadership," "...if the leader leads, he remains the leader." GM Styling, with the sole exception of the 1955-58 period of Chrysler's "Forward Look," led Detroit for half a century—from Harley Earl's very first LaSalle in 1927 to Mitchell's dramatic 1975 Cadillac Seville and the remarkably downsized GM A bodies.

MacManus also said that leaders have their detractors, and Mitchell had his share. A few of them were also-rans—spear-carriers from the profession that Mitchell dominated for two decades and influenced for four. Others were mere second-guessers who, with typical misunderstanding, viewed the chrome-bedecked late-Fifties machines of Detroit and concluded that no stylist who made a name for himself in that period was worth further discussion. (To draw that conclusion betrays ignorance of an individual's career as a whole, not to mention the enormous influence—little of it for the good—exerted by sales and top management on stylists.) Still others simply didn't like Mitchell's dress and mannerisms. In reference to Mitchell, English writer Leonard Setright recorded, "His round body clad in bright scarlet or mylar chrome coated leathers, astride one of his adolescent fantasy motorcycles, was enough to force a guffaw from Samuel Beckett." How Bill Mitchell dressed or what he drove had no bearing on his professional competence, of course. Taken as a whole, the evidence shows that William L. Mitchell was extremely competent.

When Bill Mitchell relieved Harley Earl as the head of GM Styling in 1958, he found himself with legendary shoes to fill—shoes that some said were too big for anybody. But Mitchell filled them so well that he may have invented an entire new shoe size. Admittedly,

he couldn't have succeeded to Earl's position at a better time. Harley Earl had not been on the cutting edge of car design for several years, and he had lost the styling initiative to resurgent Chrysler and Virgil M. Exner. Mitchell changed that in a hurry, bringing General Motors back to the styling pinnacle for a generation. Of course, he achieved his success by giving upper management—and more often the customers themselves—exactly what they wanted, and more so.

"If vulgarity was called for," Setright noted, "supreme vulgarity was forthcoming." What the English writer didn't say—and European prejudices aside—was that when elegance and strength of line were called for, Bill Mitchell meted them out a hundredfold. General Motors, like any other car company, has had its ugly periods. But by and large, the best cars of the Mitchell years were fresh, exciting, radical, widely imitated, and rarely uninteresting.

One of Mitchell's admirable characteristics—unusual in a field built on egos—was his candor. In an interview, he rarely failed to allude to the numerous people at GM Design who made his accomplishments possible. He was equally frank about his likes and dislikes: He compared designing a small economy car to "tailoring a dwarf." What he liked, Mitchell said, was the luxury and sports models—preferably a combination of both.

Mitchell's first great design was the 1938 Cadillac Sixty Special sedan, recognized today

as one of the most significant styling achievements of the prewar years. Later, Mitchell would be the creative force behind such memorable production cars as the 1963 Buick Riviera and stunning show models like the Corvair Monza GT and SS.

But his greatest achievement—certainly his greatest love—was the Corvette, which owed its glamour and allure to Mitchell from 1960 through the mid-Seventies. He devoted a good deal of his time to Corvette work, and of the many projects that he supervised at GM, it was his favorite by far. His penchant for the 'Vette is hardly surprising, given the personality of the man, who has been described by many of the same adjectives applied to the car itself—brash, flamboyant, even beefy. For Mitchell, as for Harley Earl before him, the Corvette was his opportunity not only to have fun as a designer, but also to make a personal statement about what a high-performance American automobile should be.

Like most pioneers in a burgeoning field, Mitchell fell into his career quite by accident. He grew up in Pennsylvania, where he fell in love with cars by visiting his father's Buick dealership. In the Thirties, he secured a job as an illustrator for the Barron Collier advertising agency in New York City. He spent his spare time drawing cars, and, in the evenings, attending classes at the Art Students League. The Collier family also liked cars, especially the racing variety, and spent many weekends in upstate New York, at the Sleepy Hollow race track—which they owned. Mitchell went with them, and one weekend his sketches came to the attention of one of Harley Earl's friends.

Harley Earl then contacted Mitchell, asking him for more sketches—wanting to know what the young designer thought cars "ought to look like in the future." Six months later, Bill Mitchell was at work at the Art and Colour Studio of GM. Six months after that, he was chief designer at Cadillac. Eventually, he became the head of GM Styling.

Controversial, highly visible, never given to halfway measures, Mitchell pulled few punches in his work, his arguments over policy with GM managers, or, as we see in this combination of several interviews with the editors over the years, in his public pronouncements.

Editor: That must have been something—from nowhere to styling head of Cadillac in 12 months.

William L. Mitchell: *It sounds great now, but there were only a hundred of us then at the whole place [Art and Colour]. When I left General Motors [in 1977], I had 1600 people.*

Ed: *How long were you with Cadillac?*

WLM: *Until I went into the Navy in the war. I came back in '49. After that, I was taken out of General Motors. Earl wanted me to run a business for his sons; he wanted to put them in design. So I took over Harley Earl Design. I did that for four years and got big accounts like Clark Equipment, General Electric, Westinghouse, Parker Pen. Oh, I really went. I didn't like the products, but the newness of it was good for me.*

Ed: *How did you return to GM?*

WLM: *Earl brought me back as director. I didn't love [Harley Earl Design], but it was good background for me, because when I came back...I didn't have to take any lip from any general manager. He [Earl] told me four years ahead I was going to take his job. He talked to [then GM board chairman Alfred] Sloan and [then president Harlow] Curtice. I guess you can't do that any more; committees have to put you in.*

Ed: *How did you first get involved with the Corvette?*

WLM: *Harley Earl—this was his idea. After the war, he was a good friend of [General Curtis] LeMay. They had these activities at the bases to keep the uniformed men happy. They started sports car racing. They got GM and a lot of different companies to put a lot of money into it to give them some fun. We built a Jeep with a Cadillac engine in it for LeMay, I remember. He said, "Harley, why don't you build an American sports car?"*

We showed the first Corvette to a group at the proving grounds, and Earl told Sloan he'd like to put it in the [Motorama] show at the Waldorf. This was a prototype—no engine, nothing. It went over so good, Chevrolet said they'd build it.

Ed: *What were some of the problems with the early Corvettes?*

WLM: *It didn't have a good engine. There wasn't a good V-8 then.*

Ed: *How did the decision to use the V-8 come about?*

WLM: *[Former chief engineer Edward N.] Cole became the head of Chevrolet, and he was a young fireball. He liked to race. He shoved that ahead. Prior to that, people started*

to try to race [Corvettes] and they weren't any good. But when you got the V-8 in it, boy, she started to go. When we beat the Jaguars—that was something. And then we beat the Mercedes...From then on it was all hell to pay. It was like a Ferrari: It looks good, but it's got to go. Performance is part of the act.

Ed: *What was the closest that the Corvette project came to being halted?*

WLM: *There were times when [James M.] Roche [distribution vice president 1960-62, later GM president and chairman] wanted to discontinue the Corvette. I raised hell. I knew Roche well, but he was a Cadillac man. I said, "...the Corvette's got far greater owner loyalty than any damn Cadillac made." And the sales manager backed me up. That was before the Sting Ray got going.*

Ed: *What was your involvement with racing?*

WLM: *I did a lot of bootlegging at GM. I had a studio right down underneath my office. I called it Studio X—[it's] where I'd bootleg all kinds of cars I wanted to do. Chevrolet was racing on a scale, and then that stopped. I knew they had three chassis they didn't use [after the 1957 Sebring race]. So I went to Cole, and he gave [one] to me for 500 bucks. I did [the racing Stingray] down in Studio X; nobody knew about it.*

Ed: *Tell us how you liked it.*

WLM: *I always liked its looks. It's my favorite Corvette. That strong shadow underneath makes it very photogenic. The early Corvettes were too rounded, too soft. The Sting Ray has that sharp body edge, and that makes it work.*

Ed: *When did you have to take the Corvette SS chassis out of GM?*

WLM: *I raced it first in Washington with [Dr.] Dick Thompson [in early 1959]. At the engineering policy committee, [then president John F.] Gordon made a statement: "I thought everybody realized we're not going to do any racing." After the meeting I said, "Were you talking to me?" and he said, "I sure as hell was." He was tough. Instead of taking it lying down, I got a couple good friends of mine who could write better than I could, and we wrote a letter to him saying, "I got my job racing with the Collier boys; racing is in my blood."*

In those days, they'd come out in those big limousines. He came out one day and I said, "Jack, did you get my letter?" And he said, "You're a pretty damn good salesman. Go

ahead." But he said, "Keep it off [GM Tech Center] property and spend your own money." So I did, and I raced for two years until he said, "Stop it, they're getting back after me for racing." So I had a little bit of my own way, and on my income tax I got away pretty good.

Ed: *Where did you keep the race car outside of the Tech Center?*

WLM: *I've got a shop on Twelve Mile Road that's just five minutes from my office, and I did the work out there. But I got GM engineers and I had a lot of talent at GM helping me. I got good mechanics to go to the races with me. I got a lot of things I wanted.*

Ed: *Did it cost you?*

WLM: *Plenty. I financed it all out of my own pocket. I couldn't afford to build and race the Stingray today. But back then, it pleased me no end to go up against Cunningham and those boys with the faster cars, and take any of them.*

Ed: *Did its body design help its performance?*

WLM: *Oh, yes. It was very slippery. It would take a D-Jag, which had a very smooth body and about the same horsepower. The Stingray would do 0-to-60 in four seconds. It had a beautiful engine—first fuel injection, then we tried four Webers with different cams. Tear your head off! The only weakness that car had was the brakes. They never did work right.*

Ed: *How did the shape translate to production cars?*

WLM: *It was the same, wasn't it? I just took all those lines and turned the Stingray racer into the production 1963 Sting Ray. That made the Corvette. And overnight, the sales just boomed. So I knew I had something.*

I went to the races in Europe and saw the cars there. I didn't want a car that looked like everything out of Europe. All their cars looked like Ferraris or Maseratis. They didn't have any sharp identifying features. I wanted a car that, by God, you'd know it a mile away. That was my whole theme. And it did have identity.

Ed: *How did the Stingray (Sting Ray) get its name?*

William L. Mitchell was GM's chief stylist from 1958-1977. His greatest love—and perhaps his greatest achievement—was the Corvette, specifically the '63 Sting Ray.

WLM: *I just did it. Jack Gordon never liked those names of mine, the fish names. They wanted everything to start with a C. But we'd get them anyway. I don't know how the Stingray got to be two words, though.*

Ed: *The Mako Shark was another of your fish names, then?*

WLM: *Yes. I love sharks because, in the water, they're exciting. They twist and turn. I caught a Mako off Bimini, and it's in my studio in Palm Beach. I've got pictures of my Corvettes below it. That's where I got the impetus to do the experimental Manta Ray. I'd do a lead car on my own. Then we built things off of it.*

Ed: *Did you object to the removal of the split window on the '64 coupe?*

WLM: *I had to admit it was a hazard. Duntov won that one. By the way, I stole that back line from Porsche. I wasn't above stealing things from European cars. Not American cars—there was nothing over here to steal! There isn't anything today, unless you want a cake of soap—then you get a Ford. You need identity on a car. If you took the antlers off a deer, you'd have a big rabbit!*

Ed: *What was your relationship like with Zora?*

WLM: *Anyone with a foreign accent can get away with arguments because they're hard to understand. He'd mumble around. But he was a good guy.*

Ed: *Did the Corvette have much influence on other cars?*

WLM: *Remember the early Pontiac Grand Prix and the 1963 Buick Riviera? When they were built, the sales people still thought that the more chrome, the better. The Corvette didn't have much chrome and it sold! So I did those two like the Corvette, and eliminated the chrome. They sold fantastically. That changed a lot of old-fashioned thinking. The European designers recognized it. They had never liked our cars before, but they liked the Corvette—and the Riviera, too. It was the same idea—trim, stylish, classic.*

Ed: *How close did the Corvair Monza GT come to being a 'Vette?*

WLM: *The Corvair was a great car— very unusual. The Monza GT and SS were the cars that might have replaced the Corvette. The GT was first. It was a rush job, done over several times, in less than 10 weeks. Engineering did a box section chassis for it, and tested it at different tracks. It outperformed the fuel injection Corvette and was very aerody-*

namic. It only weighed 1500 pounds.

Ed: *Why wasn't that a mid-engine car?*

WLM: *I wanted that, but Chevrolet said they could make the car handle the same way with the engine hanging out the back. I got Roger Penske, who was then a great Porsche racer, to drive the Monza GT. He liked it better than the Porsche. Right at that time the whole Corvair program started to wane, and I couldn't interest management in doing anything with that car. It was just no go.*

Ed: *The Monza seems like the cleanest design of that era.*

WLM: *Well, you can see where it relates to the Sting Ray shape in many ways. It could have been sold as a small Corvette and done wonderfully. It's one of the classic designs. If you've got a good design, it's timeless. If you drive a Monza GT down the street today, you'll draw a crowd.*

Ed: *The Monza GT reminds us of the Opel GT.*

WLM: *Oh, yes, of course. The Opel GT was derived from this. It relates to the Sting Ray, too, and could have been a small Corvette. It was a pretty car, with that same classic Sting Ray look. It could have sold alongside the big Corvette as a cheaper model with no problem at all. But nobody was interested.*

Ed: *It seems like a big car such as the Corvette would be easier to style than a small car like the Monza GT or Opel GT, even though the body is similar.*

WLM: *That's why today, with all the small cars on the road, it would be hard for me. I'm glad I retired when I did. After all my years of designing cars, I was being asked to make them shorter, narrower, and higher instead of longer, lower, and wider. And you*

know what I used to say: "Designing a small car is like tailoring a dwarf." That's true. It's true. It's really tough to do a good small car.

Ed: *How did the Mako Shark fit into all this?*

WLM: *That car's a real favorite of mine. We used a dark top and light underbody, and nobody had ever done that. It works very well. It's even got nice lines from the top. On so many cars, the tops just fall away. But the Mako Shark looks good from the top.*

Ed: *That car is a real goer, isn't it?*

WLM: *The Mako has the old chassis, and it's heavy. But it's got a 650-horsepower Can-Am engine. It goes like hell. And it holds the road.*

Ed: *A lot of racing cars are painted like the Mako with a dark top and light underbody.*

WLM: *They got that from me. You know why they do it? The car shows up better for photographers without a dark shadow underneath, so they get more publicity than if they had a dark car with a light top. It's true. That's why they do that. It's the same reason we painted the Mako Shark that way. That car got fantastic coverage.*

Ed: *Rumor has it that there was some thought of discontinuing the Corvette and treating the Camaro as the General Motors sports car.*

WLM: *That's very true. The first-series Camaro was done too fast. We didn't get a chance to do much. But the second-series cars [were] in production for a decade, and selling... That [was] really a hell of a package. Stirling Moss saw the first Camaro, and he said to me, "Bill, you've really got a classic. The detail...it's not all carved up. It's got a nice swoop to it." He was right. That car's*

been very popular in Europe, too. Much more than the [1968-82] Corvette[s], which they consider overstyled. No matter what we do to it, [the second-series Camaro] body always works. The Camaro Berlinetta was a show car, you remember, with brass trim. I drove it here for a few months, and everybody liked it. So I said to myself, "Maybe I've got something here."

Ed: Our favorite Stingray is the Mulsanne. That's really a nice looking Corvette.

WLM: It's the greatest Stingray ever. We used it as the pace car for all the Can-Am races, way back. It has a powerful LT-1 engine. The car's been around a lot, though. It's been red, silver, blue, and now it's back to silver again. The nicest thing about it is that you can take the whole roof off in one piece and the

flagman can stand up and see the start of the race, and everybody can see him. It's a terrific pace car.

Ed: There's a lot going on in the Mulsanne.

WLM: Yes. The big engines have to breathe in a small car like the Stingray, so you have to cut holes in the body. This car has scoops and spoilers and fins, but a lot of surface tension, too.

Ed: Is everything functional on it?

WLM: Sure. The periscope really works as a rearview mirror, for example. I took the flip-flop out and exposed the headlights like the racers do. People don't really want gadgets; they want flexible things. They don't really want headlights that flop up and down—they don't need them. So you can put the lights up

on the hood, and create more attention.

Ed: This car is getting pretty old by now.

WLM: But it's still a great show car, because it has so much animation in the styling. So many things are happening in it. If you make a show car too simple, it doesn't hold

Bill Mitchell's racing Stingray from 1959 led directly to the XP-755 Shark of 1961, which was later retitled Mako Shark I (*opposite page*). Both cars contributed to the final design of the 1963-67 Sting Ray. The Mako Shark II from 1965 in turn previewed the production 1968 Corvette. Mitchell is shown posing with the two at GM's Tech Center (*above*); the similarities between the two cars are striking.

people's interest; it's just another smooth car. If it's too simple, it's just Simple Simon.

Ed: There must be a pretty fine line between a classic design and a dull design.

WLM: Well, like they say, a designer's got to know when to lift his brush.

Ed: Let's talk about the Aerovette. Originally, it was thought to be the 1980 Corvette design, but that never came about.

WLM: What's to tell? They took the most beautiful car ever styled and let it hang around. And now, without me to sit on 'em, it's not going anywhere. It's a shame, but that car has had problems from the beginning. Originally, they were going to hire that Italian—Giorgetto Giugiaro—to do it. The Aerovette is my answer to Giugiaro. Giugiaro's cars are all full of angles. He can't draw a simple perspective, you know. He makes a side view and a top view. All his cars look like they've been cut out of cardboard.

Ed: Isn't that deliberate?

WLM: I hope not. It's horrible. Now take my Aerovette by comparison. The Aerovette has nice contours, soft curves, and still a certain sharpness. It has really good balance. It's a design you can look at from any angle. A car is like a girl, you know. You wouldn't want to see a girl from only one angle. You want to get more views.

Ed: You must have spent most of your time with the Corvette.

WLM: Well, it was my pet. Nobody bothered me. No high power in Chevrolet was interested—the volume and profit wasn't there. You could do what you wanted without anybody monkeying around. In the other divisions, when you'd have a showing, you'd have the chief engineer and six assistants plus an audience in the studio that would drive you nuts. Committees, committees, committees. The first Camaro and Firebird were so committeed that I don't remember what they look like. They were just nothing. The other ones we got done so damn fast that they never saw 'em! But with the Corvette, they would always leave you alone.

Ed: They never tried to make you build it out of steel?

WLM: With fiberglass, you can only make, say, 70,000 [units] at most [from a mold]. But you can change it. You can't do that so easily with metal. Every Corvette was different because you can do that. That's where DeLorean screwed up. That thing he

had—half metal, half plastic—you couldn't do anything with it. The Pontiac Fiero, that's [a new] beginning. Half of it's plastic. You can make a whole different car—and they ought to, because the one they have looks like a soap box.

Ed: How important were the show cars to production plans?

WLM: That's how you'd find out what people wanted. That's how the Eldorados were born and the Toronados and all that—at the Motorama. Now they don't make those anymore. Show cars were more fun to work on [because] you didn't have a bunch of committeemen telling us, "You can't do this; you can't do that." We did it, and if people liked it they'd say, "Go make it." It would do more for us in the studio to see one come out of the shop. People want to see something new.

Ed: Where do you think design is going now?

WLM: I think fins are going to come back. Even down at Daytona, at the races, your Porsches have fins on them. In that sports car class just about every car has fins. Now I don't think they'll be high. You need wings; you need that stuff on there or you've got a pickle. A Porsche to me was always—there was a word they used in Germany—like a loaf of bread. If it spun out, you didn't know which end was coming. There's a lot of stuff going on now that's called functional. But you've got to have aesthetics. You can't sell a guy a car that looks like hell and tell him it looks that way because it's aerodynamic.

Ed: What do you think of the newest-generation Corvette?

WLM: I think [it] looks like a grouper—a blunt look. I think the Camaro and Firebird are sharper. Although—I'll eat my own words—on the highway it looks pretty damn good from the front. But I don't like this lack of whip in the side view—it isn't exciting. And the big taillights look like it was done for A. J. Foyt. I think it should have been done for women as well as men. I like more interest in the car. You look at watches—there's millions of them and they look different all the time. You don't want cars all looking alike.

Ed: What would you have done differently with today's Corvette?

WLM: I'd have put more accents on it. But my day is over...[Harley] Earl never bothered me when he left. Earl was a dynamic man, more Hollywood. He looked so out of

place in Detroit it was unbelievable. He had power politically and physically. And he was a salesman like you never heard of. He could win. Styling ran the world, not design, not engineering...He made it his way. I tried to follow him, and I did a pretty good job.

Ed: Things have changed now, haven't they?

WLM: The boys that followed me are getting pushed off the map. I love 'em, but they haven't got it. Engineering is running it. The new Corvette is engineering perfect, but design? No. The engineers ran the whole damn show. They wouldn't have done that with me.

You need two things in a car: You need road value and show room value. You need a little sparkle in a car. On a little misty day they all look dull. You don't want to put chrome on with a trowel like we did in '58, but you need some. There isn't show room value in these cars today. If I had one, I'd touch it up. You have to have enough interest to keep looking at it. That goes for all the cars.

Ed: What are some specific changes you would make?

WLM: I'd put more flow in the line. I wouldn't have the sideline straight through. I know it wouldn't be as aerodynamic, but I'd put some curve in that. Like a shark is so much more interesting than a grouper because there's so many little things happening to it. This [Corvette] is a big potato. On the road, yes; but you walk up to it—blah. Black rubber around everything. It needs detail. I think the new little Pontiac [Fiero] is a dead duck; it's just a little box. I think that Fiat [X 1/9]...is much better. I shouldn't be talking about my company like that; they're still good to me.

Ed: What are some of the cars that you own now?

WLM: I've got some pets of mine I love. I've got a Jaguar roadster—the old Jaguar 12. Everything is copper on it—the body and all the chrome is copper. I've got a Firebird I did over with a Ferrari engine, and all the metal on that is gold, and it's striped in gold. My Corvette is pearl white with two fins on the back like a race car, with a blade going through it. The Corvette has a 600-horsepower Can-Am aluminum-block motor in it. I like to have a car that when I pull up, somebody says, "Whose car is that?" I want a car that, when it's stopped, people walk around it for an hour. Exciting automobiles.

CHAPTER SEVEN

1968-1977:
A Long Road
Winding

The introduction of the 1968 Corvette has been regretted by many a Sting Ray lover ever since. The '68's arrival has long been regarded as a step backward—or at least not the mighty leap forward that had been expected. After all, 'Vette folks the world over had been promised very startling things, when, inevitably, it became time to replace the Sting Ray. The fourth generation of America's sports car had literally remade the car's image during model years 1963 through 1967. So people anticipated swoopy, trend-setting designs out of Mitchell's studio—an exotic mid-engine configuration, perhaps, or even a rear-engine car developed from Corvair technology and based on Mitchell's exciting Monza GT and SS show cars. None of those expectations were met.

The new species of Corvette was a car given to more compromises than any previous generation. In terms of design, it saw the very meaning of the term *sports car* bent sharply out of synch with previous conceptions—from a dual-purpose, race-and-ride, mostly open, very fast two-seater, the Corvette had become a curvy but increasingly tame boulevard cruiser. The domestication continued rapidly after the federal government got involved in car design and many of the prime Corvette customers were sent to Southeast Asia for military duty.

The Corvette's fifth generation begun in 1968 did have staying power: It stayed, and stayed, and stayed—and stayed some more. That was mostly the result of the diminished market for high performance rather than a set policy on the part of Chevrolet Division. While the Corvette had reached a position of high profitability during the Sting Ray years, it was still a fringe product by Chevy's standards. In some corporate minds, it was more a public relations gimmick than serious business.

The degree of change witnessed in the Corvette should not be attributed completely to Chevrolet or even to General Motors. The pressures suffered by the automaker were enormous, and given the economic, social, and energy situations of the time, hardly any other scenario would be conceivable. Despite the setting in which the Corvette had to play, its newest generation was anything but uniformly dull.

A market factor of significance in determining the shape and style of the newest Corvette was the proliferation of many sporty cars—some of them called *ponycars*, as the Mustang's success saw them nicknamed—priced well below the Corvette but offering similar performance. Chevrolet itself was building the Chevelle SS 396, the turbocharged Corvair Corsa, and the new Camaro. All were impressive performers; all offered different answers to the same basic automotive problem. When the full-size Chevrolet began to turn in 0-60-mile-per-hour times that would have put the original Corvette to shame, Chevrolet Engineering was forced to play a serious game of topping the next guy's development.

The development of a rear- or mid-engine model had occupied the designers' thoughts for a long time. Chevrolet had been mass-producing one such car—the Corvair—since 1960, and when the '68 'Vette was being planned, the mid-engine approach still looked viable. For 1965, the Corvair's original swing-axle rear suspension and quirky handling were gone, and it had matured into a nice, unique little car. Its similarity to the honored marque of Porsche was obvious, and its technology intrigued not only Corvette engineers, but Corvette stylists. But the market also demanded high power. In the context of the Sixties, that virtually required a V-8 engine. Experimentally, V-8s were wedged in the back of Corvair prototypes, but they made an already tail-heavy package even more so. One preliminary design had a huge bulge necessary to clear the engine, requiring a periscope for a rear view.

Sensing correctly that the public wanted to drive cars and not tanks, Chevy discarded ideas of building a rear-engine 'Vette. Other proposals used Q-model themes, with a split front windshield and storage space provided behind the engine assembly. But no matter how hard they tried, the stylists couldn't seem to find the right look. Perhaps the search had been in vain from the beginning, because a rear- or mid-engine Corvette would have required mechanical components that just didn't exist at Chevrolet. GM had yet to produce a suitable transaxle, and the design and tooling costs for one that would only be used on a low-volume model like the Corvette would have sent prices out of sight.

But Bill Mitchell and his staff had just what they needed to make their baby considerably more exotic at the relatively low price of a new fiberglass

skin. They had prepared it in 1965, one of the most famous show cars of all time—the Mako Shark II. Its styling set it apart from anything else on four wheels, with presence, pizzazz, and the looks of a born runner. It had star quality. The Mako Shark II was not merely a showcase for GM Design's latest ideas. It was mainly a trial balloon for the next-generation Corvette. The Motorama shows were a thing of the past by the mid-Sixties, but GM was still gauging public reaction to its near-term model plans by displaying them in slightly exaggerated show car guise. In this case, the development program had been started in early 1964, more than a year before the Mako Shark II appeared. The main goal was to develop a radically different body design compatible with the existing Sting Ray chassis. Underneath, the forthcoming production model would not be very new, but Chevy was betting that a different body and high-performance engines would be enough to keep America's sports car on its upward sales course.

In profile and in the nose and fender shapes, the production prototype bore a strong resemblance to the Mako II. It was only in the roof and rear window treatment that the two differed markedly. The show car had a tapered roof in plan view and carried jazzy backlight louvers. On the 1968 prototype, the roof treatment was replaced by flying-buttress sail panels flanking an upright flat rear window. The configuration was favored for the successor to the Sting Ray coupe, and from the beginning it was intended that the backlight as well as that portion of the roof above the seats be removable. Though a convertible would also be offered, Chevy felt that such an arrangement combined the open-air appeal of the traditional Corvette roadster with the better weather protection and structural rigidity associated with closed body types. Porsche had engineered its Targa convertible in much the same way.

The styling work did not progress as smoothly as expected. One problem was that the new body turned out to have excessive front end lift at high speeds, which seriously compromised handling. A rear spoiler that held down the tail was added, but it caused even greater front lift. Duntov had already been through a similar battle

The styling of the Mako Shark II (*top*)—one of the most famous show cars of all time—set it apart from anything else on four wheels, with presence, pizzazz, and the looks of a born runner. Although the public didn't know it in 1965, it was a trial balloon for the 1968 Corvette (*opposite page*), which boasted removable roof panels (*above center*) and a new interior (*above*).

In profile and in the nose and fender shapes, the
production prototype of the 1968 Corvette bore
a strong resemblance to the Mako Shark II.
Styling work did not progress smoothly, however,
because of excessive front end lift, but additional
time in the wind tunnel led to a front end spoiler
and functional front fender louvers.

with the Sting Ray, and he was intent upon licking it before the design went into production. More time in the wind tunnel led to the use of functional front fender louvers and a front spoiler. Another problem was the Targa-style roof. Throughout the design phase, the removable section had been conceived as a single piece of fiberglass. However, engineers found that they could not make the body-and-frame combination stiff enough to prevent creaks and groans, so they added a longitudinal member between the windshield header and the fixed rear roof section—the birth of the T-top. The T-top solution came so late that it didn't appear in some early publicity photos of the new coupe. The body problems led to a one-year pro-duction delay, so the introduction of the fifth-generation Corvette planned as a 1967 model wasn't made until model year 1968.

One feature from the Mako II that survived to production virtually intact was a vacuum-operated panel that concealed the windshield wipers. It was a great idea for a show car, being flashy and attracting attention, but in

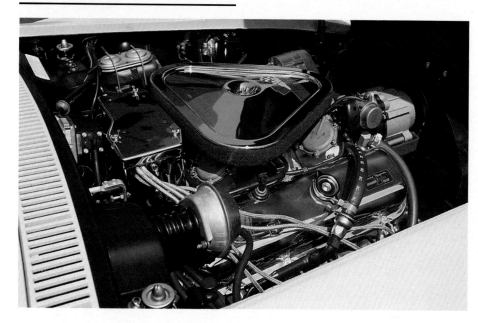

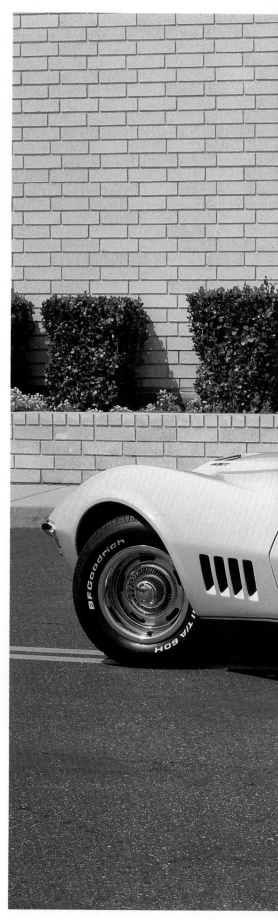

ice and snow it proved impractical. A good deal of development time went into perfecting the panel for manufacture, but the finished product was none too reliable.

Perhaps the most important problem with the Mako-inspired styling was inadequate cooling for the big-block engines that would be carried over from the Sting Ray. With the narrow engine bay and shallow grille opening proposed for the new model, radiator air flow was found to be marginal in hot weather and when the air conditioning was switched on. Duntov did what he could by cutting down the size of the front spoiler (the original had actually impeded air flow) and making front fender exhaust slots, but the cooling system was still problematic at introduction time, especially with the more powerful engines.

The Mako Shark II's styling may have been great for a show car, but it proved controversial in production form. "If there's such a thing as a psychedelic car, the 1968 Corvette is it," said *Road & Track* magazine in its initial test. Today, the styling doesn't seem that radical, so why such an uproar? The lines were definitely distinctive— exotic, really, compared to most other contemporary road cars. Even so, the '68 Corvette drew a decidedly mixed reaction. To many, the styling was wretchedly excessive. "We wish we could express more enthusiasm for the new model," said *Road & Track,* "but we feel that the general direction of the changes is away from Sports Car and toward Image and Gadget Car." The magazine had particular complaints about the interior layout, expressing the opinion that comfort and ergonomic logic had been sacrificed to styling. It praised the driver/steering wheel relationship, but deplored the

The Turbo Jet 427 V-8 (*top*) was available with three horsepower ratings for 1968—390, 400, and 435— and cars with it received appropriate hood badging (*above*). The lines were distinctive, exotic really, but to many the styling was wretchedly excessive (*right*).

difficulty of getting in and out and complained about the location of the secondary gauges in the center of the dash, away from the driver's direct line of sight. Inadequate interior ventilation was also cited despite the incorporation of windows-up Astro Ventilation with dash-mounted vents. The *R&T* testers found that not enough air was getting through the ducts to keep them cool. Luckily, factory air was available and was ordered by more than 5000 customers, who must have agreed with *R&T*.

However, auto writers had more than a few good words for the engines, all carryovers from the previous year. While many thought the big 435-brake-horsepower 427 was simply too brutish, the 300- and 350-bhp small blocks were judged quite favorably, as were the Muncie four-speed manual transmission and the new three-speed Turbo Hydra-matic. As for handling, the press seemed to like the skidpad and slalom numbers they turned out, but didn't really like the way that the car felt. Several complaints were made about a hard ride. Nobody liked the power steering and brakes much, either. *Road & Track* labeled them imprecise and suggested that potential customers skip them entirely.

The *R&T* review was downright benign compared to Steve Smith's attack in *Car and Driver*. Smith slammed everything from the windshield wipers to the ashtray. His biggest complaint was the new model's fit and finish—or, more precisely, the lack of it. "Few of the body panels butted against each other in the alignment that was intended," he wrote. "Sometimes the pieces chafed against each other, sometimes they left wide gaps, sometimes they were just plain crooked." He also complained about a chronic water leak from the T-top and claimed that one of the door locks was so stiff that it bent the key. He termed it all "a shocking lack of quality control" and declared the car "unfit to road test." Unhappily, problems were not confined to the *C/D* test car. The 1968 model is generally considered to be the low point for Corvette workmanship, with bad paint, knobs that fell off, cooling bothers, and other problems. The feeling in many quarters is that Chevrolet tried too many ideas that were not adequately sorted out and put too big of a rush on production.

As was probably inevitable, the price of the rebodied 1968 Corvette increased to $4320 for the convertible and $4663 for the coupe. Curb weight didn't change much, coming in at a little over 3000 pounds. Although the styling was all new (*bottom*), the crossed-flags insignia (*below*) and hidden headlights (*right*) were still featured on the new model.

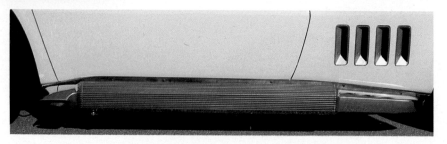

One change for 1969 was the readoption of the Stingray name (*top*), but spelled out as one word. The interior (*center*) featured a smaller steering wheel, while side exhausts continued to be an option (*above*). Exterior changes on the '69 'Vette (*opposite page*) were minimal, although the door handles were new.

Certainly the 1968 model 'Vette was far more complicated than the 1962 models that had been produced just six years before. It came in two body styles: the familiar roadster, available with optional lift-off hardtop, and the totally new T-top Sport Coupe. On the 1962 Corvette, a customer could not order power steering, power brakes, or air conditioning. All of these items were available on the '68, plus rear window defogger, three different manual transmissions, a new automatic transmission, telescoping steering column, speed warning indicator, AM/FM stereo radio, and a futuristic fiber-optic light monitoring system, not to mention the disappearing headlights and the trouble-prone hidden wiper panel. Now that the car had more gadgets, more things were likely to go wrong.

But when everything was working right, the '68 could be quite satisfying to drive. It had plenty of power on tap even with the small-block engines; the all-independent suspension was more than adequate if not exactly state-of-the-art; and, cooling problems aside, none of the glitches that cropped up were in the basic mechanicals. The gadget problems were irritating, but in the overall scheme of things, they weren't major flaws.

The 1968 Corvette could go! Ron Wakefield tested a 350-bhp 327 roadster with four-speed and the 3.70:1 final drive and came up with some impressive numbers. Top speed was 128 mph; the quarter-mile time was 15.6 seconds at 92 mph; and 0-60-mph acceleration was 7.7 seconds. The big-block engines were faster yet, if not as streetable. In any form, the new car was quite thirsty. *R&T* estimated its test car with a 327 averaged 11 to 15 miles per gallon—a figure that yielded a cruising range of 220 to 300 miles from its 20-gallon tank. Handling, too, was commendable. It was improved over previous models by the addition of wider seven-inch-wide wheels, plus the special Goodyear bias-ply tires (radials were abandoned in preproduction). Together, they provided taut cornering, though at the expense of smoothness over rough roads.

The short trips dictated by mileage figures were the order of the day, since trunk space was limited to only 6.7 cubic feet. Further, that space was again accessible only from inside the

pect. And the automaker was particularly stung by *Car and Driver's* scathing criticism. Ron Wakefield, who owned a Sting Ray at the time, had a more even-handed assessment: "The Corvette 327 remains a comfortable, fast, safe, and reliable automobile. For those who like their cars big, flashy, and full of blinking lights and trap doors it's a winner. The connoisseur who values finesse, efficiency, and the latest chassis design will have to look, unfortunately, to Europe." Yet despite all the problems and press carping, more people than ever looked to the 'Vette. Model year sales set a new record at 28,566 units, some 5000 cars better than the year before, though only fractionally ahead of the previous all-time best year 1966.

If 1968 had been the year of the Big Switch, then 1969 was the year of the Little Fixes. Duntov and his team went to work, making as many detail changes as they could in the basic design to remedy the problems noted by owners and the press. The reworking began with the cockpit. The new body was seven inches longer overall than the Sting Ray—most of it in front overhang—even though the wheel-

cramped cabin; it had no external opening. The cabin's seats were narrower and the backs raked much more steeply than before to accommodate the two-inch lower roofline. The resulting laid-back posture and the high dash with its huge tachometer and 160-mph speedometer gave the driver the impression of being locked in a cave. With the long, low nose disappearing from sight somewhere near the horizon, the driving position definitely left something to be desired.

Overall, the press was lukewarm about the '68 model—certainly not as laudatory as Chevy had come to ex-

There was no mistaking the front end of a 1969 Stingray
as it loomed ever-larger in one's rearview mirror
(*left*). Although overshadowed by the 427 (*below*),
the 327 was stroked to 350-cid and offered in 300- or
350-bhp versions. The public liked the new-generation
car so well (*bottom*) that 38,762 were built for '69.

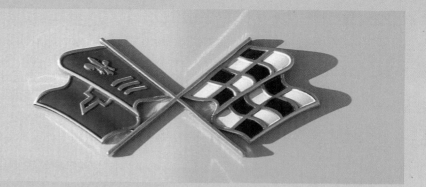

base remained unchanged at 98 inches. However, the pinched-waist styling and the lower roofline made the interior more cramped, another sore point with the writers. Accordingly, one lap-saving inch was carved from the steering wheel diameter, and Duntov pushed through a $120,000 tooling change for the inner door panels to open up a half-inch per side in extra shoulder width. Thanks in part to Ralph Nader's lobbying for safer automobiles, door handles were revamped so as to be more occupant-friendly. The dash knobs got rubberized covers for the same reason. The dash-mounted ignition switch was moved to the steering column, where it was combined with the mandated locking column for additional security, and a warning light was added to tell the driver that the headlights weren't

completely open. Attempts were also made to improve flow volume on the Astro Ventilation system, but *Road & Track* reported that the change didn't make air flow any better than it had been in 1968.

Exterior changes on the 1969 model were minimal. The most noticeable

perhaps was the return of the Stingray designation—now spelled as one word—over the front fender louvers. Another change involved the door handles. Originally, they were covered slots, with the covers releasing the door latches. But the idea ran into production delays, so the '68s had used a

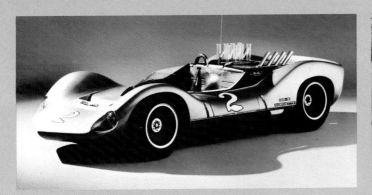

Paced by its crossed-flags insignia (*top, far left*), the
'69 Stingray seemingly could cheat the wind with its
tunneled backlight and flying-buttress pillars (*bottom*).
A mid-engine 'Vette was often rumored; Chevy show cars
such as the CERV II (*above left*) and Astro II
(*above right*) did nothing to dampen speculation.

chrome-covered handgrip with a thumb-operated external pushbutton. The intended handles finally made it on the '69s. A new headlight washer system arrived, as did a revised version of the already overengineered windshield wiper system that *Road & Track* had termed "amusing." The modification retained the hidden wipers and added washers relocated to the wiper arms and override switches so that the panel could be left up and the wipers stopped for blade changing. At the rear, the separate backup lights were incorporated into the inboard tail-lamps.

More interesting was what could be found under the hood, even though the car makers were in the second year of federally mandated—and still relatively uncomplicated—emissions controls. The famed Chevy small block was stroked about a quarter-inch to 3.48 inches, boosting displacement from 327 to 350 cubic inches on the same 4.00-inch bore. Two versions were offered for '69, with the same 300- and 350-bhp ratings as their '68 equivalents, but with compression dropped a quarter point in each case—10.25 and 11.0:1 respectively. Significantly, peak power engine speed was

also lower by 200 rpm, now 4800 and 5600 rpm, respectively. The trio of 427 big blocks returned unchanged and a fourth version rated at 430 bhp at 5200 rpm on a high 12.5:1 compression was added, though not many were built. Axle ratios ranged from a super-low 4.56:1 to a long-striding 2.75:1. Frames on all cars were stiffened to reduce body shake, and wheel rim width went up by one inch for improved handling.

Although Chevrolet was supposed

to have tightened up the Corvette's quality control, it was apparently only partially successful. In its test of a 435-bhp big-block car, *Road & Track* remarked that fit and finish was worse than on its '68 test car. Again, complaints were mostly about minor maladies like squeaks, rattles, and knobs falling off rather than major mechanical ills. But testers expected much more from Chevy's highest-priced car. The editors summed up their test thus-ly: "The Corvette 427 is an entertain-

Among the rarest 1969 Corvettes were those
equipped with the L88 engine (*opposite page*), the
aluminum-head 427 Mark IV rated at 435 bhp. Experts
reckoned actual output of the $1032 option was closer to
500; only 116 were built. The 1970 Stingray—introduced
late because of a strike—featured an egg-crate pattern
grille and side vents, and rectangular parking lamps and
exhaust outlets (*this page, top and above left*). The
Astro Vette (*above right*) was a show car of the period.

ment machine, and compared to some of the more exotic entertainment machines we drive from time to time, it's a rather crude one. But it's cheap when you compare it to other sports cars that offer performance anywhere near its own, so we shouldn't expect a great deal of refinement."

In its June 1969 issue, *R&T* published a four-way test matching a Corvette with the base 350 and Turbo Hydramatic, an automatic Mercedes-Benz 280SL, a manual-shift Jaguar E-Type, and a Porsche 911T. The comparison showed that the 'Vette still bothered the press: "In purely objective terms, the Stingray was the biggest, heaviest, most powerful, fastest, thirstiest, and cheapest of the four GTs included in this test." And none of the four testers chose the 'Vette as his personal favorite. One picked the SL and, to Chevy's likely consternation, the other three picked the Porsche with its rear-

mounted flat six. The SL was the most expensive of the foursome at $7833. The E-Type was next at $6495, followed closely by the Porsche at $6418. The Vette was priced as tested at $6392—including automatic, stereo, and air conditioning. In the eyes of some, the Corvette was no longer at the top of the sports car price/value heap. *R&T* attempted to sum up the style and character of each car, and its description of the 'Vette was telling: "The word that comes to mind is *plastic*. The image, like the styling, is flashy, with lots of deliberately eye-catching angles and gimmicks that aren't strictly necessary. Lacks finesse; like using a five-pound axe when a rapier, properly designed, could do as well. And with more grace. The personality we associate with the Stingray is the Animal, one who prefers to attain the goal with brute strength and bared chest rather than art and fast footwork." The com-

ment was far from complimentary, especially next to those about the Porsche: "The word is *serious*. The driver will take himself and his driving seriously. Damned serious in fact. Almost certain to have no more than a limited sense of humor, especially concerning Porsches...A car for the technician rather than the engineer, if you get the distinction."

Even if you don't get the distinction, it was becoming obvious that the newest Corvette design was far from perfected. Nevertheless, sales took a vertical leap, rising by over 10,000 units to 38,762—a record that wouldn't be broken until 1976. Evidently, at least a few sports car buyers disagreed with *Road & Track's* conclusion about the 'Vette's value.

Chevrolet seemed to get everything together for the 1970 model year. Because of a UAW strike, the 1969 model run was extended two months longer

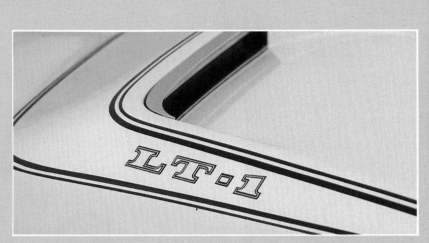

The 1971 Corvette coupe stood out in colors like Daytona Yellow (*below*). Among the options (*above left*) was the solid-lifter small-block LT-1 V-8, which boasted 370 horsepower at 6000 rpm and a hefty $447.50 price. In order to reduce stone damage, Chevy flared the aft portions of each wheel opening (*above right*).

Opposite page: In addition to the available sizzle
of the LT-1 engine (*bottom*), the seats of the 1970
Stingray were reshaped to provide more lateral support,
more headroom, and easier access to the cargo bay. They
could be had in leather, as shown (*top*). There was
still no exterior decklid for the trunk (*above*).

than usual, which may have been the time Chevy needed to make the '70 a better car. The strike was no doubt a factor in the '69 production record, but it also delayed the '70s from reaching dealer show rooms until February, and that sent Corvette production plummeting to just 17,316—its lowest point since 1962.

Corvette cosmetics were again altered only in detail for 1970. The extreme body-side tuck-under on the 1968-69 models was found to be susceptible to stone damage, so Chevy flared the aft portions of each wheel opening, which helped somewhat. The grille—actually false since the radiator air intake was on the car's underside—was changed from horizontal bars to an egg-crate pattern, and the parking lamps changed from small, round

units to clear-lens, amber-bulb, rectangular fixtures. The grille pattern was repeated on the front fender vents, replacing the four "gills" used previously. The dual exhaust outlets also shifted from round to rectangular.

Inside, the seats were reshaped to provide better lateral support, more headroom, and easier access to the still-lidless cargo bay. The shoulder belts, separate from the lap belts, got inertia storage reels, thus ending some cockpit clutter. Carried over from 1969 was a three-pocket map pouch on the passenger side of the dash, which provided more convenient small-item stowage than the hard-to-reach twin lidded bins behind the seats. A deluxe interior group was added to the options list, consisting of full cut-pile carpeting and ersatz wood trim on the

console and doors. Some people liked it, but the purists said that the fake wood made the Corvette seem too much like a Monte Carlo.

Road & Track tried a '70 'Vette with the stock 454 and automatic. It recorded 7.0 seconds in the 0-60-mph run, a 15.0-second quarter-mile at 93 mph, and a top speed of 144 mph. Though the editors described it as "one of the better Corvettes we've driven lately," they found the ride suffered from "lack of suspension travel [that] decrees too much damping in the up direction and too little in the down; the result is considerable harshness over sharp bumps but a distinct 'floatiness' over gentle undulations at speed. On bad roads the Corvette simply loses its cool, rattling, shaking and squeaking in a scandalous manner." The brakes

got only "fair" marks as they "faded more than in any recent Corvette we've tried; the extreme weight of the car [4070 pounds as tested] with the heavy engine and air conditioning, etc., are responsible."

The days of the big-inch, big-power Corvettes were already numbered. Horsepower and displacement would both fall as the Seventies wore on. As they did, America's sports car would become a more balanced package of the sort *R&T* could endorse.

Few styling changes were made on the '71s, for at least three reasons. First, the 1970 run had started late. Second, the engineers were swamped in meeting emissions limits. Third, the car still looked good, so why fool with it?

Significant for engineering, though not numbers, was the ZR-1 option—a racing package ostensibly offered for the model year. It comprised the new LT-1 370-bhp small block, heavy-duty four-speed transmission, power brakes, aluminum radiator, and a revised suspension with special springs, shocks, stabilizer bar, and spindle strut shafts. Since it was a competition option, it could not be ordered with power windows, power steering, air conditioning, rear window defogger,

Stylewise, the 1971 (*left*) and 1972 (*below*) Corvettes mainly marked time, partly because of the energy being expended on emissions tuning. After 1972, front chrome bumpers and the removable rear window would be gone.

wheel covers, or radio. Only eight examples went out the door.

After the previous year's abrupt downturn, Corvette sales made a satisfying recovery for 1971, with 21,801 units delivered for the model year. The coupe had taken the sales lead over the roadster beginning in 1969, perhaps reflecting the T-top model's greater all-weather versatility. By 1971, the gap had widened to a ratio of about five to three. Convertible popularity was on the wane throughout the industry, and the government threatened to enact a safety standard for rollover protection in a crash that would have effectively made the sale of fully open cars illegal in the United States after 1975. All of these factors conspired against the romantic 'Vette roadster, which had only a couple of years left to run.

For 1972, Corvette mainly marked time. But engines now bore the full brunt of emissions tuning, and both horsepower and performance were further deemphasized. The big-block LS-6 option was cancelled, leaving the 365-bhp LS-5 the most potent engine in the lineup. Otherwise, changes were few. The fiber-optic light monitors were scratched, which cleaned up the center console considerably, and the anti-theft alarm system previously offered at extra cost was made standard—a belated recognition of the 'Vette's high desirability among car thieves. The year 1972 would also see the last for the coupe's removable backlight—it would be fixed after the model year. Sales inched upward for 1972, scoring a gain of nearly 5200 units to reach 26,994 cars.

The LT-1 small block was also in the last of its three years of production, but for the first time it could be combined with air conditioning. Chevy engineers had been reluctant to offer the combination, fearing the solid-lifter unit's higher revving ability would pull the air conditioner belts off their pulleys. To forestall such a possibility, tachometers on cars so equipped were redlined at 5600 rpm rather than the normal 6500 rpm.

The first major styling change in the checkered history of the fifth generation of Corvettes came in 1973. In styling, anyway, technology was beginning to come up with answers to federal mandates. The '73 Corvette offered an effective answer indeed—a

The LT-1 small block was in its third—and last—year of production in 1972, but for the first time it could be combined with air conditioning (*below*). The first major styling change of the fifth-generation Corvettes came for 1973 (*right*). Chevy's answer to the federally mandated five-mph bumpers was ingenious—and attractive: a urethane plastic soft nose that could bounce back to its original shape after a parking lot bump. It added two inches to the length and 35 pounds to the weight.

This page: Corvettes for dreamers: 1970 New York show car (*below left*), Mulsanne (*below right*), Aero Coupe (*bottom left*), and Sirocco (*bottom right*). The major change for the 1974 models was a urethane body-color rear end treatment to match the front that had been revamped for 1973.

Corvette Engines: The L, LT, ZL, and LS Mega-Blocks

A mechanical-lifter small block, derived from Chevrolet's earlier 377-cubic-inch racing engine and known as the LT-1, was promised for 1969, then delayed. But fans of unusual street engines had nothing to worry about, because Chevy had two mills that were simply outrageous—the L88 and the ZL-1.

The L88 was the 435-brake-horsepower aluminum-head 427-cid Mark IV V-8 that had been introduced late in the 1968 model run. Despite its size, it weighed just 60 pounds more than its small-block brothers, not much of a penalty for an extra 85 horsepower. The claimed horsepower was reputed to be low, and some experts have suggested that a

healthy L88 would easily churn out 500 bhp. Its performance—and a formidable $1032 price—were not for the faint-hearted, though.

The ZL-1 was even wilder. It was a 427 with aluminum-alloy heads and block, derived from the engine that Bruce McLaren was running in his championship-winning Can-Am racers. The ZL-1 weighed 100 pounds less than the L88 and produced just as much conservatively rated horsepower. Both engines boasted stronger bolts and connecting rods, a modified camshaft, and cylinder heads with better breathing.

Most testers found both the L88 and ZL-1 powerhouses ridiculous for the street. They were built with just one thing in mind—acceleration, as in quarter-mile, as in drag racing. The engines accomplished heady acceleration with ease—to the detriment of virtually everything else. With their wild cams, they burped and shuddered like a colicky baby. And the

ZL-1 could not be ordered with a heater, to discourage its use on public roads—as if the $3000 price for it wasn't discouragement enough. But it was a tremendous racing machine. A typical example set up for a road course could do sub-13-second quarter-miles at 115 miles per hour. Top end was reputed to be around 170 mph—amazing for a car you could theoretically order from a local Chevy dealer.

The L88 and ZL-1 were the ultimate 1969 Corvettes, but they were predictably few and far between. Chevrolet Division records show that only 116 L88s and just two ZL-1s were completed during the year. On the other hand, thousands of Corvettes were delivered with the small blocks, both very docile engines with more than enough pep.

For 1970, the LT-1 solid-lifter small block appeared, boasting 370 bhp at 6000 rpm and a $447.50 price. It differed from the soft nose done in body color, designed to meet the five-mile-per-hour front impact protection rule that started governing all automobiles. The system was quite ingenious. A steel bumper was covered by deformable urethane plastic. It added about two inches to the Corvette's length, but only 35 pounds to its weight. It could take any kind of parking lot bump on the nose and bounce back to its original shape. Best of all, it looked good, which was more than could be said of the large black bars being wrapped over bumpers and bumper guards by less clever sports car builders. "I'm sick of these great, ugly, dirty black bumpers," moaned Bill Mitchell, who once again got his wish—to the benefit of the product. Another piece of mandated safety equipment was steel reinforcing beams in the doors that protected against side impacts.

Better still for the car were the ra-

lesser small blocks in having more radical cam timing and valve lift, larger-diameter exhaust system, and the carburetor from the big-block engines, along with special cold-air hood intake. The lesser 350 V-8s returned, unchanged from their 1969 specifications. Reflecting the increasing stranglehold of emissions requirements, Chevy stroked the big block to a full 4.00 inches for 454 cid. Output was 390 bhp at 4800 rpm on 10.25 compression. Also listed was the LS-7, a 465-bhp behemoth running 12.25:1 compression. It was ostensibly available to anyone, but it was really a competition engine and none were installed in regular production. Sports Car Graphic *did manage to get its hands on one, though, and recorded a quarter-mile time of a bit under 14 seconds and a terminal speed of near 110 mph. As with the small block of the year before, the enlarged big block produced less power per unit of displacement than its* predecessor, and its peak power speed was lower. Conversely, it had somewhat more torque and was thus more flexible at low rpm.

When GM invoked an across-the-board compression drop so that all of its engines could run on low- or no-lead fuel, the 'Vette didn't escape. The results were dramatic. The base small-block V-8 now ran a mild 8.5:1 compression and packed only 270 bhp at 4800 rpm. Compression on the LT-1 sighed to 9.0:1, and rated output sank to 330 bhp at 5600 rpm. The same compression numbers were applied to a brace of big-block engines. The LS-5 was rated at 365 bhp at 4800 rpm, and the LS-6 had 425 bhp at 5600 rpm.

None of the engines were weaklings—exactly. If they seemed to be puny at the time, it was only in relation to the prodigious power that had come to be commonplace during the muscle car era. Corvettes remained exception- *ally strong performers next to most other cars on the road. Predictably, the aluminum-head LS-6 was the top dog, capable of pushing from 0-60 mph in less than 5.5 seconds, with the quarter-mile shooting by in just under 14 seconds at 105 mph. Top speed was claimed to be in excess of 150 mph. The somewhat milder LS-5 was good for quarter-miles in the low 14s with automatic, and was only marginally slower in the 0-60-mph test.*

By 1972, the mega-block engines had been so defanged that carrying on separate discussions of them would be pointless. The American auto industry had entered the throes of its worst period in postwar history—a gray age of net bhp, seatbelt interlocks, warning buzzers, and other devices conceived in Washington. A decade would go by before the industry would accustom itself through ground-up redesign to different ways of producing high performance.

The Corvette was still called a Stingray in 1974 (*left*) and the dash still featured a three-compartment map pouch (*far left*). Shoulder and lap belts, however, were combined into a single three-point harness. Besides having an altered rear end, the '74 Corvette (*bottom*) marked the end of genuine dual exhausts and was the last of the breed able to run on leaded gasoline.

dial-ply tires being used for the first time. The Corvette had needed them for a long time. However, the radials actually delivered poorer performance than the old belted tires for the 1973 model. Road tests showed longer braking distances with an unchanged braking system and lower skidpad lateral-G figures. In addition, the radials were rated at only 120 mph while the bias-ply tires were rated at 140. But all that didn't seem to matter much in a nation that soon would see its national speed limits reduced to 55 mph in the winter of 1973-74. Corvette tires did gradually improve, and, in the long run, radials proved to be better than the bias tires had been.

Detuning and government-approved admonitions against speed were affecting the whole gamut of performance cars—both imported and domestic. But the Corvette looked worse than most because it had been such a great performer for so long. In 1973, for example, engines with mechanical lifters were not available—for the first time since 1956. Engines comprised an L48 base 350-cid unit rated at 190 bhp, L82 (350 cid) engine rated at 250 bhp, and LS-4 (454 cid) advertised at 270 bhp.

On the plus side, Chevrolet decided to concentrate on driveability and passenger comfort, both of which needed attention. An attempt was made to reduce engine roar by adding sound deadener at various points in the body and a deadening pad under the hood. Chassis mounts made of a rubber and steel combination for flexibility and strength were specified to help eliminate all but good vibrations. The problem-prone panel for the concealed wipers was junked for a simple rear hood extension. Nobody was too sorry to see it go, but some objections were raised to the permanently fixed rear window on the coupe. The attachment did, however, add a couple of inches to the small cargo compartment, since the window stowage receptacle went away as well. A new option serving both form and function was a handsome set of aluminum wheels. The only problem was that some structural problems were found in the first 800 sets, and they had to be recalled. Rumors are that some remain in service. Later 'Vette aluminum wheels used very similar styling.

Road & Track tested a four-speed L82 with 3.70:1 final drive and generally liked the changes for '73. The latest Corvette wasn't as fast as previous models and it didn't handle quite as well either, but it was a more civilized machine for long-distance touring or an afternoon's run in the hills. "For all its age, size and compromises, if the Corvette is equipped with the right options it is a pleasant and rewarding car to drive, and this 1973 example was one of the best Corvettes we've ever driven." Even considering its faults, the '73 was an extremely good buy compared to all but the really low-buck sports cars of the day. Despite less power, the 'Vette could still run the quarter in the mid-15-second range, virtually the same as a Porsche 911E or DeTomaso Pantera, but it listed at $5635 while the Porsche sold in the United States for $10,025 and the Pantera retailed at around $10,000. The Datsun 240Z, introduced for 1970, wasn't even in the same ball park with its 17.7-second quarter-mile time, though it did sport a more attractive $4600 price tag.

The *R&T* test also showed that rumors about the forthcoming Corvette still made good copy. "The '73 Corvette is not the exciting new Corvette, not the mid-engine car promised to us (and by us to you) for this year. That is still most definitely on the way, however." The mid-engine Corvette was predicted as being about three years away. As we now know, a decade would pass before a really new design of any kind would appear.

Despite the six-year-old styling and body engineering, the Corvette continued to find a steady supply of customers. Chevrolet retailed a healthy 34,464 units for 1973, an increase of about 8000 over the previous year.

Model year 1974 is not remembered very fondly by performance fans. It was the year of the Arab oil embargo, which prompted the first energy crisis in the U. S.—resulting in rising gas prices, rationing, and long lines at the fuel pumps. Suddenly, the big, heavy, thirsty Corvette looked woefully anachronistic, but Chevy could do little else than carry on with it and hope for the best.

The major change for the year was a body-color rear end treatment to match the front that was introduced for '73. Again, urethane plastic was

used, and the ensemble tapered downward instead of upward as on the original Kamm-style tail. The 1974 back bumper was a two-piece affair with a seam in the middle. In subsequent years, it would be a one-piece unit.

The '74 model marked the end of a number of items. Among them were the last genuine dual exhausts, which henceforth would be routed into catalytic converters and then to separate pipes and mufflers. The '74 was also the last 'Vette able to run on leaded gas, the unleaded requirement coming, of course, with the switch to the catalytic converter. Finally, 1974 was the last year that a Corvette could be ordered with a big-block V-8—the 270-bhp LS-4 version of the 454. The base and extra-cost small-block V-8s were still available and unaltered in output from 1973.

Other changes were extremely minor. The move to performance automatic transmissions yielded the M40 three-speed unit. Shoulder and

The 1974 Corvette (*top*) was a case where federally mandated five-mile-per-hour rear bumpers actually resulted in a better-looking car. The L82 engine (*below*) had a displacement of 350 cubic inches and cranked out 250 emissions-controlled horsepower.

lap belts were combined into a single three-point harness and the inertia-reel setup was changed somewhat. The rearview mirror became wider. Radiator efficiency improved. The burglar alarm switch was moved from the rear of the car to the left front fender. The power steering pump was altered for greater durability. And so on.

One of the all-time bargain Cor-vette performance packages appeared for 1974. It was the gymkhana suspen-sion option, code FE7, costing a mere $7. Though it was little more than the tried-and-true formula of higher-rate springs and firmer, specially calibrated shocks, it yielded a handling improve-ment all out of proportion to its paltry price. In a way, the option reflected the tenor of the times. Mammoth engines and pavement-peeling acceleration had been rendered obsolete by infla-tion, high insurance rates, and the sky-rocketing price of fuel. Then, too, buy-ers were becoming more sophisticated, beginning to demand more well-rounded cars.

Thus, the Corvette's character had changed by the mid-Seventies, and Chevy's marketing approach changed with it. The '74 was not nearly as brutal as the 'Vettes of four years

Model year 1975 saw few obvious physical changes to the Stingray (*opposite page*), but it would be the last year for the genuine Corvette roadster (for a while, anyway). Outside, small extrusions with black pads were added to the front and rear bumpers (*this page, above*). The Four-Rotor (*top*) was styled by Bill Mitchell and built on an XP-882 chassis. Its rotary engine was later replaced by a 400-cubic-inch V-8.

Despite the convertible's demise, 46,558 Corvettes were built for 1976. Few changes could be found in the engine room (*below*); the 350 V-8 came in either 180- or 210-horsepower form. Externally, the '76 'Vette (*left*) was largely a holdover from 1975. The Corvette crest is shown (*bottom*) as it appeared on the nose of the '76 Stingray.

earlier. Nor was it as light and nimble as the small-block Sting Rays. Even so, it was satisfyingly quick. With the 250-bhp small-block, it could scamper from 0-60 mph in about 7.5 seconds and top out at around 125 mph. Besides that, it could return about 14-15 mpg—not all that bad considering the performance. The 1974 was also the most luxurious

'Vette yet—still a bit noisy, perhaps, but a capable and refined grand tourer with plenty of creature comforts and far greater reliability than most of its high-buck European competitors.

Enthusiasts were about to learn that the fifth-generation Corvette had staying power in more ways than one. With the appearance of the '74 model, some began wondering if Corvette development had been frozen. It had not, of course, and rumors continued to fly about the all-new mid-engine 'Vette that was presumably just around the corner. But what most failed to notice was that the fifth generation defied industry sales trends, selling at or near its best-ever levels at a time when it should have done anything but that. The model year total for '74 was 37,502—quite close to the record figure of 1969, a year when the economy and the energy pictures were both considerably brighter. Understandably, Chevy saw no compelling need to change the Corvette's design. Apparently, neither did the buyers.

Corvette's hidden headlights are shown in the on
position (*right*). Also hidden on the '76 Corvette
(*above*) was a steel subsection in the forward part of
the body to increase rigidity and to keep out
some of the heat from the hotter-running engines.

Model year 1975 saw no obvious physical changes in America's sports car, but it would mark a milestone of sorts. This would be the last year for the genuine Corvette roadster. Since the 1953 original, the roadster body style had been a big part of the Corvette tradition. But GM was fighting against declining interest in convertibles generally and a rising chorus of consumer advocates calling for safety first. The last of 4629 ragtops came off the line in July—the end of an era.

At least the convertible was available throughout the year. The big-block V-8, which had been first wedged into a Corvette for 1965, was dropped altogether, a casualty of the oil wars. The only optional engine was the L82 small block, rated at 205 bhp, and the base 350 was detuned to a measly 165 bhp. Helping to keep the power ratings from being even more anemic was the switch to catalytic converters, a move made by most automakers in 1975. A positive note was the advent of breakerless electronic ignition, accompanied by an electronic (instead of mechanical) tachometer drive. Outside, small extrusions with black pads were added to the front and rear bumpers. A headlights-on warning buzzer was added per federal dictates. Sales hit 38,465 units.

The Corvette's hold on the public was such that it set a record the fol-

Major Specifications Fifth-Generation Corvettes

	1968	1970	1974	1977
Chassis and Body				
Frame:	Box section, welded			
Body:	Glass-reinforced plastic, two-seat coupe and convertible (except 1977)			
Front suspension:	Independent, unequal-length A-arms, coil springs, tube shocks, anti-sway bars			
Rear suspension:	Independent, lateral leaf spring, struts, U-joint halfshafts, trailing arms, tube shocks			
Wheels:	15" × 7JK steel disc	15" × 8.5" cast-alloy	15" × 8.5" cast-alloy	15" × 8" cast-alloy
Tires:	Goodyear F70-15	Michelin X 205-15	GR70-15 radials	Firestone 500 GR70-15
Dimensions				
Wheel base (in.):	98.0	98.0	98.0	98.0
Length (in.):	182.1	182.5	185.5	185.2
Height (in.):	47.8	47.4	47.8	48.0
Width (in.):	69.2	69.0	69.0	70.0
Track front/rear (in.):	58.3/59.0	58.7/59.4	58.7/59.5	58.7/59.5
Ground clearance (in.):	4.9	4.5	4.2	5.0
Weight (lbs):	3260	na	na	3450
Engine				
Type:	Ohv V-8, water-cooled, cast-iron			
Designation:	L46	LS-5	L82	L82
Main bearings:	5	5	5	5
Bore × stroke:	4.00 × 3.25	4.25 × 4.00	4.00 × 3.48	4.00 × 3.48
Displacement (ci):	327	454	350	350
Compression ratio:	11.0:1	10.25:1	9.0:1	9.0:1
Induction:	Rochester 4-bbl carburetor	Rochester 4-bbl carburetor	Rochester 4-bbl carburetor	Rochester 4-bbl carburetor
Exhaust system:	Split cast-iron manifolds, dual exhausts			
Brake horsepower @ rpm:	350 @ 5800	390 @ 4800	250 @ 5200	210 @ 5200
Lbs/ft torque @ rpm:	360 @ 3600	500 @ 3400	285 @ 4000	255 @ 3600
Electrical system:	12-volt Delco-Remy ignition			
Drivetrain				
Transmission:	4-speed manual, auto option	3-speed auto, torque converter	4-speed manual, auto option	4-speed manual, auto option
Gear ratios:				
First—	2.20:1	2.48:1	2.64:1	2.64:1
Second—	1.64:1	1.48:1	1.75:1	1.75:1
Third—	1.27:1	1.00:1	1.34:1	1.34:1
Fourth—	1.00:1	—	1.00:1	1.00:1
Rear axle type:	Hypoid semifloating			
Rear axle ratio:	3.70:1	3.08:1	3.70:1	3.70:1
Steering:	Recirculating ball (power assist 1970, 1974, 1977)			
Ratio:	17.6:1	17.6:1	17.0:1	17.0:1
Turning circle (ft):	40	37	38	38
Brakes:	Vented 4-wheel discs, 11.75" diameter, single calipers			
Brake lining area (sq. in.):	461	461	461	461
Performance				
0-50 mph:	6.0	5.5	6.3	5.5
0-60 mph:	7.5	7.0	7.5	7.0
0-100 mph:	na	14.0	18.5	19.0
Standing-start quarter-mile (sec):	15.5 @ 90-94 mph	15.0 @ 92-95 mph	16.0 @ 90-93 mph	15.5 @ 90-92 mph
Top speed (mph):	130	145	124	na
Average fuel consumption (mpg):	11-15	8-12	12-15	13-16

lowing year, even though the '76 version was mostly a holdover from 1975. Despite the convertible's demise, 46,558 coupes were sold before dealers closed their books, a reflection of the recovering market and lack of any real price/performance competition. Few changes could be found in the engine room, the bogus air extractor vents vanished from the rear deck, and rear bumper trim was slightly altered. A sport steering wheel was offered, but 'Vette fanatics were irritated by it because it was the same wheel found on the lowly Vega. To increase rigidity and to keep out some of the heat from the hotter-running engines, a steel subsection was added to the forward part of the body structure. Induction was modified so that air came in from in front of and above the radiator instead of from the cowl area near the windshield. The change was made to remedy a noise problem caused by having the air flow close to the passenger compartment.

For 1977, the fifth-generation Corvette still continued on. Once more the mechanicals were left alone, and most of the year's efforts were aimed at refinement for boulevard cruising. Naturally, the most visible ones were inside. The console was redesigned to accept a larger array of Delco music-makers, including an AM/FM stereo radio with integral tape deck, a first-time option. Also new were a revised sport steering wheel with leather-wrapped rim and a steering column stalk control for headlight dimmer switch and windshield wiper/washer. The steering column itself was redesigned to allow driving with arms extended. The redesign also made entering and exiting easier. A related modification lengthened the manual transmission lever for easier use of the handbrake. Leather upholstery was now standard, and cloth seats with hide bolsters became an extra-cost item. Power steering and brakes were both standardized. Again, the alarm switch was relocated—this time incorporated with the left door lock button. Rearview mirror position and sunvisors were revamped, and the console gauges and heater controls were restyled for a more contemporary look.

Outside, the optional rear deck luggage carrier was reworked so that the twin lift-off panels could be carried there instead of in the luggage com-

Serial Spans, Production, and Base Prices

Year	Serial Prefix	Serial Span	Prod. Units	Price
1968	194378S	400001-428566	9936 coupe	$4663
	194678S		18,630 roadster	$4230
1969	194379S	700001-738762	22,154 coupe	$4781
	194679S		16,608 roadster	$4438
1970	194370S	400001-417316	10,668 coupe	$5192
	194670S		6648 roadster	$4849
1971	194371S	100001-121801	14,680 coupe	$5536
	194671S		7121 roadster	$5299
1972	1Z37K2S	500001-520486*	20,486 coupe	$5472
	1Z67K2S	500001-506508*	6508 roadster	$5246
1973	1Z37K3S	400001-424372	24,372 coupe	$5921
	1Z67K3S	400001-406093	6093 roadster	$5685
1974	1Z37J4S	400001-432028	32,028 coupe	$6372
	1Z67J4S	400001-404629	4629 roadster	$6156
1975	1Z37J5S	400001-433836	33,836 coupe	$7117
	1Z67J5S	400001-404629	4629 roadster	$6857
1976	1Z67J6S	400001-446558	46,558	$7605
1977	1Z67J7S	100001-149213	49,213	$8648

*proportional figures

A new numbering system took effect in 1972. Using the prefix 1Z37K2S as an example, the numerals and letters designate the following:
1 = Chevrolet Division
Z = Model
37 = Coupe (67 would be Convertible)
K = Base engine 1972-73
J = Base engine from 1974
2 = Model year, where 2 is 1972
S = St. Louis plant

Opposite page: The bogus air extractor vents vanished from the rear deck of the '76 Corvette and rear bumper trim was slightly altered (*top and bottom left*); the interior (*bottom right*) changed little. The 1977 Corvette (*this page*) featured refinements geared to improve boulevard cruising.

1977

Power Teams

The combinations of engines, transmissions, and axle ratios available to Corvette buyers skyrocketed in the late Sixties. The following chart attempts to sort out some of the confusion. It was compiled from factory records through 1974, after which combinations shrank back to manageable size. The chart does not take into account certain mid-year changes, such as the advent of the 350-cubic-inch V-8 in January 1968. All specs are for engines without air conditioning, which had the effect of altering availability.

Engine	Disp	Bhp (@ rpm)	Transmission	Axle Ratio Standard	Optional
Model Year 1968					
Turbo-Fire V-8	327	300 @ 5000	3-speed manual (2.54:1 low)	3.36:1	3.08:1
			4-speed manual (2.52:1 low)	3.36:1	3.08:1
			Turbo Hydra-matic	3.08:1	—

Engine	Disp	Bhp (@ rpm)	Transmission	Axle Ratio Standard	Optional
Model Year 1968					
Turbo-Fire V-8	327	350 @ 5800	4-speed manual (2.52:1 low)	3.36:1	3.55:1
			4-speed manual (2.20:1 low)	3.70:1	4.11:1
Turbo-Jet V-8	427	390 @ 5400	4-speed manual (2.52:1 low)	3.08:1	3.36:1
			4-speed manual (2.20:1 low)	3.36:1	3.08:1 3.55:1 3.70:1
			Turbo Hydra-matic	3.08:1	2.73:1
Turbo-Jet V-8	427	400 @ 5400	4-Speed manual (2.52:1 low)	3.08:1	3.36:1
			4-speed manual (2.20:1 low)	3.36:1	3.08:1 3.55:1 3.70:1
			Turbo Hydra-matic	3.08:1	2.73:1
Turbo-Jet V-8	427	435 @ 5800	4-speed manual (2.20:1 low)	3.55:1	3.36:1 3.70:1 4.11:1

partment, where they were less convenient to stow. Glass roof panels were listed as an option at the start of the model year, but GM cancelled them in a reputed dispute with the supplier over sales rights. The vendor eventually marketed them itself—and Chevy promptly went to another source for 1978. One final exterior change would be noted instantly by car spotters: The Stingray nameplate came off the front fenders, replaced by the traditional crossed-flags insignia, and the car was simply called a Corvette.

Sales continued to climb, with 46,558 units retailed for the model year. Not bad for a design that had been in production for 10 seasons— the longest run of any Corvette generation to date, and eloquent testimony to its near-universal appeal. The Corvette's longevity also said a great deal about GM's knack for being able to update a design successfully in light of new federal requirements without any major alterations and without detracting from aesthetics or performance— as much a factor in the resurgence of the Chevrolet Camaro and Pontiac Firebird ponycars as it was in maintaining the popularity of the Corvette.

The fifth generation had done exceptionally well indeed, prospering during one of the most difficult periods in the history of America's automaking industry. But it was far from finished. It was about to be rejuvenated with some special revisions for a very special year. America's sports car was about to celebrate its Silver Anniversary.

While engine choices remained the same for 1977,
Corvette's interior came in for some revisions
that year. The console, for example, was redesigned
to accept a larger array of Delco music-makers and
a revised sport steering wheel with leather-wrapped rim
appeared, as did a steering column stalk control
for headlight dimmer switch and windshield wiper/washer.
Leather upholstery became standard. Production spurted
to a record 49,213 units, indicating that America's
love affair with the Corvette was as strong as ever.

Model Year 1968

Engine	Disp	Bhp (@ rpm)	Transmission	Axle Ratio Standard	Axle Ratio Optional
Turbo-Fire 350	350	300 @ 4800	3-speed manual (2.54:1 low)	3.36:1	3.08:1
			4-speed manual (2.52:1 low)	3.36:1	3.08:1
			Turbo Hydra-matic	3.08:1	—
Turbo-Fire 350	350	350 @ 5600	4-speed manual (2.52:1 low)	3.36:1	3.55:1
			4-speed manual (2.20:1 low)	3.70:1	4.11:1
Turbo-Jet 427	427	390 @ 5400	4-speed manual (2.52:1 low)	3.08:1	3.36:1
			4-speed manual (2.20:1 low)	3.36:1	3.08:1 / 3.55:1 / 3.70:1
			Turbo Hydra-matic	3.08:1	2.73:1
Turbo-Jet 427	427	400 @ 5400	4-speed manual (2.52:1 low)	3.08:1	3.36:1
			4-speed manual (2.20:1 low)	3.36:1	3.08:1 / 3.55:1 / 3.70:1
			Turbo Hydra-matic	3.08:1	2.73:1
Turbo-Jet 427	427	435 @ 5800	4-speed manual (2.20:1 low)	3.55:1	3.36:1 / 3.70:1 / 4.11:1
			Turbo Hydra-matic	3.08:1	2.73:1 / 3.36:1
Turbo-Jet 427 L88	427	430	4-speed manual (2.20:1 low)	3.36:1	3.08:1 / 3.55:1 / 3.70:1 / 4.11:1 / 4.56:1
			Turbo Hydra-matic	3.08:1	2.73:1 / 3.36:1

Model Year 1970

Engine	Disp	Bhp (@ rpm)	Transmission	Axle Ratio Standard	Axle Ratio Optional
Turbo-Fire 350	350	300	4-speed manual (2.52:1 low)	3.36:1	3.08:1
			Turbo Hydra-matic	3.08:1	3.36:1
Turbo-Fire 350	350	350	4-speed manual (2.20:1 low)	3.70:1	4.11:1
			4-speed manual (2.52:1 low)	3.36:1	—
Turbo-Fire 350	350	370	4-speed manual (2.20:1 low)	3.70:1	3.55:1 / 4.11:1
			4-speed manual (2.52:1 low)	3.55:1	3.36:1 / 3.70:1
			4-speed manual (2.20:1 low)	3.36:1	3.08:1 / 3.55:1 / 3.70:1
Turbo-Jet 454	454	390	4-speed manual (2.52:1 low)	3.08:1	3.36:1
			Turbo Hydra-matic	3.08:1	2.73:1
Turbo-Jet 454	454	460	4-speed manual (2.20:1 low)	3.36:1	3.08:1 / 3.55:1
			Turbo Hydra-matic	3.08:1	3.36:1

Model Year 1971

Engine	Disp	Bhp (@ rpm)	Transmission	Axle Ratio Standard	Axle Ratio Optional
Turbo-Fire 350	350	270/210*	4-speed manual (2.52:1 low)	3.36:1	3.08:1
			Turbo Hydra-matic	3.08:1	3.36:1

Model Year 1968

Engine	Disp	Bhp (@ rpm)	Transmission	Axle Ratio Standard	Axle Ratio Optional
Turbo-Fire 350	350	330/275*	4-speed manual (2.20:1 low)	3.70:1	3.55:1 / 4.11:1
			4-speed manual (2.52:1 low)	3.55:1	3.36:1 / 3.70:1
Turbo-Jet 454	454	365/285*	4-speed manual (2.20:1 low)	3.36:1	3.08:1 / 3.55:1 / 3.70:1
			4-speed manual (2.52:1 low)	3.08:1	3.36:1
			Turbo Hydra-matic	3.08:1	3.36:1
Turbo-Jet 454	454	425/325*	4-speed manual (2.20:1 low)	3.36:1	3.08:1 / 3.55:1
			Special 4-speed (2.20:1 low)	3.36:1	3.08:1 / 3.55:1 / 3.70:1 / 4.11:1
			Turbo Hydra-matic	3.08:1	3.36:1

Model Year 1972**

Engine	Disp	Bhp (@ rpm)	Transmission	Axle Ratio Standard	Axle Ratio Optional
Turbo-Fire 350	350	200	4-speed manual (2.52:1 low)	3.36:1	3.08:1
			Turbo Hydra-matic	3.36:1	3.08:1
Turbo-Fire Special	350	255	4-speed manual (2.52:1 low)	3.36:1	3.55:1
			4-speed manual (2.20:1 low)	3.70:1	—
			Turbo Hydra-matic	3.36:1	—
Turbo-Jet	454	270	4-speed manual (2.52:1 low)	3.08:1	3.36:1
			4-speed manual (2.20:1 low)	3.36:1	3.55:1
			Turbo Hydra-matic	3.08:1	3.36:1

Model Year 1973

Engine	Disp	Bhp (@ rpm)	Transmission	Axle Ratio Standard	Axle Ratio Optional
Turbo-Fire 350	350	190 @ 4400	4-speed manual (2.52:1 low)	3.36:1	3.08:1
			Turbo Hydra-matic	3.08:1	3.36:1
Turbo-Fire Special	350	250 @ 5200	4-speed manual (2.52:1 low)	3.55:1	3.36:1 / 3.70:1
			4-speed manual (2.20:1 low)	3.70:1	3.55:1
			Turbo Hydra-matic	3.55:1	3.36:1 / 3.70:1
Turbo-Jet	454	275 @ 4400	4-speed manual (2.52:1 low)	3.08:1	3.36:1
			4-speed manual (2.20:1 low)	3.36:1	3.55:1

Model Year 1974

Engine	Disp	Bhp (@ rpm)	Transmission	Axle Ratio Standard	Axle Ratio Optional
Turbo-Fire	350	195 @ 4400	4-speed manual (2.52:1 low)	3.36:1	3.08:1
			Turbo Hydra-matic	3.08:1	3.36:1
Turbo-Fire Special	350	250 @ 5200	4-speed manual (2.52:1 low)	3.55:1	3.70:1
			4-speed manual (2.20:1 low)	3.70:1	3.36:1 / 3.55:1 / 4.11:1
			Turbo Hydra-matic	3.55:1	3.70:1
Turbo-Jet	454	270 @ 4400	4-speed manual (2.52:1)	3.08:1	3.36:1
			4-speed manual (2.20:1 low)	3.36:1	3.08:1 / 3.55:1
			Turbo Hydra-matic	3.08:1	3.36:1

* Gross/net
** All bhp figures net after 1972

CHAPTER EIGHT

1978-1982: The Silver Lining

The Corvette's silver anniversary inspired questions as to General Motors' goals for the car. Where was it going? Except at GM, the answer seemed shrouded in mystery.

The Corvette was going in the same direction that it had been heading for the past decade—up and over the 50,000-unit-a-year mark in sales, the height of acceptance for a car that the corporation never thought would sell half as much. And the model would do so despite any impediments that the government, the safety lobby, or the Arabs could throw at it. By the late Seventies, the Corvette was nowhere near its original concept of a dual-purpose sports car. But as a show room traffic builder and high-profit personal car, it was indispensible. GM decided that the old beast still had plenty of life left in it.

An all-new Corvette was still a few years away, and sooner than Chevrolet could imagine, it would need all the traffic building that it could muster. Signs of impending problems for GM had been discernible since 1973. Perhaps the most important factor—the turning point—was the Arab oil embargo of that winter, which triggered a series of events that had enormous impact on the entire industry. As Lee Iacocca would say later, "The market flip-flopped by 40 percent, literally overnight. That had never happened before, not even in the Depression." Sales of big Detroit cars, heretofore that city's staple good, were stunted, while buyers paid premium prices to get into compacts and subcompacts that they would not have used even for a run to the grocery store in 1972. Lines grew at gas stations and states adopted various laws intended to ration the limited supply of fuel.

The embargo had one positive result, though. The perils of 1973-74 made the nation energy-conscious in a way that it never had been before, highlighting the need for a type of car that buff magazines had been requesting for years—a car that was smaller, more efficient, and better built. For a couple of years, the American public focused on that very kind of car. As a result, the Japanese automakers established themselves as major competitors. Up to the early Seventies, they had made only a small dent in the American market, in which the Volkswagen Beetle was still the dominant import. Toyota and Datsun were suddenly serious competition for VW. Driving a Japanese car became chic, just as driving a Beetle had been in the Fifties.

Then the oil started flowing again. Many buyers forgot everything that they had just experienced. The ones who didn't, however, continued to buy foreign cars. Japanese makes had impressed people with their quality, if not their long-term durability, and they ultimately overcame league-leading VW. The Japanese had focused on Americanized styling and accessories, plus they offered a high value per U.S. dollar.

Did all of this affect the Corvette? Yes and no. The economy craze was not all that significant, because 40,000 or more people each year would be willing to pay whatever price to drive a large, V-8-powered sports car. But the quality issue was something else. For the first time, testers, buyers, and even long-time fans were complaining that the Corvette was poorly assembled out of shoddy materials. *Ergonomics* became a familiar word if not a household one, and the Corvette was judged to have low marks in that category. In fact, it ranked poorly indeed with the gymkhana suspension, which was about as sophisticated as that found on a snowmobile.

But critics remained in the minority for the time being, and sales continued to be strong. In model year 1979, for instance, Chevrolet would build its sales to 53,807 Corvettes—the first 50,000-unit year in the car's history. "In 1970," said *Road & Track's* John Lamm, the St. Louis plant "...reached 32,000 and they said no more, that is the utmost capacity. [Now] with the same facility and the same floorspace, we ended up eventually producing 44,000 Corvettes."

Another factor affecting the auto industry bears mentioning: By the late Seventies, inflation coupled with mandated equipment was sending the prices of new cars into the stratosphere, making new car ownership increasingly difficult for a growing number of Americans. More and more people began to forsake the traditional habit of trading their cars for new ones every two or three years. GM looked at the situation and decided that it called for more timely products. The 1975 Seville broke new ground as a compact luxury car, and the 1977 down-sized standard cars were extraordinary for having trimmed hundreds of pounds and many inches without losing interior space or comfort. Such were the first stages in a massive program to revamp GM's entire fleet. All of the company's future cars would be smaller, lighter, and more economical, and an increasing number of them would employ space-saving front-wheel drive. After the 1977 down-sizing, the intermediates were trimmed for 1978, and the X-body front-wheel-drive compacts debuted two years later. The subcompact J-body was planned for 1982.

Through the turn of the decade, the Corvette soldiered on without much change. However, making the conclusion that it was forgotten would be a mistake. It just didn't have the highest priority at the time. It sold well enough, so it was left alone. The major alternative, if and when a new 'Vette became necessary, was generally agreed to be a mid-engine car. The mid-engine project had been postponed often—once when Ford killed its own mid-engine Mach I program, then again when continued good sales of the current car rendered a radically new design useless. The potential future Corvettes—XP-882 and the Aerovette—and the idea of a Wankel powerplant never quite reached fruition.

On March 15, 1977, at precisely 2:01 PM, Chevrolet general manager Robert D. Lund drove the 500,000th production Corvette off the assembly line in St. Louis, Missouri. It was an historic occasion, paralleling that day in late June nearly a quarter of a century earlier when the very first one had rolled out the door of the small plant in Flint, Michigan. The event signaled a time for looking back to reminisce and for looking forward to plan. The Corvette's future remained uncertain, with the decision as to its direction being based on all of the conflicting and, in some cases, baffling influences of the time.

The immediate problem facing GM was the 1978 Silver Anniversary Edition of the car. Chevrolet Division wanted something dramatic. But how could it be dramatic with a 10-year-old design? Styling proposed a significant change that helped—a fastback roofline for the 1978 model. It was a relatively inexpensive alteration that gave the car a fresh appearance. The fastback line was created by a wide expanse of glass that wrapped around to the car's sides, improving rear-quarter visibility while contributing a feeling of interior spaciousness. Emblems front and rear cited the model as com-

memorating the Silver Anniversary. The luggage area was now larger and more accessible, but a hinged backlight would have made it even better—an idea rejected on grounds of cost.

Among minor changes for the '78 were squared-up housings for the speedometer and tachometer to match the restyled center console gauges that had appeared in 1977. The interior

door panels were redesigned, with new armrests and integral door pulls. A glove box with a real door and a fuel tank with greater capacity (24 gallons, up from 17) were positive changes. Moving the windshield wiper/washer control from the steering column stalk back to the dash was not. By 1978, Corvettes were the most stolen cars in America, and the standard anti-theft

The Corvette celebrated its Silver Anniversary in 1978.
In honor of the occasion, it received a new fastback
roofline with a wide expanse of glass that wrapped
around to the car's sides, improving rear-quarter
vision while contributing a feeling of interior
spaciousness. Emblems front and rear cited the
model as commemorating the Silver Anniversary.

system was now wired into the lift-out roof panels, which had an unfortunate habit of disappearing on dark nights. Likewise, because the new "glassback" exposed the luggage area, a security shade was mounted at the rear of the compartment. It could be rolled forward to cover anything stored underneath. The roof panels were available in glass as well as steel, and both were modified to provide more headroom and simpler locking procedures. The three-point seat belts were given a single inertia reel, and belt guides were eliminated.

For the first time, 60-series tires were available, necessitating some inner fender shearing. According to division public relations, Chevrolet "put the most aggressive tire on the car as possible." The HR60s (225R/60-15 metric) were an option to the standard GR70s. In addition, the FE7 gymkhana suspension package cost $41.

The historical importance of the 1978 model prompted the factory to produce two specials—the Silver Anniversary model and the Pace Car Replica. The 'Vette had paced the 62nd running of the Indianapolis 500 in 1978. Demand for the Pace Car was so high that a few bogus ones appeared, and dealers asked up to $28,000 for them.

Performance seemed to lose out in deference to the other events. The old standby 350-cubic-inch V-8 was back again, in two forms with marginally revised power settings. The base L48 with 185 brake horsepower (175 bhp in California) pulled a 3.55:1 final drive for better acceleration. The optional L82 developed 220 bhp and cost $525 extra, having dual-snorkel air intake and a revamped exhaust system behind its catalytic converter to reduce back pressure.

Sales were apparently recovering from the depressing levels reached from 1973-75. Although production dipped by about 2500 units, the total count for the model year was still well over 45,000. What did the numbers signify for the future? Despite the fastback restyle, the Corvette was beginning to look a bit dated. With Dave McLellan now in charge of Corvette engineering, work had begun on an eventual replacement that bore a more conventional look than had been anticipated for so long. But no one was sure when the replacement would

The Silver Anniversary Corvettes were offered in coupe form. As 'Vettes were a favorite among car thieves, the standard anti-theft system was wired into the lift-out roof panels, which had an unfortunate habit of disappearing on dark nights. The roof panels were available in glass as well as steel, and both were modified to provide more headroom and simpler locking procedures. Likewise, because the new "glassback" exposed the luggage area, a security shade was mounted at the rear of the compartment.

Since 1978 was a special year for Corvette, all cars received Silver Anniversary emblems with crossed flags (*above*) front and rear. Chevrolet wanted something dramatic for the occasion, but what? Styling proposed the answer—the fastback roofline—as a relatively inexpensive alteration that gave the 10-year-old design a fresh appearance and an altogether racier look (*right*).

enter production. The 1979 model continued with few changes, and the division relaxed when it set a sales record of over 50,000 units. The high sales relieved the pressure on the replacement project, too.

Changes for 1979 were minor. Lightweight bucket seats from the 1978 Pace Car Replica appeared, with more rearward travel plus different inertia seatback locks. The passenger's seatback folded forward to create a longer open area for carrying awkward cargo, but the reclining seatbacks that many had come to expect even on Japanese economy cars were still not an option in the Corvette.

All engines now had the L82-type twin-snorkel air cleaner, while the base L48 engine gained 10 more horsepower. Shock valving was standardized, whereas previously the rates had varied depending on the transmission. The final drive ratio was lowered

from 3.08:1 to 3.55:1 on models with automatic transmissions.

Other items: Pace-Car-style front and rear spoilers became optional. Tungsten-halogen high-beam headlamps were phased in. The base AM/FM radio was standardized. A final touch was the return of the crossed-flags insignia to the nose and sides.

Drag racer Doug Nash developed an interesting five-speed manual transmission as an aftermarket item, even though Corvettes weren't campaigned as they had been at one time. The five-speed was intended for use on the drag strip. It had a light magnesium-alloy case that was split to make gear changes and servicing more convenient, and it had straight-cut spur gears for higher strength and lower friction than conventional helical-cut gears, with a choice of 17 different ratios. Called the 4+1 Quick Change, Nash's

Chevy dubbed it a "Limited Edition" (*below*) and indeed the Pace Car Replica (*right*) was just that with a total production run of 6200 units. In addition to the silver and black paint job and the Pace Car lettering on the sides, Pace Cars received dramatic spoilers front and rear and a host of power and luxury extras. Base price started at $13,653.

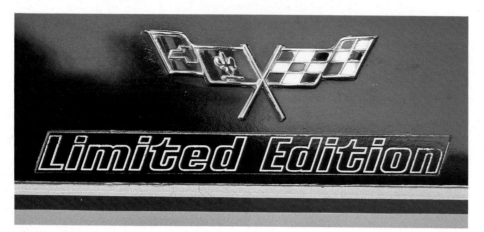

box was available at $995 for street use and at $1000 for the drag strip. *Road & Track* said, "the combination of a low numerical axle ratio and high numerical transmission gearing will live longer than the reverse combination, because as the final drive ratio increases numerically the size of the pinion gear decreases and the number of pinion teeth increases...And because most of today's cars are being built with low numerical axle ratios for reasons of improved fuel economy and lower emissions, it means no change in final drive ratio is necessary to take advantage of the Nash five-speed." *R&T* found that the new gearbox raised the 'Vette's top end from 116 to 130 miles per hour compared with the factory four-speed. Though no difference could be found in quarter-mile performance, the Nash unit posted a gain of about 1.5 miles per gallon in fuel economy, plus it reduced noise levels. The most interesting aspect of the Nash transmission was that it forecast

Special 1978s: Anniversary Edition and Pace Car Replica

Chevrolet needed something dramatic with which to celebrate the Corvette's 25th anniversary in 1978. No spectacular new car was in the works, and not much could be done to improve the engineering of the old one. GM Styling was given the job of saving the day.

Styling's biggest improvement was the fast-back rear window, which finished off the looks of the car the way that it should have been all along. Finally the Corvette had a reasonable amount of luggage space and reduced aerodynamic drag. To accommodate the modification, the interior was restyled—something else that was long overdue. In addition, Chevrolet picked up a cue from the aftermarket and fitted its car with tinted glass roof panels from the factory. They not only looked racy, but they increased headroom. As a final touch, Goodyear GT radial tires were installed.

Chevrolet also wanted to change the appearance of the car through a stripe package that would not be too expensive to produce, could be marked up significantly, and would be viewed as a desirable option. Bill Mitchell suggested that a Silver Anniversary Corvette be painted his favorite color—silver. The Anniversary package appeared as an option for any Corvette sold in 1978. In addition to the 25th anniversary emblems, the treatment included the first factory two-tone paint on a Corvette except for the early removable hardtops, having a silver upper body and a gray underbody, highlighted by a pinstripe along the dividing line. Except for the paint, however, the Silver Anniversary Corvette was depressingly stock for a celebration car.

In another move that had similar ramifications, Chevrolet negotiated with the Indianapolis Motor Speedway to have a modified Corvette chosen as the Indy pace car for 1978—a decision announced in October 1977. Chevy advertising always liked the added publicity of having a car chosen to pace the Indy 500. One such campaign involved the orange and white Camaro convertibles of 1969. Besides the pace car itself, Chevrolet wanted to build 2500 replicas for sale to the public on a first-come, first-serve basis—100 units for each year of Corvette production. However, Chevrolet had 6200 Chevrolet dealers in the United States, and General Motors was very

sensitive to charges of favoritism. So any special Corvette would have to be built to a minimum order of 6200 units. Therefore, Limited Edition Indy Pace Car Replica Corvettes made up about 15 percent of the total 1978 production to come off the St. Louis line—not really all that limited of an edition.

The Indy Pace Car order number was RPO-Z78. Like the Silver Anniversary Corvette, the Pace Car had two-tone paint treatment, with black on the upper body and silver metallic on the lower. The pinstripe between them was bright red. Alloy wheels were standard, along with huge radial tires. The roof panels were glass. The Pace Car interior reflected Bill Mitchell's influence, with silver leather or silver leather and gray cloth, and with gray carpets. Chevrolet was planning to

restyle the Corvette seats for 1979, so the program was rushed to completion so that the 1978 Indy Pace Cars would have silver versions of them.

The most dramatic additions to the Pace Cars were the spoilers. At the front was one similar to what could be found on contemporary Firebird Trans Ams. It wrapped under and around to blend into the wheel wells. At the rear, an obviously tacked-on spoiler wrapped down the body sides part way.

Further, all Pace Car Replicas came equipped with power windows, rear defogger, air conditioning, sport mirrors, tilt steering wheel, heavy-duty battery, power door locks, and an AM/FM stereo with either eight-track tape player or CB radio. The final touch was a package of decals that could be attached

to the doors. They read "Official Pace Car, 62nd Annual Indianapolis 500 Mile Race, May 28, 1978."

The base price of the Indy Pace Car was $13,653, compared with the $9351 sticker for a stock 1978 Corvette. But not one Pace Car sold at list. Most of them went for at least $15,000. Many dealers were asking $22,000, and some people paid as much as $75,000 for one! Chevrolet got more publicity out of the Indy Pace Cars than it ever dreamed possible, since many newspapers reported on the astronomical prices asked for them. A booming business began creating bogus cars.

For better or worse, the Indy Pace Car Replica was one model that would be remembered for a long, long time.

207

OFFICIAL PACE CAR
62nd ANNUAL INDIANAPOLIS 500 MILE RACE
MAY 28, 1978

This page: Some details from the 1978 Corvette Pace Car highlight the 350-cubic-inch L82 engine and the new-for-1978 60-series radial tires. The interior (*opposite page*) received squared-up housings for the speedometer and tach, redesigned door panels and armrests with integral door pulls, and a glove box with a real door.

a radically new manual production transmission being developed for the still-distant sixth-generation Corvette.

During 1978, *R&T* matched the 'Vette in a comparison test against the Mazda RX-7, Datsun 280-ZX, and Porsche 924. The American sports car came in last overall, and the editors jumped all over its harsh ride, buried driving position, minimal cargo space, and indifferent workmanship. But in summing up, they said, "Much loved and still very desirable, it's quick, has excellent brakes, a superb automatic transmission, and is filled with many appreciated amenities...all of which make it an excellent value."

With the advent of the government's corporate average fuel economy (CAFE) standards for 1978, Chevrolet decided that the Corvette needed to go on a diet. The first evidence of the weight loss could be found on the 1980 models. Curb weight was pared by about 250 pounds by using aluminum instead of steel for the front frame cross member and differential housing. The car also made greater use of plastics. The aluminum intake manifold previously used on the L82 engine was extended to the base L48. In federal trim the base engine lost five bhp to emissions tuning—190 bhp at 4400 rpm and 280 lbs/ft torque at 2400 rpm. The L82 returned with five more horsepower—230 bhp. Californians had to settle for a special 180-bhp 305-cid small block, available only with automatic transmission.

In the interest of better mileage, the previously optional front and rear spoilers were made integral with the surrounding bodywork, and the grille was raked back slightly. The result was a drop in the coefficient of drag from a Cd of 0.503 to a more respectable 0.443. While the rating wasn't great, it was a welcome improvement all the same. Air conditioning and tilt-telescope steering wheel were now standard; the power door lock button was relocated; and the two storage compartments behind the seats were combined, with the battery remaining in a separate cubbyhole behind the driver. A depressing sign of the times was that the speedometer was now calibrated to only 85 mph, in line with another government mandate.

A second fuel crunch happened in early 1979. The bottom fell out of the

American car market in the ensuing economic chaos. Yet the Corvette sailed on. Though volume was down by some 20 percent, the model year total of 40,614 units was still quite respectable for a heavy, thirsty, specialty car that had become almost too expensive (about $13,140 base) to be affordable for those people most interested in buying it.

For model year 1981, weight was reduced even further through some clever materials substitutions. Heading the list was a new transverse monoleaf rear spring made of reinforced plastic instead of steel. It pared 33 pounds from the cars equipped with automatic transmissions. Other weight-saving engineering measures included the use of thinner glass for

the doors and roof panels, and the installation of a stainless-steel exhaust manifold. The car had only one engine option—a reworked version of the familiar 350 called the L81. It featured magnesium rocker covers and an auxiliary electric cooling fan to supplement the regular engine-driven fan. In line with other 1981 GM cars, the 'Vette gained the firm's new Com-

Originally, Chevy wanted to build only 2500 Limited Edition Indy Pace Car Replicas on a first-come, first-serve basis. But since Chevy had 6200 dealers, it was decided to build one per dealer (*above*). Most sold at well over list. The Pace Car decal package, which included a winged Indianapolis Motor Speedway logo (*right*), was not factory installed—its use was at the owner's option.

The 1979 Corvette (the Stingray label had disappeared the year previous) soldiered on with few changes, but it hardly mattered as production expanded to another record: 53,807 units. New on the '79s (*above and left*) were lightweight bucket seats and extra-cost spoilers, both from the Pace Car Replica, and a base AM/FM radio. Tungsten-halogen high-beam headlights were phased in during the year, and the crossed-flags insignia returned to the nose and sides.

puter Command Control electronic emissions control system. It provided more precise fuel metering and governed the lockup of the automatic transmission's torque converter clutch, which was adopted as a fuel-saving measure. The interior was spiffed up with a six-way power driver's seat and quartz clock as standard, and all factory radios acquired electronic instead of manual tuning. Prices, pushed by inflation, rose again, with the base window sticker now a bit over $15,000. Despite a generally dismal sales year for the industry as a whole, Corvette once again showed well, selling 45,631 units.

Perhaps the biggest Corvette news of the year was the transfer of production from the old St. Louis plant to a brand-new high-tech facility in Bowling Green, Kentucky. Many of the loyal workers from Missouri were re-located to the sleepy college community that would be the 'Vette's next home. An interesting historical footnote is that for two months during the summer of 1981 the cars were built simultaneously in both places. A key advantage of the Bowling Green plant was its more advanced paint shop. St. Louis had used lacquer exclusively, but Bowling Green would apply more durable enamels and clear top coats, emulating European and Japanese practices. The Kentucky factory also had much more automated manufacturing hardware in the quest for tighter quality control. The plant had been expensive, but Chevy evidently considered the Corvette worthy of the investment. How things had changed!

With the opening of the Bowling Green facility, some observers concluded that Chevy was preparing for the arrival of an all-new Corvette model. The observers were right, of course. The existence of the next design was more or less an open secret by that time. Said *Road & Track* in November 1982: "...after all these years of rumors, conjecture, glimpses of exotic mid-engine project cars, hearsay, and slightly blurred photos shot through knotholes in the Milford Proving Ground fence, we can swear with confidence...that there really is an all-new 1983 Corvette in the wings." But testing machinery and working out assembly procedures made more sense with a familiar design than with a new one, so the fifth generation would put in one final appearance.

Using the existing platform to gain field experience with the future model's drivetrain also made sense, so the 1982 Corvette was, as *R&T* put it, "truly the last of its series...a transition car [with the] new drivetrain in the old body." The engine was still the time-proven 350-cid V-8, but with a newly developed twin throttle-body fuel injection system—called Cross-Fire injection—instead of a carburetor. For the first time since 1965, injection appeared on a production 'Vette. The system consisted of an injector unit for each cylinder bank plus cross-over intake manifolding to speed up the velocity of the air/fuel mixture. Computer Command Control electronics governed duration of injector opening in response to signals from various engine-mounted sensors. The revised power unit—intriguingly dubbed L83—was rated at 200 bhp at 4200 rpm, with a peak torque of 285 lbs/ft

The 1979 Corvette (*left and above*) featured a number of under-the-skin improvements. All engines adopted the L82-type twin-snorkel air cleaner, while the base L48 engine gained 10 horsepower, to 195. Shock valving was standardized, whereas previously it had varied depending on the transmission. The final drive ratio was lowered from 3.08:1 to 3.55:1 on models with automatic transmission for quicker acceleration. Time—and Corporate Average Fuel Economy regulations—were catching up with the Corvette by now, however, and Chevy would soon have to put its sports car on a diet.

developed at 2800 rpm. For the first time since 1955, no manual gearbox was available. The standard transmission was a four-speed automatic with torque converter lockup that was effective on all forward gears except first and governed by the engine's electronic control unit. Other changes included an in-tank electric fuel pump and a solenoid-operated trap door in the hood that opened at full throttle. The air filter, which had previously contained charcoal, reverted to paper. The exhaust system was extensively redesigned around a significantly smaller and lighter catalytic converter, dictated mainly by emissions standards.

To commemorate the last of the big 'Vettes, Chevrolet issued a special Collector Edition model for '82. However, recalling its experience with the bogus 1978 Pace Car Replicas, the division

Chevrolet claimed the 1980 Corvette (*below and bottom*) had "a recognizably new, aerodynamic appearance, plus extensive weight-reducing changes. Front air dam and rear spoiler are integrated into bumper covers." The coefficient of drag (Cd) thus dropped from 0.503 to 0.443 and the dieting took off 250 pounds. *Opposite page*: Four-Rotor XP-882 (*top*), Turbo Vette 3 (*bottom*).

XP-882, Aerovette, and Wankel: The 'Vettes that Weren't

XP-882 was an experimental program begun in the late Sixties that fueled persistent widespread speculation that the next Corvette would have a mid-engine design. The original full-scale running prototype surfaced in late 1969 as a curvy, low-slung coupe with mechanicals borrowed from the front-drive Oldsmobile Toronado and modified by Duntov for a mid-ships production installation. By mid-1970, the car was plastered all over buff books like Road & Track, which said in its July issue, "We'll stake our reputation on this being the Corvette of the future—but don't expect it until 1972 at the earliest." A January 1971 story forecasting a 1973 announcement would prove equally misguided, though the car now bore Corvette script and looked close to being production-ready.

But General Motors had something else in mind. At the enthusiastic urging of president Ed Cole, the company was busy developing a rotary engine patterned after Felix Wankel's pioneering design in Germany. Originally, it was intended as an option for Chevy's subcompact Vega to provide a domestic alternative to the rotary NSU and Mazda models then arriving in the United States. With its light weight and compact size, the Wankel was also deemed ideal for a sports car. Cole ordered two prototypes based on the XP-882 chassis: One used the basic two-rotor unit being readied for the Vega, having a sleek body styled and built by Pininfarina in Italy. Sometimes called the Two-Rotor car, it carried the XP-987GT project designation. The other car was an arresting gullwing coupe created by Bill Mitchell and powered by a pair of two-rotor engines bolted together and producing some 420 brake horsepower. Both of the cars toured the show circuit and got wide press coverage. Again, everyone assumed that here was tomorrow's Corvette. But then the energy crisis hit, exposing the Wankel's comparatively poor fuel economy. Mazda sales took a nosedive, and GM abruptly stopped further work on its own rotary—including the mid-engine Corvette designed around it.

But Bill Mitchell was nothing if not persistent. At his request, a 400-cubic-inch small-block V-8 was slipped into the four-rotor coupe and the car was retitled Aero-

vette. It again went on tour, and again the rumors started flying. Mitchell began lobbying at Chevrolet for the car's production. As usual, if he wanted something badly enough, he got it. GM chairman Thomas Murphy actually approved the Aerovette for the 1980 program. By the end of 1977, clay models were complete and tooling orders were about to be placed. For the moment, the Aerovette was the next Corvette.

However, the project lost its most influential supporter when Mitchell retired in 1977. Duntov had supported it, too, but he had retired at the end of 1974. Also, Ed Cole was gone. A further blow came from Duntov's successor, David R. McLellan, who preferred the front mid-engine concept—inaugurated with the 1963 Sting Ray—over a pure midships layout for reasons of packaging, manufacturing, and per-

formance. In addition, Chevy looked at some of the Aerovette's design elements—especially the radical V shape of the windshield and the gullwing doors as well as the mid-engine mechanicals—and concluded that the entire enterprise would be simply too expensive given the Corvette's sales volume. Another argument was that while manufacturers like Porsche and Lotus had offered mid-engine production models, none had sold very well. Meanwhile, Datsun couldn't build enough of its front-engine 240Z, though it was admittedly less costly. The mid-engine layout had been expounded as the wave of the future for road-going sports cars, but the car makers weren't bearing out that conclusion. Porsche only confirmed Chevy's move away from a mid-engine design with its 1976 introduction of the 924—a front-engine automobile.

handled the 1982 series differently. It was built only as needed to satisfy customer orders, not as a fixed proportion of scheduled production. To prevent someone from turning a standard car into a Collector Edition, Chevy also fitted special vehicle identification number plates. In many ways, the Collector Edition was the best of the fifth generation. Setting it apart were cloisonné emblems on hood, rear deck, and steering wheel; a unique silver-beige metallic paint scheme; graduated shadow-like contrasting paint stripes on hood and body sides; bronze-tint glass roof panels; and finned, cast-aluminum wheels styled like the ones first seen on the 1963 Sting Ray. Inside were special silver-beige cloth upholstery, leather door trim, leather-wrapped steering wheel, and luxury carpeting. The most obvious external difference was the Collector's frameless lift-up glass hatch, postponed from the 1978

Weight reduction continued as a priority for the 1981 Corvette (*left*). A reinforced plastic monoleaf transverse spring saved 33 pounds and thinner glass helped, too. The interior (*below*) was spiffed up with a six-way power driver's seat and quartz clock as standard.

Although the price of the '81 Corvette (*above*) had crossed the $15,000 mark, 45,631 units were built. The '82 (*opposite page, top*) came only with automatic transmission. The Collector Edition (*bottom*) featured cloisonné emblems, special paint, and lift-up hatch.

Corvette Performance Comparisons 1978-82

	1978	1979	1982
Engine (cid):	350	350	350
Induction system:	Carburetion	Carburetion	Fuel injection
Bhp:	220	220	200
Axle ratio:	3.70:1	.3.55:1	2.87:1
Transmission:	4-speed manual	3-speed automatic	4-speed automatic
Weight (lbs):	3490	3655	3425
Acceleration (sec)			
0-30 mph:	2.3	2.5	2.7
0-60 mph:	6.5	6.6	7.9
0-100 mph:	17.9	18.5	24.8
Quarter-mile:	15.2	15.6	16.1
Speed @ quarter-mile:	95	91	85
Top speed (mph):	132	130	125
Average fuel consumption (mpg):	15	12	21

restyle and, incidentally, not included on base models.

Performance gains over the previous L81 engine were made by the injected L83 V-8, with its 10 extra horsepower. The L83 showed a definite performance gain despite its automatic transmission. *Road & Track*, comparing the 1982 with its 1981 four-speed car, said, "the power shows in quicker dragstrip numbers. The new car ran the quarter-mile in 16.1 seconds at 84.5 mph and accelerated from 0-60 in 7.9 seconds. The pre-wundermotor did it in 17.0 at 82 mph and 9.2 seconds. At last relief from years of backsliding. And throttle response is excellent. In the 1983 Corvette, predicted to be at least 500 pounds lighter than this year's 3425-pound car, it should be a very nice engine." The injection also improved economy a little, and it certainly deterred owners from making anything remotely close to hot-rod modifications.

The long-running fifth generation had seen many, many changes. The Collector Edition earned the dubious distinction of being the first Corvette to break the $20,000 price barrier, listing at $22,538. That was a far cry from the $4663 price of a nicely equipped

At $22,538, the '82 Collector Edition earned the distinction of being the first Corvette to break the $20,000 price barrier. To discourage the building of bogus Collector Edition cars out of standard Corvettes, Chevrolet wisely fitted special vehicle identification plates. Perhaps because of the faltering economy, and perhaps because a new model was known to be close, the last of the fifth-generation 'Vettes saw production of 25,407 units, the lowest since 1967. Of these, only 6759 were Collector Edition models.

1968 model. Besides rising prices, the intervening 15 years had seen two restyles, the demise of the big-block engines, significant performance losses and slight performance gains, and the addition of more and more creature comforts. Yet for all that, the essential character of America's sports car had survived. Said *R&T:* "No matter how much luxury...you pack into a Corvette, the basic honesty of the car rises above its own image. It tells you this is an uncompromised two-seater with a big engine and that it's made to go around corners and come out of them

fast. The car has its own particular flavor and appeal, and the automotive world would lose a great deal if the Corvette were to become too much like other automobiles."

Chevy was not about to let that happen, of course, but the time for change was definitely at hand. Perhaps because of the faltering economy, and perhaps because a new model was known to be close, Corvette production fell to its lowest point since 1967, a disheartening 25,407 units. Of these,

continued on page 227

Serial Spans, Production, and Base Prices

Year	Serial Prefix	Serial Span	Prod. Units	Price
1978	1Z67J8S	100001-147667	47,667	$9645
1979	1Z87A	400001-453807	53,807	$12,313
1980	1Z87A	100001-140614	40,614	$13,956
1981	1G1Y87L	100001-145631	45,631	$16,259
1982	1G1Y87*	100001-125407	25,407	$18,290
	1G1Y07**			$22,538
1983	No model year production			

* coupe
** hatchback

In many ways, the 1982 Collector Edition was the best of the fifth-generation Corvettes. Given its unique features and small production, it seems destined to live up to its name in the very near future.

These pages show a number of detail shots of the
1982 Collector Edition, which marked the end of an era
for Corvette. The long awaited sixth-generation Corvette
was finally ready, and a *new* era was about to begin.

continued from page 223

only 6759 were the Collector Edition—indicating that every one of them seems destined to live up to its name in the very near future.

The 1982 model was the end of a remarkable motorcar and a remarkable era. Now a new Corvette was ready. The long wait was over.

Major Specifications 1982 Corvette

Chassis and Body
Frame: Box section steel, ladder type with 5 cross members
Body: Glass-reinforced plastic, two-seat coupe
Front suspension: Independent, unequal-length A-arms, coil springs, tube shocks, anti-sway bar
Rear suspension: Independent, lower lateral arms, axle halfshafts as upper lateral arms, trailing arms, transverse leaf spring, tube shocks, anti-sway bar
Wheels: 8″ × 15″ cast-alloy
Tires: P55/60R-15 Goodyear Eagle GT

Dimensions
Wheelbase (in.): 98.0
Length (in.): 185.3
Height (in.): 48.4
Width (in.): 69.0
Track front/rear (in.): 58.7/59.5
Ground clearance (in.): 5.0
Weight (lbs): 3425

Engine
Type: Ohv V-8, water-cooled, cast-iron block
Main bearings: 5
Bore × stroke: 4.00 × 3.48
Displacement (ci): 350
Compression ratio: 9.0:1
Induction system: GM Throttle-Body fuel injection
Brake horsepower @ rpm: 200 @ 4200
Lbs/ft torque @ rpm: 285 @ 2800

Drivetrain
Transmission: 4-speed automatic
Gear ratios: First—3.06:1
    Second—1.63:1
    Third—1.0:1
    Fourth—0.87:1
Rear axle ratio: 2.87:1
Steering: Power-assisted recirculating ball
Turns lock-to-lock: 2.6
Brakes: Vented discs, 11.75″ diameter front and rear
Brake lining area (sq. in.): 461

Performance
0-50 mph (sec): 5.8
0-60 mph (sec): 8.0
0-90 mph (sec): 19.0
Standing-start quarter-mile (sec): 16 @ 83 mph
Top speed (mph): 125
Average fuel consumption (mpg): 19-21

CHAPTER NINE

1984-1988: Driving Into Tomorrow

Few cars have been more eagerly anticipated than the 1984 Corvette. It was not just another new model, but the latest expression of what had become an automotive institution. It would be the first really different version of America's sports car in 15 years. As such, it couldn't help but generate intense scrutiny and widespread debate among enthusiasts and members of the automotive press even before it appeared.

The new model had been a long time coming, indeed. So great things were expected of it. The automotive world had made leaping changes since the last generation was born: Fuel economy standards were now a fact of life—and law. Materials, labor, and petroleum products had become more expensive. America's sports car had long since ceased being the ultimate wheeled possession financially for many people. Cars like the Datsun Zs, the Mazda RX-7s, and the Porsche 924s and 928s had raised considerably the standards by which sports cars were being judged. How would the Corvette compare against such respected rivals? Equally important in the minds of many was how the sixth generation would compare with its illustrious predecessors. Would it be worthy of the hallowed tradition that it had inherited? Would it be able to maintain that tradition in the brave new world of the Eighties?

After several delays, which only served to heighten the anticipation, the new Corvette was at last unveiled publicly in the early spring of 1983. The reaction was generally a mixture of relief and unrestrained excitement. The sixth generation was, thank goodness, still a Corvette in appearance and mechanical layout. Yet it was startling and entirely new, completely up to date and oozing high technology from every pore of its fiberglass being. In some ways, it was not exactly the car that had been predicted, but it was obviously a car to be respected.

The press was quick to give the '84 its due. Said *Car and Driver* in March 1983: "You have waited long enough. So let's get it over with: the new Corvette is a truly stout automobile. It is all that the fevered acolytes so desperately wanted their fiberglass fossil to be—a true-born, world-class sports car loaded with technical sophistication...The roadholding on this new machine is so advanced that we recorded the highest skidpad lateral acceleration—0.90 g—ever observed with a conventional automobile by this staff. That figure practically trivializes the previous high-water marks...generated by such exotics as the Porsche 928 and assorted Ferraris...It is the hands-down fastest American automobile, capable of 140-mph top speeds, 0-60 mph times under seven seconds, and 15.2-second quarter-mile forays...one of the half-dozen fastest production automobiles in the entire world."

That same month, *Motor Trend* echoed: "All the qualities it needed to have, it has in great abundance. Stylish appearance? Obviously. Fresh engineering? Just look. Proper comfort? But of course. Formidable performance? Stand back. There may be no better way to see the USA. Mission accomplished."

Said *Road & Track:* "There's a great deal of thoughtful design evident in this new Corvette, quite enough to bring it to the attention of those who felt the previous versions had become increasingly tacky. Is it now the best exotic car in the world? The best exotic car value? Its performance levels... stack up very well with those of the Ferrari 308GTSi or Porsche 928. Or should we measure the tremendous market pressure the Corvette puts on less expensive high-performance cars ...Resolution of these questions awaits proper comparative testing, but three things are clear: the new Corvette is abundantly more than an updated clunker to any of us, the questions posed are far from trivial, and the car's enthusiast appeal is immensely broad."

The development program for the 1984 design began in earnest in mid-1978, shortly after General Motors management cancelled plans for a production version of the mid-engine Aerovette. The effort involved the closest collaboration between Engineering and Design yet seen at GM. The chief collaborators were Corvette engineering head David R. McLellan and designer Jerry Palmer, head of Chevrolet Studio Three at that time. Their close liaison was vital if the new model was to be built with a high level of quality—important because it would sell for considerably more than the last of the fifth-generation cars.

According to Palmer, the keynote for the '84's design was "form follows function." While many automakers have paid only lip service to that traditional dictum over the years, both Palmer and McLellan deemed its wisdom essential for the Corvette to make it competitive with more recent-

Although the new Corvette had been a long time
in coming, few cars have been more eagerly anticipated
than the sixth-generation 1984 model. As the first
really different version of America's sports car in 15
years, it generated widespread debate among enthusiasts.

ly designed sports cars. Specifically, the task was to eliminate the deficiencies for which the fifth generation had been criticized while at the same time maintaining the traditional Corvette look and driving feel. The car would have to have superior aerodynamics, more passenger room, and—most important for a driver's car—even better handling than earlier models.

Accordingly, the sixth generation was engineered literally from the ground up. Both design groups began with the T-point—the position of the seated driver's hip joint relative to the interior and the rest of the car. The T-point was raised an inch and moved an inch or so rearward compared to the previous Corvette. Doing so opened up more legroom and also put the driver in a higher position relative to the road, contributing to better visibility. Further, raising the T-point allowed the chassis to sit higher than before for more ground clearance, though the choice of 16-inch rather than 15-inch wheels and tires also played a part.

With the car's handling a major consideration, the chassis was engineered around contemporary Pirelli P7 radials—then the state of the art for tires. However, the Corvette would be introduced on Goodyear Eagle VR50 tires, developed specifically for the 1984 model and sized at P255/50VR-

16. The VR indicates the tires' speed rating, which was in excess of 130 miles per hour. Mounted on cast-alloy wheels of 8.5-inch width front and 9.5-inch width rear, the tires were notable for their "Gatorback" tread design—a V-shaped pattern with horizontal gaps cut perpendicular to the tread that gave the tires the appearance of an alligator's back. The Gatorbacks were developed so that they would shed water more effectively to resist hydroplaning in wet weather. The design was based on technology developed for Goodyear's Formula 1 and Indy car rain tires. The wheels would be unidirectional because of the Gatorback tread and because of the shape of their radial cooling fins—specific left and right/front and rear wheels were not interchangeable.

Complementing the tire and wheel technology was a considerably revised chassis. The old perimeter-type ladder frame was abandoned for a steel backbone design not unlike the one pioneered by Lotus of England. For the Corvette, the spine took the form of a C-section beam that carried the driveshaft and was rigidly connected to the differential. The benefits were less weight and more cockpit room through elimination of the transmission and differential cross members. The steel backbone also allowed the exhaust system to run under the

The development program for the 1984 Corvette (*both pages*) began in earnest in mid-1978. Chief collaborators were engineering head David McLellan and designer Jerry Palmer. The keynote for the '84 design was "form follows function," deemed essential to make the new Corvette competitive with newer—and more sophisticated—sports cars from Germany and Japan.

"I really believe we've designed a car without compromises," said designer Jerry Palmer regarding the completely restyled '84 'Vette (*above*), "but we've managed to retain the Corvette identity."

Major Specifications 1984 Corvette

Chassis and Body
Frame: Skeletal steel
Body: Glass-reinforced plastic, two-seat coupe
Front suspension: Independent, unequal-length A-arms, transverse fiberglass leaf spring, tube shocks, anti-sway bar
Rear suspension: Independent, upper and lower trailing arms, lateral arms, tie rods, halfshafts, transverse fiberglass leaf spring, tube shocks, anti-sway bar
Wheels: Unidirectional cast-alloy, 8.5" × 16" front, 9.5" × 16" rear
Tires: Goodyear Eagle VR50, P255/50VR-16

Dimensions
Wheelbase (in.): 96.2
Length (in.): 176.5
Height (in.): 46.7
Width (in.): 71.0
Track front/rear (in.): 59.6/60.4
Ground clearance (in.): 5.0
Weight (lbs): 3200

Engine
Type: Ohv V-8, water-cooled, cast-iron block
Main bearings: 5
Bore × stroke: 4.00 × 3.48
Displacement (ci): 350
Compression ratio: 9.0:1
Induction system: GM Throttle-Body fuel injection
Brake horsepower @ rpm: 205 @ 4300
Lbs/ft torque @ rpm: 290 @ 2800

Drivetrain
Transmission: 4-speed automatic
Gear ratios: First—3.06:1
             Second—1.63:1
             Third—1.0:1
             Fourth—0.70:1
Rear axle ratio: 3.31:1
Steering: Power-assisted rack-and-pinion
Turns lock-to-lock: 2.0
Turning circle (ft): 40.0
Brakes: 4-wheel vented discs, 11.5" diameter front and rear
Brake lining area (sq. in.): 330

Performance
0-50 mph (sec): 5.0
0-60 mph (sec): 7.0
0-90 mph (sec): 16.0
Standing-start quarter-mile (sec): 15.5 @ 88 mph
Top speed (mph): 140
Average fuel consumption (mpg): 16-20

driveshaft instead of alongside it. Welded to the frame was what Chevy called an "integral perimeter-birdcage unitized structure"—"uniframe," for short—making it the first Corvette to employ unit construction instead of body-on-frame. The birdcage formed the windshield and door frames, lower A-pillar extensions, rocker panels, rear cockpit wall, and front subframe. It also included the hoop at the rear of the cockpit that acted as the connecting point for a new lift-up rear window. The entire structure would be galvanized inside and out for corrosion resistance. In effect, it was a skeleton over which the major fiberglass body panels would fit. Completing the basic assembly were an aluminized bolt-on front suspension carrier and a bolt-on extension for the back bumper.

The more rigid platform allowed McLellan's staff to rework the suspension. The front end retained the familiar unequal-length upper and lower A-arm arrangement of previous years, though modified. Instead of a coil spring on each side, the '84 had a single reinforced-fiberglass leaf spring mounted transversely between the two lower arms. A 20mm anti-roll bar would be standard, while a 25mm bar would be included in an optional handling package—RPO Z51. The big change came about at the rear. Zora Arkus-Duntov's old three-link geometry was replaced by a five-link setup consisting of upper and lower longitudinal links mounted between the hub carriers and the body, twin lateral strut rods connecting the differential with the hub carriers, another transverse plastic leaf spring as used since 1981, plus U-jointed halfshafts and rear-mounted tie rods. Steering was changed from GM's usual recirculating-ball mechanism to rack-and-pinion. It featured a forward-mounted rack for greater precision and a standard high-effort power assist for better control at high speeds. The normal steering ratio was set at a constant 15.5:1, quite fast for an American car. It was raised to 13:1 in the Z51 package. A tilt-and-telescope steering wheel would be standard.

As before, stopping power would be supplied by large vented disc brakes at each wheel, hydraulically assisted. The brakes themselves were a newly designed creation by Girlock, an American offshoot of the British Girling company. Making extensive use of aluminum, the brakes had 11.5-inch rotors and featured quick-change semimetallic pads (held by a single bolt) with audible wear indicators.

Dave McLellan claimed that "even in base suspension configuration, the new Corvette…is absolutely superior to any production vehicle in its part of the market." An extra margin of superiority was the rationale behind the Z51 option, a $51 bargain. It had the Eagle VR50 tires plus heavy-duty shocks front and rear (RPO F51) and the FE7 Sport Suspension with heavy-duty lower control arm bushings, uprated front and rear springs and stabilizer bars, plus the faster-ratio steer-

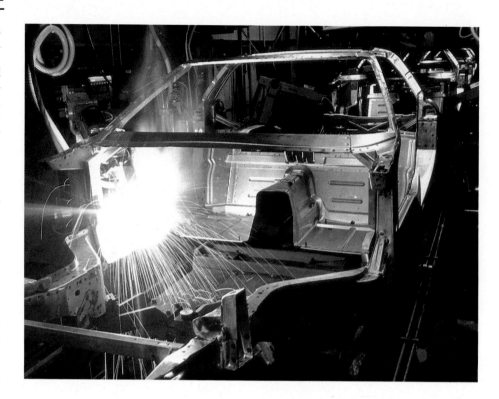

The 1984 model was the first Corvette to employ unit construction (*above*), referred to by Chevy as an "integral perimeter-birdcage unitized structure." The more rigid platform (*top right*) gave the engineers the freedom to rework the suspension with transverse fiberglass leaf springs front *and* rear. Aerodynamics played a major role in the development process (*bottom right*).

ing. The Z51 package also included a shorter 3.31:1 rear axle ratio.

More evidence of Design and Engineering teamwork was found under the clamshell hood—a part of the design concept from the beginning. The hood included the tops of the front fenders and lifted to a near-vertical position to facilitate service access. Underneath was a familiar friend in somewhat different dress—the trusty L83 5.7-liter/350-cid V-8 that was used for 1982, with twin throttle-body electronic fuel injection and the Cross-Fire induction system with dual ram-air intakes. Rated output was boosted by five brake horsepower to 205 at 4300 rpm and by five lbs/ft of torque to 290 at 2800 rpm, reflecting the adoption of a more efficient radiator fan and accessory drive. The underhood area was dominated by a flat-top silver-finish air cleaner created by Palmer's crew and made of die-cast magnesium. The air cleaner had sepa-

rate vacuum-modulated doors that regulated air flow from ducts molded in on the underside of the hood. The ducts connected to the air cleaner when the hood was closed. A single air intake under the nose, below the bumper, fed outside air to the underhood ducts—making it a bottom-breather. The entire engine compartment was color-coordinated in silver and black. Palmer even persuaded GM's AC-Delco Division to develop a matching battery.

For the first time since 1981, the Corvette's standard transmission was a four-speed manual unit, but it was nothing like any previous gearbox. Basically, it was a normal unit with a second planetary gearset attached, actuated by the engine's Computer Command Control electronics. The auxiliary gearset sat at the rear of the transmission and engaged through a hydraulic clutch in all ratios except first. The effect was to provide a step-

down or overdrive reduction of 0.67:1 in each of the top three gears to improve part-throttle fuel economy. At wide throttle openings the overdrive was automatically locked out. Overdrive could also be disengaged via an override switch. Standard final drive was 3.07:1, with 3.31:1 gearing available for better standing-start performance. Returning from 1982, but now as an option, was the four-speed overdrive automatic—the GM 700-R4 unit with lockup torque converter clutch effective in all ratios except first.

Production delays forced postponement of the 4+3 Overdrive manual until early 1984, so the first of the new Corvettes were equipped only with the automatic. Dennis Simanaitis, engineering editor for *Road & Track,* called the 4+3 "a gearbox smarter than your average driver," and he liked the way it worked. But he noted that "even with all [its computerized] wizardry, [fuel economy] is little different from that with the automatic. We recorded 15.0 mpg versus 15.5 for the car with the Turbo Hydra-matic, and that sounds

The '84 model (*top*) still had a Corvette "face" even though fog and turn lamps were located where the air intakes used to be. Underneath the clamshell hood (*above*) lurked the familiar 350-cid L83 V-8 (*top right*), now rated at 205 bhp. The interior (*bottom right*) was completely redone—and roomier.

like a wash." Originally, the overdrive override switch was reserved for a special export version of the new model, owing to vagaries of the EPA's fuel economy test procedure. Had the car been tested without the automatic overdrive engagement, it could easily have fallen under the dreaded gas guzzler tax mandated by CAFE. McLellan stated that the overdrive lockout was intended for U. S. sale all along, even though the first manual cars shown to the press didn't have it.

Still, the transmission situation brings up a telling point: Despite Chevy's considerable effort to keep weight as low as possible, the Corvette emerged heavier than most had expected—by a good 300 pounds. Nevertheless, the 1984 Corvette did emerge 250 pounds lighter than a comparably equipped 1982 model, which was a

worthwhile gain. The weight loss was the result of numerous subtle tricks. Besides the ones already mentioned, others included some industry firsts in the use of lightweight materials. For instance, the driveshaft and supporting yokes were made of forged aluminum, welded together. The radiator support was made of plastic sheet molding compound (SMC). The reinforced-fiberglass transverse springs weighed half as much as four steel coil springs of comparable size. They were also claimed to be more durable, capable of withstanding 5,000,000 full cycles versus about 75,000 for steel springs. The cooling system had twin expansion tanks made of plastic, as were the radiator fan and shroud. Aluminum figured extensively throughout the car, with the front suspension control arms and knuckles and

the rear suspension lateral arms all consisting of aluminum forgings. So was the chassis spine. The automatic transmission torque converter housing was formed from aluminum sheet. The brakes' splash shields were aluminum rather than steel, and the calipers were an iron-aluminum alloy for greater strength with less weight.

While McLellan's engineers busied themselves with technical intricacies, Palmer's staff was shaping the car in Production Studio Three. The program moved along quite rapidly once the designers shifted their efforts back to a front-engine configuration. A full-scale theme clay model based on a Palmer sketch was completed in September 1978. By mid-November of the following year—a scant 14 months later—the new design was more or less final except for taillamps, front

Although some of the dimensional changes on the 1984 Corvette (*below*) weren't all that large, the car's proportions were definitely fresh. Overall length was down a significant 8.8 inches despite only a minor cut in wheelbase—from 98.0 to 96.2 inches— and a mere 1.7-inch reduction in front overhang. The secret was a 5.3-inch chop in rear overhang, which gave the effect of a longer hood even though it was actually shorter. Contributing to the sleekness was a 64-degree windshield angle as measured from the vertical—the steepest of any American production car in history.

fender trim, and the shape of the nose.
Though the wheels and tires were the
dominant design element in all the
various sketches and clay models,
Palmer's staff wrestled with the overall proportions as much as with surface
detailing. As Palmer told *Car and
Driver's* Jean Lindamood: "The evolution...was a very slow, methodical
one. It wasn't bangety-bangety-bang.
We made incremental changes—very
slight. I'm talking about 1/8-inch
movements, just enough to change the
accent of a form or the loading of a
line."

The design brief was a tall order:
First and foremost was the demand
that the car must look like a Corvette.
In other words, it couldn't break with
traditional Corvette appearance
"cues." Drivelines would be carried
over, and though the car could be a bit
smaller outside, it had to have more
room inside. Other goals were that it
have improved visibility and less aerodynamic drag. A key change affecting
room, drag, and visibility came when
Engineering relocated the steering
linkage further forward than originally envisioned. The move allowed the
small-block V-8 to be lowered in the
chassis, thus achieving a lower hood
line for better forward vision and reduced frontal area—the latter a big
factor in reducing air drag.

The resulting all-new design was
still very much a Corvette. Said
Palmer: "I really believe we've designed a car without compromises, but
we've managed to retain the Corvette
identity. The car still, for example, has
folding headlamps. It has a Corvette
'face,' even though there are foglamps
and turn lamps where air intakes used
to be. The front fender vents are still
there, as is the large backlight and the
functional rear spoiler. The first time
people see this car, they're going to
know what it is...[Yet] the new car's
massive surfaces, such as the hood, are
deceiving. On first glance you probably wouldn't believe it is smaller than
the previous year's model in every di-
mension except width."

Though some of the dimensional
changes in the '84 weren't that large,
the car's proportions were definitely
fresh. Overall length was down a significant 8.8 inches despite a minor cut
in wheelbase—from 98.0 to 96.2 inches—and a mere 1.7-inch reduction in
front overhang. The secret was a 5.3-

With its striking exterior, whose real change came from
the increase in width (*top right*), the new Corvette
needed an equally striking cockpit. It got one (*above*).
Dominated by a space-age instrument panel and the usual
high center tunnel/console, the interior featured a
whopping 6.5-inch increase in shoulder room. A perimeter
rub strip completely encircled the car (*bottom right*).

inch chop in rear overhang, which gave the effect of a longer hood even though it was actually shorter. Contributing to sleekness was a 64-degree windshield angle as measured from the vertical—the steepest of any American production car in history. Compared to the fifth generation, the base of the windshield sat 1.5 inches lower and forward a bit further. In turn, the shift allowed the beltline to be dropped, giving the '84 a glassier appearance.

As Palmer suggested, the real change in the car's looks came from the increase in width. The old pinched-waist midsection was gone, along with the bulged front and rear fender lines. In their place was a smoother, more organic contour, especially when viewed from the front or rear three-quarter angle. The car retained its predecessor's flared wheel arches, which combined with the fat tires to accentuate the hunkered-down look. The fenders had no more conflict with the beltline, which rose uninterrupted from the windshield toward the near-vertical Kamm-style tail with the traditional quartet of lights. In profile, it had a discernible wedge shape that was pleasing and functional in the GM idiom.

One styling element new to the Corvette was a perimeter rub strip that completely encircled the car, and it served visually to link the tops of the front and rear bumpers. It also concealed the shut lines of the clamshell hood along the body sides.

After 15 years of Corvettes with T-tops, the '84 hardly could have reverted to a fixed roof. But the T-bar was gone, replaced by a one-piece removable panel with four attachment points—two on the windshield header, and two on the roof hoop. Unlike recent contemporary 'Vettes that had their twin roof panels riding on the rear deck, the '84 stowed its panel in special slots built into the top of the luggage bay. For added protection against vandals, the top could be removed only with a special wrench. Buyers had a choice of either a body-colored panel or a tinted transparent top made of scratch-resistant acrylic. The acrylic top was an option that was delayed until well after the model's introduction. Either top was far lighter and easier to wield than the awkward glass panes of old.

Chevy boasted that the '84 Cor-

The exterior appearance of the 1985 Corvette (*opposite page*) remained unchanged, except that the Cross-Fire Injection script was replaced with Tuned Port Injection. Although the engine remained at 5.7-liters displacement, horsepower was boosted from 205 to 230 (*below*). A more rigid platform allowed for a suspension redesign (*center*). Not everybody liked the electronic instruments (*bottom*).

vette's shape was partly refined in the wind tunnel. A wrinkle in that aspect of the car's development was the use of a sensor to compare pressure differences at various points on the car as it sat in a moving airstream versus pressure in other parts of the tunnel. According to Chevrolet, the technique yielded a detailed picture of the "actual pressure variants and vortices created by passage of the vehicle. Such an image is far more useful than is a picture of surface flow only, and Corvette is believed to be the first sports car ever designed with the assistance of such a tool." While the resulting drag coefficient was only average by today's standards—0.34—the reduced frontal area made the Corvette much slipperier than that often-misleading value suggested. And it represented a useful 23.7 percent drag reduction compared with the 1982 Corvette's 0.44 Cd.

With its striking exterior, the Corvette needed an equally striking cockpit. As the creation of GM's Interior Design group directed by Pat Furey, it was dominated by a space-age instru-

After a decade's absence, the convertible returned to the lineup for 1986 (*below*). It featured a strengthened chassis and a softer suspension. All soft tops that year were considered Indy Pace Car Replicas, in honor of the real thing, which was driven by General Chuck Yeager at the Brickyard (*right*).

ment panel and the usual tall center tunnel/console. Occupants sat a bit lower in the '84, but the cockpit looked more spacious and open than in the fifth generation. Appearances were not deceiving. Despite the shorter wheelbase and a 1.1-inch reduction in overall height, the '84 offered fractional gains in head and leg room and a whopping 6.5-inch increase in total shoulder room—an area where the old car was decidedly lacking. Cargo room was also greater, by a useful eight cubic feet or so, and it was more accessible thanks to the lift-up hatch window.

All instrumentation was now directly ahead of the driver—no more minor dials in the center of the dashboard. In fact, the dash held no dials at all—the car used an all-electronic display supplied by GM's AC Division. It featured digital and analog graphic displays for speedometer and tachometer, plus numerical engine function readouts in a smaller panel flanked by the two main displays. A switch panel in the vertical portion of the center console allowed the driver to select which functions would be monitored. The functions included instantaneous and average miles per gallon, trip odometer, and fuel range, as well as engine temperature, oil pressure and temperature, and electrical system voltage. The console also housed the heat/vent/air conditioning controls and the much

acclaimed GM-Delco/Bose sound system—an $895 option.

Standard seats in the '84 were especially designed high-back buckets with prominent bolsters on both cushion and backrest, manual fore/aft adjustment, and, at long last, reclining backrests. Full cloth trim was standard, with leather upholstery optional. Also offered at extra cost was the latest in super seats—supplied by Lear-Siegler. They provided electric adjustment for backrest angle and cushion bolster in/out, plus a powered three-stage lumbar support adjuster using inflatable bladders that could be individually air-bled to achieve the proper contour.

Shortly after the '84 went on sale a couple of running changes were announced. An oil cooler became standard equipment, and the base 15-inch wheel/tire package was deleted, thus making the 16-inchers a mandatory option with the base suspension.

Meanwhile, auto magazines were subjecting the '84 models to their first full road tests, and, as a result, the initial enthusiasm of some writers cooled. *Car and Driver* was the most critical. Most everyone described the ride as harsh, but the Z51 package earned special scorn from technical editor Don Sherman: "The problem...is that it's a balls-out calibration that ruins the car for day-to-day use...Really bad pavement sent its wheels bounding, and even minor bumps or irregularities threw the car off on a momentary tangent...In exchange for these hardships you get lightning reflexes...and imperceptible body roll." *Motor Trend's* Ron Grable was more charitable. He praised the quick acceleration and phenomenal handling of his manual-transmission example, then noted: "This level of cornering performance does not come totally without cost, however, and the Corvette can be a harsh environment at times, on certain surfaces. For instance, you definitely want to stay out of the far right lane on freeways that have seen lots of heavy 18-wheeler traffic. The 'Vette will jiggle your eyeballs on any surface the big rigs have roughed up." CONSUMER GUIDE® magazine testers also criticized the "tough" ride. Though the test car had the softer base suspension, the editors

continued on page 251

Three shots (*opposite page*) depict Corvette assembly
and inspection at the Bowling Green, Kentucky factory.
The 1986 Corvette (*above and top*) saw the advent of a
Bosch-designed anti-lock braking system, a more
sophisticated theft-deterrent system, and a
revised dual exhaust system.

The 1986 Corvette roadster (*left*) featured 9.5-inch wheels at all corners, a 10mm increase in ride height, and deflected-disc Delco shock absorbers. Following tradition, its top folded under a special hatch and was manually operated—a castback to earlier times. The interior (*below*) looked like something out of the twenty-first century when it was all lit up. The convertible listed for $5000 more than the coupe.

continued from page 246

felt that even it was too stiff and jar-ring most of the time on patched city streets. They also found "exhaust and road noise are loud at anything above idle speed, though the exhaust settles down when cruising in OD. The automatic transmission is sensitive to throttle changes in city driving, so it seems to be changing gears almost constantly. It's also slow to come out of high gear unless you really pour on the throttle."

Most testers shared an initial dislike for the flashy instrumentation. *C/D's* Sherman described it as "purposely too futuristic to be appreciated by anyone mired in the twentieth century," while his fellow staffer Patrick Bedard quipped that "everything about the cockpit is so George Lucas, from the glow-winkie dash to the g-couch seats." CONSUMER GUIDE® noted that "the instrumentation is complete and entertaining, but the bar graphs are just for color; they're too hard to read to be useful...The test car's panel was dimly lit on one side, and the en-

Corvette sales had taken a plunge to under 40,000 units for 1985, probably due in part to a $3000 increase that pushed starting prices to around $25,000. Even with the advent of the convertible for 1986 (*top row*), sales slipped further to just over 35,000 units for the model year. The 350-cid V-8 (*left*) cranked out 230 horses at 4000 rpm in 1986.

Convertible production was underway by January 1986. Since all ragtops were considered Indy Pace Car Replicas, each one was shipped with pace car decals, but the buyer made the decision whether or not they should be applied. The cars were available in the full range of standard colors, although the actual car that paced Indy was painted bright yellow. The convertible sold well enough, but some felt that, considering its cost, it lacked refinement.

tire display is hard to read in sunlight."

Despite such carpings, the press had nothing but good things to say about the '84 Corvette's acceleration and roadholding. Most reports showed 60 mph available from rest in around seven seconds and handling numbers that were nearly untouchable by any other series-production automobile. CONSUMER GUIDE®'s verdict: "More sophisticated and technically up to date than its predecessor, and a world-class sports car with few rivals

in performance. You have to live with a bump-and-grind ride and plenty of noise to enjoy it, but it provides motoring thrills in potent doses." Said *MT's* Grable: "The '84 Corvette is…taut, responsive, predictable, and desirable. The running changes…have addressed—and improved—a couple weak areas, areas that had been uniformly criticized. Does this mean Chevrolet is listening? We certainly would like to think so, because that bodes well for the future of this out-

standing American representative in the GT arena."

The exterior appearance of the sophomore year 1985 model remained unchanged, except that the Cross-Fire Injection script was replaced with Tuned Port Injection. That modest alteration signaled big changes under the hood. While the displacement of the Corvette's long-lived small-block V-8 remained the timeworn 350 cubic inches, the multi-port fuel injection increased horsepower drastically—from

205 to 230 bhp. In addition to the resultant 150-mph top speed and improved acceleration, Chevrolet also claimed better fuel economy, which may have been doubtful. Few test results bore out the claim.

In response to the complaints about the harsh ride of the 1984 model, Chevy changed spring rates on both the standard and Z51 performance suspensions. The Z51 now included 9.5-inch wheels in front as well as rear, plus gas-pressurized Delco-Bilstein shocks and a revised heavy-duty cooling system. Instrument panel graphics were revised to improve clarity, and models with the four-speed manual gearbox received a heavy-duty 8.5-inch ring gear differential for improved durability.

Testers who were able to drive the '85 version on a track found it a spectacular performer and a terrific handling car—at speeds well over 100

Opposite page: The sixth-generation Corvette continued the tradition of utilizing hidden headlights (*bottom right*), but sported the crossed-flags theme in a modified form (*bottom left*). The big wheels and full wheel cutouts gave the '87 'Vette a hunkered-down look (*top*). Seen from above (*below*), the hood looked quite expansive.

Major Specifications 1987 Corvette

Chassis and Body
Frame: Skeletal steel
Body: Glass-reinforced plastic, two-seat coupe
Front suspension: Independent, unequal-length A-arms, transverse fiberglass leaf spring, tube shocks, anti-sway bar
Rear suspension: Independent, upper and lower trailing arms, lateral arms, tie rods, halfshafts, transverse fiberglass leaf spring, tube shocks, anti-sway bar
Wheels: Unidirectional cast-alloy, 9.5" × 16"
Tires: Goodyear Eagle VR50, P255/50VR-16

Dimensions
Wheelbase (in.): 96.2
Length (in.): 176.5
Height (in.): 46.4
Width (in.): 71.0
Track front/rear (in.): 59.6/60.4
Ground clearance (in.): 5.0
Weight (lbs): 3325

Engine
Type: Ohv V-8, water-cooled, cast-iron block
Main bearings: 5
Bore × stroke: 4.00 × 3.48
Displacement (ci): 350
Compression ratio: 9.0:1
Induction system: Bosch Multi-Port fuel injection
Brake horsepower @ rpm: 240 @ 4000
Lbs/ft torque @ rpm: 345 @ 3200

Drivetrain
Transmission: 4+3-speed manual overdrive
Gear ratios: First—2.88:1
  Second—1.91:1, 1.30:1 OD
  Third—1.34:1, 0.91:1 OD
  Fourth—1.0:1, 0.68:1 OD
Rear axle ratio: 3.07:1
Steering: Power-assisted rack-and-pinion
Turns lock-to-lock: 2.4
Turning circle (ft): 40.5
Brakes: 4-wheel vented discs, 11.5" diameter front and rear
Brake lining area (sq. in.): 330

Performance
0-50 mph (sec): 4.9
0-60 mph (sec): 6.5
0-90 mph (sec): 13.8
Standing-start quarter-mile (sec): 15.0 @ 93 mph
Top speed (mph): 135, 150 overdrive
Average fuel consumption (mpg): 16-18

mph. Steering response was now razor-sharp, and the chassis was perfectly tuned for race track workouts. But the vast majority of Corvettes are not driven on tracks—the writers recorded that more work was needed on the suspension. Not only was the car still stiff, even with standard suspension, but it was still quite noisy for a grand tourer in its price range.

Then Corvette sales took a steep plunge, dropping to under 40,000 for the 1985 model year—the first time that had happened since the grim year

of 1975. The drop was a shock to many at Chevrolet Division—after all, this car may have to last until the millennium. But they partially explained it by the whopping price increase for the year—from about $22,000 to about $25,000. It would rise even higher.

The advent of a Corvette convertible in 1986—the first in 11 years—didn't do anything to improve sales, either. Sales slipped to just over 35,000 for the model year. However, the convertible's return was good news for those who respect tradition. Some-

For 1988—the 35th anniversary of the Corvette—America's sports car looks much the same as the 1984-1987 models. The only difference between it and the '87 is the redesign of the wheel slots, which complements an increase in wheel size to 17 inches as an optional package and as part of the Z51 option. The wheels remain unidirectional, with a second row of slots on the 17-inch version. Larger brake rotors, modified suspension, and 245 bhp are features of the '88.

how, not having a roadster in the line just hadn't seemed right. Its reappearance signified to many the Corvette's coming to light from the dark days of car design caused by decrees from the federal government. The change from coupe to convertible had entailed some attention to the car's stiffness, with reinforcement added under the fiberglass body shell. The extra support was applied to the forward frame cross member, the K braces connecting the cross member to the frame rails, the steering column and its mounts, and the front torque box. A crossbeam was placed behind the seats and a strong X brace under the car at midsection. The seatback riser was double steel panel, and the door latch mechanism was strengthened. The convertible was tighter than the coupe! Wrote Steve Kimball in *Road & Track*, "When body engineer Bill Weaver was asked if these reinforcements could be added to the coupe, he smiled and said it's being looked into." The coupe received the same treatment in 1987, and was a much tighter, more rattle-free car as a result.

Following tradition, the roadster's top folded under a special hatch, and it was manually operated—a castback to earlier times, but also to less expensive Corvettes. No Z51 handling suspension was offered for the roadster, which had its own suspension—including 9.5-inch-wide wheels on all four corners, lower recommended tire pressures, a 10mm increase in ride height, and deflected-disc Delco shocks. The softer suspension "allows some wallowing at high speeds," reported Kimball, "but this is only in comparison with the Corvette coupe."

Convertible production at the Kentucky factory began in January 1986, and all of them for the 1986 model year were considered Indy Pace Car Replicas, with the usual round of decals shipped with each car. The buyer decided if they should be attached. The cars were available in the full range of standard colors, though, whereas the actual car that paced Indy for 1986 was bright yellow. The Corvette convertible sold well enough, but at $5000 more than the coupe, it was beginning to enter territories occupied by very esoteric competition. Many felt that the car still lacked the necessary refinement that such a market demanded. A Bosch-designed anti-lock

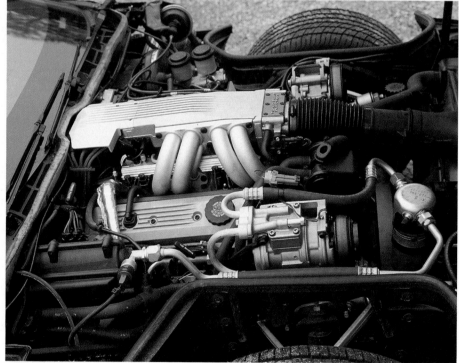

This page: While the interior (*top*) continues as before, the engine (*above*) boasts modified cylinder heads for improved breathing and a new camshaft for better performance. From the front, the '88 Corvette (*right*) looks like the '87.

The sixth-generation Corvette is a sophisticated
American exotic that has taken to the tracks and proven
that it is capable of winning races as well as cruising
the nation's highways—a true ride-and-race car.
Note the missing wheel trims on this '88 (below).

braking system, a more sophisticated theft-deterrent system, and a revised dual exhaust system were further changes for the 1986 model year.

Reunited again, the coupe and convertible models were revised slightly for 1987. Most of the work happened under the hood, as it had in 1985.

Roller lifters reduced friction losses. Rocker-arm covers had raised rails to forestall oil leaks. The spark plugs were moved closer to the center of the combustion chambers to improve burning capabilities and to retard knock. Horsepower was up to 240 bhp, but the real improvement in 1987 was

found in the engine's digging capacity—it had 345 lbs/ft of torque, compared to only 290 in the previous edition. An optional electronic system monitored tire pressure to warn the driver of low air pressure in any one of the four tires. A drop of as little as one pound below a preset limit would trig-

Among the improvements to the 1988 Corvette (*left*) is
a suspension with modified geometry front and rear,
providing enhanced stability when stopping.
The optional 17-inch aluminum wheels (*above*)
feature a second row of slots (wheel trim lacking).

ger a warning light on the dashboard. Altogether, the sensors, transmitters, and other parts of the system weighed less than two pounds. More attention, too, was given to the interior. Porsche-like seats that grab and grip a driver and passenger were added, with Recaros optional for the more particular. A side bolster switch was also added.

For 1988—the 35th anniversary of the Corvette—America's sports car looks much the same as previous sixth-generation cars. The only visual difference between it and the 1987 model is the redesign of the wheel slots, which complements an increase in wheel size to 17 inches as an optional package and as part of the Z51 option. The wheels remain unidirectional, with a second row of slots on the 17-inch version. Larger brake rotors accompany the base package's 16-inch wheels, while rotors that are an inch larger yet are fitted with the 17-inch

wheels. In addition, the car has a modified engine and suspension. The geometries of both the front and rear suspensions have been changed, in particular to enhance stabilization when stopping. On the engine, modified aluminum cylinder heads feature improved breathing, and the new camshaft provides better performance. Horsepower has increased to 245 bhp.

The sixth-generation Corvette is a sophisticated American exotic that has taken to the tracks and proven that it is capable of winning races as well as cruising the nation's highways—a true ride-and-race car. Where is it going in the future? Look to higher performance yet, along with some of the styling cues to be found on the Corvette Indy and ASC Corvette Genève show cars. The latest model proves that America's sports car is one for which the nation's enthusiasts can feel proud.

Corvette Indy

In 1986, Chevrolet showcased a street version of its Indy-car V-8 engine in a concept vehicle called the Corvette Indy. The Corvette Indy's introduction was called "an early look at a project under development" by Chevrolet's chief engineer Don Runkle. The Corvette Indy promised to be the testbed for many contemporary automotive features, many of which were not operative at the concept car's introduction to the public.

The Corvette Indy was striking in its outward appearance, looking somewhat like a bubble and having a full canopy top that covered not only the interior but the engine compartment that rested amidships. The middle section of the canopy removed for open-top motoring. Visible through the canopy was the engine—a 2.65-liter dual-overhead-camshaft V-8 modified to run on gasoline instead of the racing version's alcohol fuel. The multiport fuel injection system worked in combination with two turbochargers and two air-to-air intercoolers. The shovel-nosed car had a front slit from side to side. Hidden headlights led each fender, and a Corvette insignia was

centered on the hood. The curves of the canopy flowed in conjunction with those of the rest of the body, which featured intake scoops in front of the rear wheels. In the rear, spoilers crossed the top and the bottom of the rear deck.

As compelling as was the exterior design, the mechanicals of the Corvette Indy showed how the vehicle was being used for research by Chevy's engineering staff. Chevrolet called its engineering work a Total Wheel Control System, and all-wheel drive, all-wheel steering, anti-lock braking, traction control, and active suspension were all part of it. All-wheel drive was a full-time four-wheel-drive system. All-wheel steering could be selected as an alternative to steering only at the front of the car. Four-wheel steering gave the vehicle improved low-speed cornering and maneuverability, and it gave body designers more flexibility in working on interior space because the wheel wells did not intrude as much. Monitored and controlled by microprocessors, steering from the rear wheels promised high-speed advantages as well. Anti-lock braking was not new to the Corvette insignia, with ABS being a

part of the 1986 Corvette's equipment list. Traction control was monitored by computer, utilizing sensors that read relative acceleration between the four wheels, balancing the drive electronically for maximum control. Hydraulics replaced the more conventional springs, shock absorbers, and stabilizer bars for the active suspension part of the Total Wheel Control System. Computer controls enabled the system to meet the immediate needs of the car as it encountered different types of roads and handling situations.

Interior controls of engine speed through the gas pedal were electronic, in keeping with the computer-controlled nature of the rest of the car. Electronic sensors of the drive-by-wire operation read the position of the pedal, and the engine would respond accordingly via computer. It was a fitting adjunct to the Total Wheel Control System. Other interior features that reflected the electronic nature of the vehicle included the dashboard and environmental controls for both the driver and passenger. The steering wheel housing supported a thin electronic panel that delivered

engine and road speed. In the center of the dash was a cathode-ray tube that displayed the view to the rear as photographed by an aft-facing camera. Furthermore, cathode-ray tubes in each door panel displayed information about the car and its navigation, and each door had individual climate and radio controls.

Chevrolet claimed that the Corvette Indy wasn't bound for production. Neither was the Aerovette of several years earlier—a concept car that has had so much influence on the shape of things named Corvette ever since. The engine and the technology are here, and so is the Corvette Indy research vehicle that points to the future.

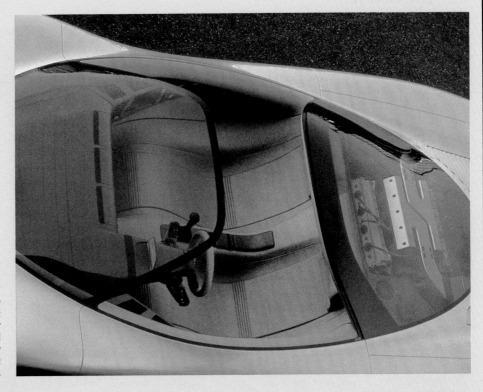

In speculating on what the Corvette of the future will be like, one need only look at the Corvette Indy (*both pages*), a show car and research vehicle that Chevrolet debuted in 1986. Chevy described it as "an early look at a project under development." It serves as a testbed for future technology.

Corvette Genève

ASC Incorporated is a specialty company that supplies sunroofs and other aftermarket automotive products, and it builds limited-production automobiles and one-off concept cars that demonstrate its capabilities. The company's Corvette Genève is "a three-dimensional demonstration of how advanced design elements can be integrated with pure practicality to create a car that surpasses the expectations of either," according to ASC. The Genève was "developed as a hybrid of ASC's advanced design concepts and the current production-model Corvette...a one-of-a-kind study in engineering possibilities."

ASC's primary work was in the body and interior. Some of the design is reminiscent of the Corvette Indy, particularly in the rear, where ASC employs two spoilers—one above and one below the tail. As the rear deck begins to slant down, the upper spoiler's leading edges continue horizontally above the fenders, then turn transversely into the spoiler itself. In the center is the high-mounted center stoplight, utilizing high-intensity LED for lighting. The lower rear spoiler is an extension of the side skirts, which slant up behind the rear wheels and then go across the lower part of the tail end. The four round stoplights are mounted flush to the body. The Genève's sloped nose also sports an integrated spoiler. Along the sides, the air extractor vents are functional, and the side molding is color-keyed. Mirror housings have been restyled. ASC integrated the door handles and LED front and rear side markers into the molding. Behind the cockpit, a hard tonneau covering protects the lowered black Cambria cloth top.

The restyled interior features a significant amount of leather upholstery. ASC considers the interior "sculptured," with contoured black leather seats having charcoal suede inserts. The word Genève crosses the leather in red on the upper part of the seats. Black leather wraps the steering wheel, instrument panel, and console. The console's shape takes it behind the back part of the cockpit, where it meets the partition between the seats and the storage shelf underneath the tonneau at a 90-degree angle.

The production model aspects of the Genève are its engine and running gear. The 5.7-liter V-8 engine has aluminum heads and tuned port fuel injection, and it develops 230 brake horsepower. It drives through a four-speed automatic transmission. ASC added Kelsey-Hayes 17-inch aluminum wheels that carry special Goodyear tires—275/40ZR-17 front and 315/35ZR-17 rear. Other stan-

The Corvette Genève (*both pages*) was built off a production chassis by ASC Incorporated to test their "advanced design concepts" on both the exterior and interior of the sixth-generation Corvette.

dard production features include Bosch anti-lock brakes and an anti-theft system.

ASC's Director of Design D. Mark Trostle: "Our objective was to combine the excellent engineering characteristics of the present-day Corvette chassis with a new evolutionary exterior and interior design. With the cooperation of General Motors design staff, we were able to take creative license in merging our interpretation of the future design trends of Chevrolet with the chassis of a car that has proven to be world class."

From the rear, the Corvette Genève has overtones of both the current production car and the Corvette Indy show car. It sports two spoilers—one above and one below the tail. The four round taillights are mounted flush to the body, while the high-mounted center stoplight is fitted unobtrusively into the top spoiler.

Major Specifications
Corvette Genève

General: Front-engine, rear-drive, two-seat, two-door roadster. Unit construction. **Manufacturer:** Chevrolet Division, General Motors Corporation; ASC Incorporated

Dimensions and Capacities
Wheelbase (in.): 96.2
Overall length (in.): 184.0
Overall width (in.): 76.0
Overall height (in.): 48.0
Track front (in.): 66.8
Track rear (in.): 72.5
Curb weight (lbs): 3350

Drivetrain
Engine type: Ohv V-8, aluminum heads
Displacement (l/ci): 5.7/350
Compression ratio: 9.0:1
Fuel delivery: Tuned port fuel injection
Net bhp @ rpm (SAE): 230 @ 4000
Net lbs/ft torque @ rpm (SAE): 330 @ 3200
Transmission type: 4-speed automatic
Final drive ratio: 3.07:1

Chassis
Front suspension: Unequal-length upper and lower control arms, transverse single leaf springs, stabilizer bar
Rear suspension: Independent, five links, upper and lower control arms, transverse single-leaf springs, stabilizer bar
Steering: Power-assisted rack-and-pinion
Turns lock-to-lock: 2.4
Turn diameter (ft): 40.1
Brake system: 4-wheel discs, Bosch ABS
Wheels: Kelsey-Hayes 9.5" × 17" front, 11" × 17" rear
Tires: Goodyear 275/40ZR-17 front, 315/35ZR-17 rear

Profile:
David R. McLellan

David McLellan replaced Zora Arkus-Duntov as the head of Corvette engineering in 1975. Like many of the other people who have been involved with the Corvette over the years, McLellan is a unique personality. The 1984 model was the first Corvette to reflect that personality fully. With his tousled, sandy hair, McLellan has an almost elfin look that belies his technical expertise.

McLellan was born in the Upper Peninsula of Michigan in the mid-Thirties, about the time that Harley Earl was designing LaSalles and Cadillacs. His family then moved to Detroit, where Dave McLellan grew up. He remained there for his college education at Wayne State University, where he majored in mechanical engineering. He went to General Motors in 1959, fresh out of school, and worked first at the corporation's Milford proving grounds. He spent the better part of a decade there, during which he obtained a master's degree in engineering mechanics from Wayne State.

In 1968, McLellan was transferred to Chevrolet Division, where he worked on the second-generation Camaro. He was also involved with John DeLorean's proposal for a common chassis intended for the Camaro, the compact Nova, and possibly, he says, the Corvette. Fortunately for the two-seater, the common chassis never came to be. But McLellan did contribute to the X-body Nova/Camaro chassis.

McLellan's next career step came in 1973—a year's sojourn at MIT as a Sloan Fellow sponsored by Chevrolet. The year was an important experience. It gave him the opportunity to learn about the automotive industry in other countries. He returned to Chevrolet in 1974, and was given his first Corvette assignment as a staff engineer under Duntov. Just six months later, Duntov retired and McLellan was named chief Corvette engineer.

Though the proposed mid-engine production car derived from Bill Mitchell's Aerovette design was nearly ready at that point, McLellan favored the traditional front-engine/rear-drive configuration for the next-generation Corvette. Significantly, a series of owner surveys supported his position. By now, McLellan had clearly established himself as a clever and capable designer. He had to be. He had the challenge of engineering and overseeing development of the first all-new Corvette in some 20 years.

Here are excerpts from interviews with McLellan by the editors shortly after the introduction of the 1984 Corvette.

Editor: What was the first Corvette model you worked on?

David R. McLellan: The first program I had any impact on was the '78. As chief engineer there are some aspects that are under my direct control, some things not under control. The engine and transmission are not under direct control. The '78 program involved many things besides moving on emissions and fuel economy. From a design standpoint, we had devised a hatchback Corvette which was never approved. That was a hatch with a large frame around it. For '78 we reassessed why we were having problems getting stuff like that approved. The '78 design was originally conceived as a frameless hatch design. This was the one that appeared in the Collector Edition in 1982, its first production appearance.

Ed: When did you realize you would be able to build a new Corvette?

DRM: We realized in that 1977-78 time frame [that] we had to do a new Corvette or the product would be in serious jeopardy. There was general recognition it was time to take a major step with the Corvette. The big issue in that time frame was what should that step be? The options ranged from carrying out the midships V-8 Aerovette-based design to doing a V-6 midships car to taking the front/mid-engine design we had and doing a thorough reassessment of it. We started the process with the midships variation as our mainstream. It

occurred to us only as we got into detailed assessment to look into the front/mid-engine design again. About that time, Porsche came out with the 928—a front-engine V-8 sports car. We looked again at the benefits and it emerged as a very strong candidate and...ultimately emerged.

Ed: What was the downfall of the mid-engine Corvette?

DRM: After all this energy Chevrolet had poured into convincing everybody that a midships car was the way to go...But when you get to a high-performance-engined car that carries two people and has some kind of creature comforts, the mid-engine gets very tough to deal with. Nobody had—and still hasn't—come up with a mid-engine design that is a fully marketable car. All these mid-engine cars are not without their difficulties.

Ed: Is this also true of the Pontiac Fiero?

DRM: The Fiero has a little bit different market. It has to do with the smaller engine. We were showing these aerodynamic low cars and saying these are mid-engine cars. There is a certain amount of cubic volume that is consumed by all those functions to transport two people and achieve a level of creature comfort. To make the midships cars look so slick, we had been ignoring the people issue. There was no utility or luggage space at all in those cars. That's where you get into trouble with the larger engine. The front/mid-engine design offers more benefits at that point. Then it comes down to what can we do to reconfigure [it]. So we set about doing that by repackaging the details, putting the front suspension around the engine, putting the engine in at a completely different attitude, designing the rear suspension to configure it around the occupant requirements. Generally, we were able to make the car a little bit shorter and lower, though a little bit wider.

Ed: What was important to change on the Corvette?

DRM: As we analyzed the old car, a lot of things, we felt, were right...That was reflected in its performance in the marketplace. We really look at this new Corvette as an ultimate performance statement by Chevrolet. What I mean by that is, in all respects that are important to a Corvette, the car needs to be king of the hill. If it's worth doing, it's worth doing better than anybody else. With the old Corvette, we had kind of let things slip a little bit. We had not been pounding the table with our management as hard as we should have. We certainly are today. In fact, we are being pressed by our own management.

Ed: *What changes in automotive technology have affected the Corvette?*

DRM: *It has been updated year by year. It progressed dramatically in '81 and '82 when we moved production from St. Louis to Bowling Green. It was Jerry Palmer and the design team who worked closely together. One of the first things we laid down [for the '84 model] was the tire size. For the kind of performance we wanted, the only tire available in that size was a Pirelli P7. Much of the design was done around that tire. We brought Goodyear in early in [the program] and gave them the specifications, and they worked hard on it. We're very pleased with the results. The tires have been trouble-free. [Even with the wider footprint] they have better hydroplaning performance than previous tires. Goodyear is X-raying 100 percent of the tires for quality control and is testing a sampling using a holographic technique.*

Ed: *Why the use of the unidirectional wheels on the '84?*

DRM: *Basically for aesthetics. It's kind of a non-issue. If that is what the designer wanted and it's reasonable to give it to him, then we'll give it to him.*

Ed: *Is your relationship with Design much like it was between Bill Mitchell and Zora Arkus-Duntov? Mitchell told us that he thinks Engineering is running the show more now than he let them when he was in charge. Is that happening?*

DRM: *Certainly Bill Mitchell is a very flamboyant guy. The only way we really got our act together on this car was by waiting until Bill Mitchell retired. The previous car was never really accepted outside the U. S. The new car carries the cues that make people recognize it as a Corvette, but [are] not so exaggerated. As we got into the aero aspect of it, this car was really designed in the tunnel. [It] has a coefficient of drag of 0.34, and we know how to get it down to a 0.31 or even 0.30 in honest production trim.*

Ed: *What effect did the wind tunnel have on the '84's styling?*

DRM: *Top speed and fuel economy have a lot to do with aero design. Probably the most critical piece of the car from an aero design standpoint was the backlight and the way the taillights were formed. We looked at a variety*

of ways to terminate the rear of the car.

I can't think of any great disagreements we had with Palmer. The only thing I recall was that we had to redo the taillamps without visible screws. Once we laid down where the engine and people were, it was Jerry fine-tuning the design. I think Jerry was very satisfied with the design, and so were we.

Ed: *Why is the Corvette still as heavy as it is?*

DRM: *I can't tell you how many pounds are tied up in open [Targa-roof body] design, but it's a lot. Structural integrity is important. For light weight, coupe construction is the way to go. To my way of thinking, a . . . ragtop design is a throwback. We wanted an open feeling, in contrast with the DeLorean. That's the ideal of a closed-in car.*

Ed: *Was any material other than fiberglass ever considered for the sixth generation?*

DRM: *We never considered anything other than reinforced plastic. It has the ability to absorb minor impacts, and is nearly as light as aluminum.*

Ed: *Why aren't other cars made that way?*

DRM: *It's expensive. But you are seeing more and more use of reinforced plastics. Cars such as the Fiero and Honda CRX are using it.*

Ed: *Will the Corvette continue to employ plastic or fiberglass construction?*

DRM: *Yes! I see the plastic family of materials evolving themselves. There's a great revolution going on in . . . composites.*

Ed: *The 1984 Corvette took a lot of criticism for being a hard-riding car. Why was it made that way?*

DRM: *There are two schools of thought in the press, and we obviously don't side with those who say the car is too harsh. It is a tough car. It was never intended as anything else. It was intended to allow you to get out on a race track and not wallow all over the place. It was intended to enable you to get out and set lap records, and the car has set a number of production lap records at various race tracks. That's one aspect of the car we wanted to optimize and—no question about it—we did.*

When you get onto some of the terrible concrete we have in the frost zone, the car gets kind of tough. In response to those kind of inputs, we are looking into softening up the ride. But we're doing it very carefully so as not to jeopardize the handling performance that is inherent there. It's going to be evolutionary,

and it's going to be done without degrading the handling performance we've already demonstrated.

Ed: *What is the rationale behind having a separate export model for the first time?*

DRM: *The car was designed not just for Canada and the U. S. market but for the export market from the ground up. The export requirements were taken into consideration very early in design, so changes were kept to a minimum. We're producing the export car in the Bowling Green plant so it doesn't have to be retrofitted at point of sale. The car is export-certified for or is now in final stages for (and I think I'll get all the countries here, but I may miss a few): Germany, France, Switzerland, Austria, the low countries, Sweden, England, Spain, Italy, Saudi Arabia, and that whole Middle East area, and Japan. The initial export volume will be low—around 1000 cars. The continuing demand in this market is so high we would have to forego deliveries here to get the car to Europe. With the dollar so strong and all the economic barriers, the price in Europe will be at 928 levels. That car is cheaper there, so the two converge.*

Ed: *Will we see much factory support of Corvette racing?*

DRM: *Our support of racing is a technical support, a position we have taken for a long time. We won't be out there racing the car ourselves.*

Ed: *Do you think racing is still important to the success of the Corvette?*

DRM: *I think it's a very important adjunct to it. There's the overall statement on Chevrolet performance we're making with the Lola turbo V-6 GTP car project. That's a joint venture between ourselves and Ryan Falconer, who is doing the turbocharged V-6 motors. We did the aero work on the car . . . That car . . . will be a testbed development tool to wring out the vehicle system as a competitive prototype vehicle. Then it's up to various private racers to take replicas of that car and turn them into successful racing cars. We're doing the part of that venture that we do best, which is supporting engine development and doing the aerodynamic development.*

Ed: *Will we see twin-turbocharged, aluminum-block V-6s in racing 'Vettes?*

DRM: *That's certainly a possibility. But that's up to [the private racers] given the rules of the series. We really feel the production car is itself a viable competitor. At this point in* time the SCCA and their production racing class has not recognized any of the high-performance sports cars. It's kind of a spooky situation. I think they're pretty close to doing that. We've encouraged them to come up with a classification that recognizes the Corvette, 928, [Ferrari] 308, and the Lotus Esprit Turbo, because all of those cars are roughly equal competitors. We're fairly comfortable that the [Corvette] just driven to the race track is competitive.

Ed: What is the purpose of the bulge on the dashboard facing the passenger seat? Was it originally designed to house an air bag?

DRM: The car is designed around an interior concept to make the car more "friendly" to the occupant in the event of a crash situation. It was developed somewhat like the driver's side, where you have a steering wheel in front of you that absorbs some of that energy. That's why the instrument panel comes out in that padded area the way it does. It was not designed to house an air bag.

Ed: Will we see a different engine—such as a V-6—in the production Corvette anytime soon?

DRM: Probably not. We're not going to see them in the short run, period. We'll see them only if we see a benefit. If we can see a V-6 turbo that would outgun the V-8 and had fuel economy and what other benefits it would need to have to be viable, we would consider it. Part of it is that we have such a damn good engine in the small-block V-8. Its evolutionary progress outstrips anything we can demonstrate in a competing alternative... That engine in NASCAR form is putting out over 600 horsepower. We are continuing to evolve the engine. You'll see an evolutionary process over the next few years where you'll look back and say, "Step by step, they radically changed that engine."

Ed: How long will the sixth generation's production life be?

DRM: You have to look at the viability of the configuration. As long as fuel prices do not become outrageous in terms of [buyer] income, and all other things being equal, the current configuration has a long potential life. We will continue to evolve the present configuration. If there is some dramatic shift in consumer demand, we'll have to reconsider what we're doing.

Ed: Do you see the Fiero becoming a serious competitor?

DRM: We've designed the Corvette with drivetrain robustness that will make it a serious ultimate competitor in the marketplace. I look at the Fiero as a very complementary car at best. I don't see the Fiero outgunning the Corvette. There is nothing they can do that we can't do or do more of.

Ed: Are there any mid-engine or rotary-engine Corvettes still in development?

DRM: No. Not at all.

Ed: What sort of Corvettes might we see further down the road?

DRM: There may be turbine powerplants by then that are viable. That would open up dramatic new opportunities in terms of design.

Ed: Many manufacturers are looking at four-wheel-drive for road cars. Is there a four-wheel-drive Corvette in the future?

DRM: Duntov did a four-wheel-drive Corvette back in the Sixties. In fact, the first of the mid-engine production designs was conceived such that it could have a four-wheel-drive variation. It's not out of the question, [but] it's not very pertinent to the short term.

Ed: Why was the first sixth-generation Corvette designated a 1984 model and not a 1983, leaving out a 30th anniversary model?

DRM: Well, [Chevrolet General Manager Robert C.] Stempel said it. He had two choices: He could have the last '83 into the marketplace or the first '84. Everything we built [on an experimental basis] we called an '83. Bob made the decision that, nope, it's going to be the first '84. The government rule is that you can have only one January 1 in your model year...Since we were not going to sell the cars to the public until March 24, we fell within that criteria.

We went out of production with the old one back in mid October [of 1982]. We had shut down production and cleared the plant out and rebuilt the assembly facility to handle the '84 Corvette. The first production car that was a salable vehicle—VIN00002—is in the Sloan Museum in Flint. VIN00001, which is the lowest serial number, was raffled off by the National Council of Corvette Clubs for charity. It was car number one of '84 production, but it was not the first car built. It was built a couple days later, after they had the production line up and running smoothly. VIN00002 was part of a family of cars, about the first 70, we are not selling because we use those cars to get the build of the vehicle up to standard.

Beginning with the 1984 model, the Corvette's future would be entirely in the hands of a younger—yet no less capable—generation of General Motors professionals. Jerry Palmer is one of the most important members of the new breed. Since 1974, he has been the head of Chevrolet's production Studio Three, where the 1984 Corvette took shape. More importantly, he has had overall responsibility for Corvette design since his redoubtable predecessor, William L. Mitchell, retired as GM's vice president of design in 1977. Thus, Palmer inherited an exciting yet formidable job in much the same way that Dave McLellan did in taking over for Zora Arkus-Duntov on the Engineering side. Both men and their respective teams faced the challenge of not only maintaining the tradition of America's sports car, but improving on it. Judging from the results, Palmer is admirably suited for the job.

Never assume that the job was easy, however. For one thing, Palmer is an articulate, thoughtful, soft-spoken man succeeding one of the most flamboyant and outspoken designers in the industry. Second, Mitchell had been the sole arbiter of Corvette styling for more than 20 years, in itself a very tough act to follow. Although the fifth-generation 1968 design had remained quite popular through its extraordinarily long production run, it was also quite dated by the mid-Seventies. Clearly, its replacement would have to be more modern both in appearance and in function. Yet as development work proceeded on what would become the 1984 model, it was equally clear that any new Corvette would still have to be instantly recognizable as a Corvette. Palmer also faced the problem of giving the car enduring style—a look that would seem fresh in the 1990s, for instance—because the next generation would almost surely be in production for about as many years as its long-lived predecessor.

Finally, Palmer had to face the thorny question of how to update the future. GM had tantalized Corvette fans with the dream machines of the early Seventies, including the mid-engine experimentals and the Aerovette. In fact, Mitchell's stunning Aerovette had been readied for 1980 production, only to be canceled at the last minute. All the concept cars still looked wild and exotic some 10 years later, and many enthusiasts still remembered them. So Palmer had to come up with styling

that would not only be practical for production but also be as eye-grabbing as the show cars. Anything less could have been detrimental to sales. That Palmer managed to reconcile these issues in the 1984 design is a tribute to his creativity and artistry. In fact, he and his staff produced what may well be the most handsome car of the Eighties. Certainly, few would disagree that the 1984 model is one of the best-looking Corvettes ever built.

Jerry Palmer claims to be one of the few designers in the domestic auto industry who is a native Detroiter. His experience with GM Design goes all the way back to 1964, when he spent a summer there as a student. After graduating from the Center of Creative Studies in Detroit the following year, he joined GM permanently, completed the company's internship program, and then served briefly in the Advanced Studios at Design Staff. After a stint in the Army during 1966-67, he returned to Chevrolet and has been with that division ever since, except for brief assignments at GM subsidiaries in Europe and Japan. His first Corvette involvement came in 1969 when he assisted Mitchell in creating several show models. Most recently, Jerry Palmer has been appointed executive designer of Advanced Design, reporting to Charles M. Jordan—head of Design Staff.

Jerry Palmer's affable, easygoing personality belies an intense enthusiasm for his work, about which he is uncharacteristically modest for such a high-ranking executive. He's always eager to talk about Corvettes despite an always hectic schedule. Following are excerpts from interviews with the editors.

Editor: When did you first get involved with the Corvette?

Jerry Palmer: My first production involvement came in the '73 and '74 car. I was the assistant chief designer, and we were doing only the front and rear of the car.

Ed: What were your thoughts about the previous Corvette design?

JP: I thought it was an exciting car. I was really enamored by the show cars, such as the Mako Shark, that led into that body style. Even today you see an '81 or '82 on the road—I know they're dated, but they're still exciting and have a lot of personality. They are definitely Corvettes.

Ed: When did you start working on the new Corvette?

JP: We're always working on a new Corvette. We started on [the sixth generation] in 1977, but there were designs before that which were part of the program. We literally laid out the package starting with a clean sheet of paper. The only thing that was a given was the engine and transmission and need for additional ground clearance. We really started with a package. There's a lot of time and effort spent finalizing the rest of the architecture.

Ed: At this point, were there any further thoughts concerning a mid-engine design?

JP: When the decision was made to go front-engine, the mid-engine responsibility went downstairs to the Advanced Studio. [Studio Three] had mid-engine responsibility until that time. We are the production studio, so when the decision to go front-engine was made, the mid-engine design went downstairs to an Advanced studio.

Ed: Would you have preferred a mid-engine car?

JP: A mid-engine design offers different proportions, more unfamiliar proportions. Based on the components available at that time, we made the right decision. The P-car was essentially what we were looking at—V-6 powered. I also had [1982] Camaro responsibility, and we were going to come out with a pretty wild Z28 package. There's no way a 60-degree V-6 Corvette in the form we were working on could compete with the Z28 we were working on. Then Porsche came out with

their front/mid-engine [928] design. All those decisions made back in that late-Seventies time frame fortified Chevrolet's direction. The mid-engine car is an exciting car, but the [latest] Corvette is a fantastic car for the money in handling, braking, performance. It's right there. We didn't have to apologize for anything. The car is very forgiving. It's hard to screw up in a Corvette; you can screw up in a Ferrari or a rear-engine Porsche very easily. Those considerations were very strong on the engineering side. Plus, the mid-engine car offers less packaging flexibility.

Ed: What is your working relationship like with Dave McLellan?

JP: We have a very good relationship. Dave knows enough about what we [designers] do to understand or challenge. We are very knowledgeable about each other's bailiwick and can challenge each other. I would say Chevrolet was very creative in helping us achieve the package we wanted. To come up with the idea and make it look good is one thing; to make it work is another. There is more integration between the two [disciplines] than there was...years ago. We have a better understanding of what has to be done to make the product people are demanding out there. We're getting closer together.

Ed: Bill Mitchell has criticized the 1984 Corvette in some respects. What is your reaction?

JP: We've talked about it. Bill and I are still good friends. He really didn't like the car at first and said so. Then, after he saw the car out in the real world and saw it in motion, he called me up and said, "I gotta tell ya, that thing really looks aggressive. I still don't quite like the back end, but it looks like a Corvette." I think the thing is [becoming more familiar to] Bill. It doesn't have the exaggerated statement that the previous Corvettes had, but I'm sure if Bill were running the studio I don't think the Corvette would be a lot different than it is today. The shapes are Corvette, but the shapes are also aerodynamically tuned. We didn't conceive the design to aero, but we certainly had aero in mind. We had to meet targets.

Ed: Mitchell told us he thought the '84 was more an engineer's car, not a stylist's car.

JP: I was not controlled at all by Engineering. In fact, Engineering bent over backwards to give us what we wanted. I think Bill would have probably done things a little differently.

However, I don't think it would be a lot different. The 16-inch wheels, the 65-degree windshield—those things are all designer's wants, like the flip-open front end, the T-less T-top. Engineering didn't make those things. They made them happen, but the concepts originated here at Design Staff. For some of those design features we paid penalties...in cost and in mass. But the appearance or aura of that car is the thing we wanted. Engineering didn't back off. In fact, I can't think of anything Engineering demanded we have that we're not happy with. I think the days [are gone when Engineering compromises] what we want. They want as exciting a car as we do.

Ed: *What is the limiting factor in production numbers with the current car?*

JP: It gets down to how many people you want to employ at Bowling Green and how many shifts. We are very reluctant to go into a double shift until we are satisfied the demand is there, not an artificial demand because of the newness of the car. If the demand is there, I'm sure Chevrolet will consider another shift. I feel with a double shift we can make 60,000 cars with the quality the car has to have. We will not pump out cars and detract from the quality. We are still gaining on the quality of the car. I see the car leveling out at around 40,000 units a year. That's a gut reaction.

Ed: *The previous body design lasted 15 years. How long do you think this new one will be around?*

JP: I don't think it's going to last anywhere near that long. But I think it will take us into the Nineties; in fact, I know it'll take us into the Nineties. That's not to say the car will not be injected with new technology wherever possible or [if] we discover something better appearance-wise or function-wise. We'll implement that, but it won't be a total new design.

Ed: *Do you have a favorite Corvette of the past?*

JP: I have several. The 1956 [and] '57 are favorites of mine. Of course, the '63 split-window coupe has been identified as the classic Corvette, and I have to agree with that. The '65 convertible, '68, [and] '69 cars. Didn't like the rounded-off rear end [on] the '61. I think the '80 car was an improvement over the 1974-79 car. Those are some high points.

Ed: *Do you keep an eye on the aftermarket to see what other designers do with the Corvette?*

JP: Sure, but there hasn't been anything

The sixth-generation Corvette, which has been improved continually since 1984, proves that "America's Sports Car" is one for which the nation's auto enthusiasts can feel proud.

that's gotten me to say, "Hey, look at what they've done here. Let's try that." We've been through this thing for so many years [and] we've tried a lot of things. I really get a kick out of seeing the competition cars, because [altering the design] becomes functional.

Ed: *What is your opinion of the Pontiac Fiero?*

JP: I think it's a neat car. The car looks good on the road, better than I thought it would. It's not a Corvette, and I don't think it has to be a Corvette. For the money, it's a hell of a car.

Ed: *Would you be interested in working on the Fiero?*

JP: I guess I'd like to work on anything that presents a challenge.

Ed: *Could the Fiero ever threaten the Corvette?*

JP: If they start to up the power of that to the point where they become a threat to the

Corvette, we also have the ability to turn the wick up.

Ed: *Do you foresee a V-6 Corvette?*

JP: It's an interesting package. I'm sure it's one of the options we'll be looking at in the Nineties if the gas guzzler problem stays with us and we have to maintain or achieve higher performance levels.

Ed: *Would a V-6 work in the current chassis, and what kind of styling options would that offer you?*

JP: I really don't know, because when you get the V-6 to put out the kind of power needed to match or surpass the performance levels we know now, all that room vacated by the two cylinders will be absorbed by intercoolers. The secret to the V-6, obviously, is turbocharging. I don't think there's any question the V-6 is going to be the performance engine of the future. But we're not planning any styling changes around that possibility now.

CHAPTER TEN

Corvettes in Competition

Although sports cars are supposed to be capable of racing, the original Corvette sports car wasn't conceived specifically with racing in mind. Harley Earl thought people might race it: After all, it was spartan, light, and pretty hot—for a six. But in fact the original '53 developed into more of a boulevard sports car like the Kaiser-Darrin than a racer. The original two-seat Thunderbird had a more spectacular racing career than the first Corvettes.

Nothing in the records of the Sports Car Club of America signifies that the six-cylinder Corvette won anything in particular. The first win was by a 1955 V-8, which took the stock car class at the annual Pikes Peak Hill Climb in Colorado. It was an unofficial victory, however, because the sanctioning body that would eventually record annual performance—the United States Auto Club—hadn't been formed yet in 1955.

The temptation to tape the headlights, add numbers to the doors, and go racing really surfaced when the first V-8s were tucked under the hoods of the 1955 and '56 models. Once the urge was born, it stuck, and grew. In the meantime, Zora Arkus-Duntov was saying that winning cars would sell very well from the show room. That was the experience of other sports car builders. By 1955, management was ready to try anything to make the Corvette more attractive. Duntov had done some racing himself, though he was by no means a distinguished driver. He had even failed twice to qualify at Indianapolis. What he did have was the technical expertise to fashion serious competitors out of the basic car, and he knew that the Corvette had potential once the high-winding V-8 arrived. Management told Duntov to proceed, and that was all he needed to hear.

The V-8 made the car buffs take the Corvette seriously for the first time, especially after Duntov himself set a record for the Daytona flying mile in late 1955—150.583 miles per hour. A few weeks later—in January of 1956—at the Daytona Speed Weeks, Betty Skelton set an American sports car speed record, and John Fitch drove a Corvette to victory in the sports car class in the standing-mile run. All the car needed, the performances suggested, was a little research and development, backed by plentiful aid from the factory.

The restyled 1956 Corvette looked more purposeful than the '55, and a young dentist from Washington, D. C., took a shine to it. Dr. Richard Thompson began campaigning in SCCA Class C Production that spring, aided by Duntov and Chevrolet. By the end of the season, he held the C-Production championship. The SCCA immediately bumped the 1957 Corvette with its larger engine up to B Production for the season, but Thompson won that, too. Part of Dick Thompson's winning formula was a special cam developed by Duntov, the same camshaft used in the Daytona cars.

In the mid-Fifties, the most important international event for sports cars, aside from the legendary Le Mans 24-Hours, was the 12 Hours of Endurance run on the old airport course at Sebring in central Florida. It attracted competitors from around the world, and the most prestigious marques were usually well represented, all vying for the acclaim and notoriety associated with a Sebring win. Duntov knew that a good showing at this one event would help the Corvette's image. He wanted more than anything else for the car to be taken seriously, and not to be thought of simply as a toy—which is what some had called the 1953-55 car. In early 1956, Duntov immersed himself in a purpose-built racer, which became known as the Corvette SS (Super Sport). The inspiration for the experimental project (XP-64) was the racing D-Type Jaguar, which would be one of its track competitors. At one point, GM considered sneaking one of its own V-8s into the D-Type chassis and actually racing it with new bodywork. Ultimately, however, approval was given to Chevy's own design.

In final form, the SS looked a bit like the Jaguar—a smooth, cigar-shaped body sporting a rear dorsal fin. But GM couldn't resist giving it some Corvette styling flourishes, so the SS appeared wearing a wide, toothy smile plus a modified version of the body-side cove indentations from the production '56. Underneath the slick exterior was a complex multi-tubular space frame, de Dion rear suspension, and a hopped-up, fuel-injected version of the just-released 283-cubic-inch small-block V-8, putting out 307 brake horsepower at 6400 rpm. Bodywork and many chassis components were made of lightweight magnesium, and the whole car was quite a bit smaller than the production 'Vette. The SS wheelbase, for instance, was just 72 inches, versus the road car's 102 inches, and overall length was a com-

continued on page 278

In early 1966 Zora Arkus-Duntov immersed himself in a
purpose-built race car project, which resulted in
the Corvette SS (Super Sport). The inspiration
for experimental project XP-64 was the racing D-Type
Jaguar, which would be one of its competitors on the
track. Chevy hoped that winning races would sell cars.

continued from page 275

pact 168.6 inches. The SS stood just 48.7 inches high with its removable bubble canopy, designed for long-distance events. In open form it sat about three feet high.

The SS was entered in the prototype class at the 1957 Sebring race, along with a brace of production models running in the sports car category. John Fitch was selected as team manager, though Duntov was on hand to supervise the entire operation. Preliminary track testing got underway in mid-February. Originally, the incredibly talented Juan Manuel Fangio had been signed to drive the SS, but he asked to be released from his contract when he found that the car wouldn't be ready on time. However, Duntov had been reworking a test car mule, driving it around the airport course himself to sort out handling problems. Fitch and his mechanics had prepared the SS, though it would have to run without

In final form, the SS (*below*) looked a bit like the
Jaguar D-Type—a smooth, cigar-shaped body sporting a
rear dorsal fin. But GM couldn't resist giving it some
Corvette styling touches, so the SS appeared wearing a
wide, toothy smile (*bottom left*) plus a modified version
of the body-side cove indentations from the '56 'Vette.

the magnesium body initially planned. Fangio saw the car with the large number one on its flanks and was intrigued. He asked to drive it in practice, and promptly went out and unofficially beat the Sebring lap record. Suddenly, the pits were buzzing about the Corvette racer.

Duntov's long-range game plan was to use Sebring as a shakedown for the SS, then to go on to Le Mans in June. But his plans didn't work out. The SS was forced to retire at Sebring after completing only a few laps—the victim of an over-torqued bushing. Victory also eluded the production entries, though both finished respectably enough. In fact, Thompson and co-driver Gaston Andrey managed 12th overall and first in class. The second team car, driven by Bill Kilborn and Jim Jeffords, took the checkered flag in 15th position. America's sports car had proven to be a true dual-purpose machine, and one to reckon with. As if to confirm that, Dr. Thompson won another SCCA championship in 1957, this time in the B-Production class where the 'Vette now qualified owing to its larger-displacement standard engine. J. R. Rose captured the B-Sports/Racing crown with his modified Corvette the same year.

Due to the AMA racing ban, the

continued on page 285

Underneath the slick exterior of the SS was a complex multi-tubular space frame and a de Dion rear suspension (*right*). The engine (*below*) was a hopped up version of the just-released 283-cubic-inch small-block V-8, putting out 307 brake horsepower at 6400 rpm. Bodywork and many chassis components were made of lightweight magnesium, and with a 72-inch wheelbase and overall length of 168.6 inches, the whole car was quite a bit smaller than the production 'Vette.

A bubble canopy was designed for the SS for use in long-distance racing events. With it, the SS stood just 48.7 inches high (*below*). Zora Arkus-Duntov is at the wheel. The tag on the rear (*bottom*) labels the SS as "experimental," while the overhead view (*left*) shows off the car's sleek racing-inspired design.

continued from page 280

spotlight shifted to the privateers beginning with the 1958 season. As in the stock car field, most racing Corvettes for the year were more competitive 1956-57 models, not the bulkier, heavier '58s. The 'Vette's notable wins were highlighted at the Sebring classic, where a near-stock Corvette finished 12th overall. The car, driven by Jim Rathmann and Dick Doane, also scored first in the GT class, sprinting

to the line 20 laps ahead of the nearest Mercedes-Benz 300SL. At the Pikes Peak Hill Climb, Ak Miller took his 'Vette to a first-place win in the sports car division with a time of 15 minutes, 23.7 seconds and a speed of 48.392 mph for the 12.42-mile course, which rises from 9402 feet to 14,110 feet through 230 curves. Jim Jeffords gave the 'Vette its second consecutive B-Production crown in SCCA with his "Purple People Eater" car—actually one of two SR-2 racing machines

created for Sebring. Built during the summer of 1956, the car featured a rounded nose, a single central rear tail fin with faired-in headrest, and paint reminiscent of the kind used on racing airplanes. A highly modified stock model, it was raced by Curtis Turner, Dr. Thompson, and Harley Earl's son Jerry before Jeffords acquired it. In 1959, Jeffords again took the national B-Production crown.

The 1960 season witnessed several Corvette triumphs. The first came at

Zora Arkus-Duntov (to the right) examines the Sebring SS in 1957 (*top left*). Famed racing driver Juan Manuel Fangio drove the SS in practice at Sebring, and promptly went out and unofficially beat the Sebring lap record (*far left*). The 283-cid V-8 was fuel injected (*left*). The SR-2 (*above*) was created for Sebring. Two copies of this highly modified stock model were built during the summer of 1956.

Bill Mitchell's Stingray racer, the XP-87 (*both pages*),
was painted red initially, but it's shown here in
its silver show car form as seen in early 1961.
It rode the 1957 SS chassis, but sported a new body,
and took the SCCA C-Modified championship in 1960.

Sebring, where Chuck Hall and Bill Fritts added another class win for America's sports car in the 12-hour endurance race. But the man who gave the Corvette the moral victory for which Duntov had longed was Briggs Cunningham. He provided a good showing at Le Mans. Cunningham—no stranger to the French circuit after having competed there with various cars for about a decade—entered three Corvettes in the maximum-displacement GT class, along with a Jaguar prototype. Although one of the 'Vettes retired during the race—spinning out on the rain-soaked track—the Fitch/Grossman Cunningham Corvette came in eighth overall, completing 3782 kilometers. At one point, Fitch was timed at over 151 mph as he drove down the long Mulsanne Straight.

The Stingray racer (*above*) could reach 60 mph
from a standing start in four seconds. At one point
it was equipped with four Weber carburetors and could
"tear your head off," according to Bill Mitchell. Late
in 1961 Zora Arkus-Duntov began work on yet another
Corvette racer he hoped would be a world-beater.
This was Chevy's last "openly" supported factory
competition car, the fearsome Grand Sport (*right*),
Duntov's reply to Carroll Shelby's Ford-powered Cobra.

Though the winning Ferrari of Oliver Gendebien and Paul Frere was considerably faster at 170 mph, the Corvette had conclusively proven its mettle in the world's most demanding long-distance endurance. In another arena, Dr. Dick Thompson was campaigning Bill Mitchell's Stingray Special. The Stingray, which would go on to influence the succeeding generation of Corvettes introduced in 1963, won SCCA's C-Modified National Championship in 1960.

Corvette wins were abundant in 1961. On July 4, Ak Miller repeated a 1958 win in the Pikes Peak Hill Climb by hurtling his 'Vette up the mountain in 14:28.6 minutes, an average speed of 51.5 mph. Third through sixth places at the Peak were also taken by

Corvettes. At Sebring and in SCCA races, Corvettes were all-powerful.

Late in 1961, Duntov began work on yet another Corvette racer that he hoped would be a world-beater. It was Chevrolet's last openly supported factory competition car—the fearsome Grand Sport. Designed by Duntov, along with Walt Zeyte and others, the GS was Chevrolet's reply to the challenge of the Ford-powered Cobra—a lightweight rocketship created by ex-racer Carroll Shelby that employed a British AC roadster body stuffed full of Ford 289 V-8. It was an engine that was already beginning to show its muscle on the tracks. Duntov had hoped to complete 125 Grand Sports, the number needed for it to qualify as a production sports car under interna-

tional racing rules. The Grand Sport program was carried out in great secrecy, deep within the confines of GM and away from disapproving managerial eyes.

The Grand Sport appeared in late 1962 bearing a specially built woven fiberglass body with lines very close to those of the recently released Sting Ray split-window coupe. The chassis was a special tube-ladder affair with stock suspension mounting points. The drivetrain consisted of a four-speed gearbox designed to hook up to a special 377-cid racing version of the Chevy V-8, which would have an aluminum head and block, along with two spark plugs per cylinder. Power output was reported to be 550 bhp, though the actual figure was probably higher. Duntov took the first proto-

Zora Arkus-Duntov had hoped to build 125 Grand Sports
(*left*) to qualify it as a production sports car, but
only five were built before GM axed it. The
instrument panel (*top*) clearly indicates that this
was a race car. Its 377-cid V-8 (*above*) boasted 550 bhp.

After GM axed the Corvette Grand Sport (*both pages*), all five fell into private hands. One car went to Grady Davis, a Union Oil official; Dick Thompson drove that car to a victory at Watkins Glen in 1963. Texas oilman John Mecom, Jr., got three of them and took them to the 1963 Nassau Speed Weeks, where they took first and third in class in the main event. Overall, however, their racing careers were spotty.

type to Sebring in December 1962 to test the car's general competitiveness and its brakes in particular, which he hoped to improve. Some question remains today over whether the tests and the car itself were actually approved by Duntov's superiors. Apparently, they were not, because when word of the tests reached GM headquarters, the company publicly restated its opposition to racing in January 1963, and the entire project was halted after only five cars had been built—all of which had been completed the previous summer. None of them had engines.

The Grand Sport program wasn't dead yet. Two Corvette enthusiasts—Grady Davis and Dick Doane—managed to obtain two of the cars. They were purported to have been delivered in unmarked trucks. Davis, a Union Oil official, and Doane, a Chevrolet dealer, dropped in stock Corvette engines, and Dick Thompson raced the Davis car through the 1963 season,

winning at that year's Watkins Glen race. The other three cars wound up in the stable of Texas oilman John Mecom, Jr., who took them to the Nassau Speed Weeks in 1963. Roger Penske led virtually all the way in the 25-lap Governor's Trophy Race in one, finishing third overall and first in the prototype class in a field of 58. In the main event, the Nassau Trophy Race with its 56 laps and 62 entries, Grand Sports finished fourth and eighth overall and first and third in class.

In early 1964, the Davis and Doane Grand Sports were returned to GM to be prepared for the Daytona Continental, at which time they were converted from coupe to roadster configuration. But management decreed that the roadsters be moved to a warehouse, where they sat for three years before being purchased by Penske and George Wintersteen in 1966. Meanwhile, the Mecom cars contested Sebring in March 1964, but the results proved disappointing. Delmo Johnson and co-driver Dave Morgan endured numerous mechanical breakdowns to finish 32nd, while Penske and Jim Hall put their white GS across the line 18th overall. It was a sad finale for the Grand Sport. The roadsters saw limited action in 1966, but without a major victory. Perhaps the point had

Corvette's dominance in racing was stymied during the mid-Sixties as most of the truly important events went to the Cobras, even though they were far from the "production" sports cars Carroll Shelby claimed them to be. But they had the SCCA's blessing, and *that's* what counted. Nonetheless, privateers raced 'Vettes—often successfully—as shown here (*both pages*) at the Mid-Ohio race track in 1966-68.

Racing Corvettes (*this page*): An Owens-Corning team car in pre-race trials at Daytona, 1971 (*top*); J. Marshall Robbins running a 427 Corvette in A-production at the Mid-Ohio Nationals in 1973 (*above left*); J. Marshall Robbins in the 1973 Road Atlanta Trans-Am (*above right*). *Opposite page*: Jack Broomall in a much modified B-Production Stingray at the Charlotte Bonus National in 1979.

been made, though. The GS would serve as a reminder that full-scale factory involvement in racing wasn't easy.

At the same time, numerous privateers continued to put production Corvettes into victory circles across the country. Dick Thompson took the A-Production championship in SCCA with his newly homologated 327, which the SCCA considered too overwhelming to stay in Class B. Class B meanwhile was dominated by the 283 'Vettes of Yenko and Dominianni through 1964. And, after a dry spell from 1962 to 1963, the 'Vettes returned to dominate their class at the Sebring 12-Hours.

The highlight of the 1963 season was Yenko's repeat B-Production championship and Roger Penske's prototype class victory at Nassau. The following year, Penske's 'Vette ran first in the GT class at the Daytona Continental, driven by Wintersteen, Guldstrand, and Moore. Such victories were heartening for Corvette fans, who really had very little to cheer about in the mid-Sixties. Most of the truly important events now fell to the Cobras, even though they were far from the production sports cars that Carroll Shelby said they were. But they had the SCCA's blessing, and that's what counted. So the Corvette's dominance in road racing was stymied for a few years. Duntov knew the score: "It was clear as day to me that the Cobra had to beat the Corvette. The Cobra was very powerful and weighed less than 2000 pounds. Shelby had the configuration, which was no damn good to sell to the people, except a very few. But it had to beat the Corvette on the tracks." Cobra production would cease after 1967, and by the end of 1968 those cars still racing were tired and worn out. Until then, Corvette pickings were slim, though the car would roar back in the Seventies.

But even the Cobra era had a few Corvette bright spots. For example, the Sting Ray entered by Roger Penske finished 12th overall and first in the GT class at the 1966 Daytona Continental and ninth overall and first in GT at that year's Sebring 12-Hours. The following year, Don Yenko teamed up with Dave Morgan for another Sebring win in GT. And at Le Mans in 1967, the Corvette of Bob Bondurant and Dick Guldstrand ran a strong first in class until its engine failed toward the end of the marathon. A little-reported triumph came at the Bonneville Salt Flats, where Bob Hirsch ran to a record-setting 192.879 mph. Model year 1968—with all its apparent heaviness and clumsiness—saw class wins at Sebring and Daytona.

The rebound in SCCA came in 1969, after the Cobra had gone out of production. Chevy engineer Jerry Thompson and driver Tony De-Lorenzo teamed up to take the A-Production National Championship, ending the Corvette's drought that had begun back in 1962. The year 1969

also saw Allan Barker capture the B-Production title, which would continue through the next three seasons. After 1972, Barker sold his 'Vette to Texas racer Bill Jobe, who won the class with it in 1973 and 1974, giving the car six consecutive national B-Production titles. As recently as 1978, the car was still being campaigned.

In 1970, Corvette repeated as A-Production champ, with a young John Greenwood doing the honors. He won again in 1971. He also teamed up with TV personality Dick Smothers to come home first in GT at Sebring for 1972. At that year's 24 Hours of Daytona, DeLorenzo and Yenko scored yet another GT victory while finishing a

Jim Moyer campaigned a Corvette in the IMSA Camel GT in 1975 (*top left*), while Budweiser sponsored a fleet of sixth-generation Corvettes racing in the SCCA Trans-Am series (*top right*). Morrison-Cook-prepared Corvettes also participate in SCCA-sanctioned show room stock endurance racing, and John W. Heinricy, product engineering manager for Camaro and Corvette, enjoys slipping behind the wheel of these race-going 'Vettes (*right*). It's clear that the Corvette has much more competition history to write since the cars are still running well in both SCCA and IMSA.

surprising fourth overall. Greenwood moved on to Le Mans, where he qualified faster than any other GT contender. He led the class for hours during the race itself until a blown engine forced him out. Filling in for Greenwood as SCCA national A-Production title holder was Jerry Hansen.

The energy crisis put a temporary damper on racing in 1974, but by 1975 things were more or less back to normal. Like the Sting Rays before them, the fifth-generation Corvettes were too big and heavy to compete effectively against the likes of Porsche and BMW in international endurance events. And Corvette campaigners couldn't hope to match the large sums of money spent by the European companies. So the 'Vette's biggest successes continued to come in SCCA club racing. America's sports car would be A-Production champion from 1973 through 1978, B-Production champ from 1973 through 1974 and from 1976 through 1979. Corvettes also did well in the new sport of autocross, winning the B-Stock Solo II crown every year from 1973 through 1979, except for 1975.

Trans-Am competition in the Seventies had its share of good show-

continued on page 305

Corvettes entered in SCCA's Showroom Stock endurance racing division (*this page*) have done extremely well, fighting tooth-and-nail against the Porsche 944 Turbos in the SS class and winning every race through the 1985 and 1986 seasons. In competiton sponsored by the International Motor Sports Association, the Corvette has likewise been a consistent contender and frequent winner in the GTO division (*opposite page*).

For the past few years, Chevrolet has been
involved in the role of providing technical assistance
for an exciting mid-engine prototype racing car, the
Lola-based, Chevy-powered Corvette GTP (*both pages*)
that competes in IMSA's Camel GT series.

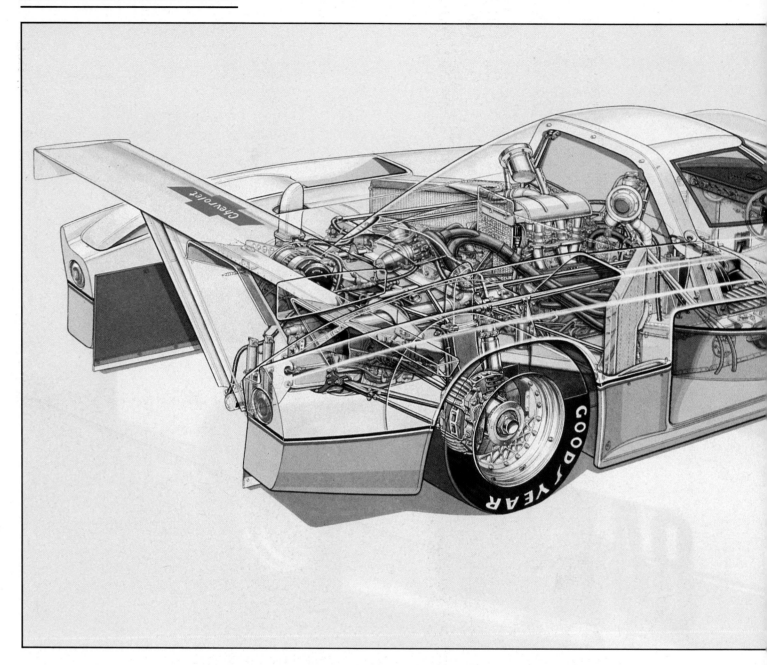

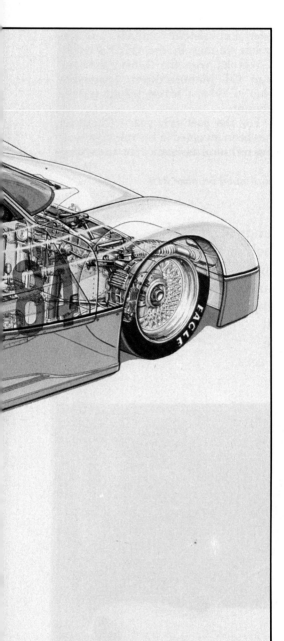

continued from page 300

ings by Corvettes. In 1973, the 'Vettes of J. Marshall Robbins, Greenwood, and Jerry Thompson finished third, fourth, and fifth overall. In 1975, Greenwood was the overall winner, while 'Vettes driven by Babe Headley, Jerry Hansen, and Paul Misuriello came right behind him in second, third, and fourth position. Two lean years followed, but then in 1978 Corvette claimed the Trans Am's Category II championship, with Greg Pickett's wild racer. Headley finished a distant

second to Bob Tullius' Jaguar, heavily backed by its U.S. sales subsidiary, in Category I.

Jaguar was not so fortunate in 1979. Gene Bothello's Corvette was the Category I winner, with the 'Vettes of Frank Joyce and Gary Carlen in third and fourth places. Pickett finished second in the 1980 consolidated series. Then, in 1981, Eppie Wietzes ended up the point leader in a season described as one of the most exciting and competitive in the Trans Am's history.

More recent Trans Am seasons have been ruled by Capris, XR4Tis, Ca-

A cutaway (*left*) shows the location of the main components of the Corvette GTP. Its V-6 engine is turbocharged (*below*). Three drawings (*bottom row*) compare the GTP with a production sixth-generation Corvette, emphasizing the GTP's long-tail body.

maros, and Nissan 300ZXs. But usually a Corvette can be found toward the top of the points standings. Phil Currin's car ran third in points for 1982, although Phil never won a race outright—an example of consistency, if nothing else. In 1984, Darin Brassfield and David Hobbs were the sixth- and eighth-place point-scorers, with the year including Brassfield's outright wins at Road America and Riverside.

Meanwhile, Corvettes entered in SCCA's Showroom Stock endurance racing division have done extremely well. The sixth-generation cars have fought tooth-and-nail against the Porsche 944 Turbos in the SS class, with the Corvette winning every race through the 1985 and 1986 seasons.

In competition sponsored by the International Motor Sports Association (IMSA), the Corvette has likewise been a consistent contender and frequent winner in the GTO division. Chevrolet won the IMSA All-American GT Manufacturers Championship in 1978, a fitting tribute for the division.

For the past few years, Chevrolet has been involved in the role of providing technical assistance for an exciting

continued on page 310

Driven by Sarel Van Der Merwe and Doc Bundy, the Corvette GTP (*both pages*) has proven itself by starting on the pole for several races during the past few years, as well as winning a good number of races for the Hendrick Motorsports racing team and its GM Goodwrench sponsor. It serves to add luster to the Corvette name, helping to sell (hopefully) regular production cars.

Chevy calls its Indy V-8 engine (*both pages*) "a purebred
racing powerplant." It features dual overhead cams
and four valves per cylinder. Needless to say,
it's turbocharged. Also contributing to its
performance are eight throttle butterflies, tuned
intake runners, and a short-stroke crankshaft. John
Heinricy, product engineering manager for Camaro and
Corvette, expects to see some rub-off from the Indy
V-8 to production Corvette engines as time goes by.

Mario Andretti is shown here studying Chevy's
Indy V-8 (*right*). He races that engine in Number 5
(*above*), a Lola-based car shown here at the 1987 CART
(Championship Auto Racing Team) Long Beach Grand Prix.
He also raced it at the 1987 Indianapolis 500. A fuel
system failure cost him that race, but he started
from the pole and led for most of the race.

continued from page 306

mid-engine prototype racing car that
competes in IMSA's Camel GT series.
The Lola-based, Chevy-powered car
features a long-tail body with ground
effects skirting and a nose vaguely
reminiscent of that of a current production Corvette. The turbocharged
V-6-powered GT prototype, driven by
Sarel Van Der Merwe and Doc Bundy,
has proven itself by starting on the
pole for several races the past few
years, as well as winning a good number of races for the Hendrick Motorsports racing team and its GM Goodwrench sponsor.

Recent racing victories are all very
heartening. The Corvette is, after all, a
car that depends on selling 30,000 or
40,000 copies a year for its survival.
Without full factory-authorized support such as one finds in the Porsche
and Ferrari efforts, the Corvettes with
their winning record on the race tracks
of the world are an impressive testimony to their worth as true sports
cars.

Profile:
John W. Heinricy

Top left: John W. Heinricy, Product Engineering Manager for Corvette and Camaro. Chevrolet believes that racing *does* improve the breed, and proves it by running Corvettes in SCCA Showroom Stock (*top right*) and IMSA GTO competition (*above*).

Presently the Product Engineering Manager for Corvette and Camaro, John Heinricy has worked intensely with the Corvette program since 1984. Heinricy earned a BSME degree from South Dakota School of Mines in 1970 and added an MBA from Michigan State in 1985. He has been employed by Chevrolet since 1970 and served as a test engineer and development engineer before becoming the Corvette's engineering manager. He also races the cars on which he works, as he indicates in the following interview with the editors.

John W. Heinricy: *In looking at the books [on our cars], one of the things that I always like to see in both the Corvette and Camaro books is [that] they cover the special models real well. We talked about the Indy Corvette. They've got a lot of coverage of Stingrays and Corvette Grand Sports, CERV I, and that sort of thing, and I wanted to be sure you were aware of what's been going on during the last several years along the same lines. There are special one-off race cars that have been out there racing. I wanted to be sure you were covering those. I'm not sure they're very publicly known, just like when I was in high school and college I never heard of a Stingray Corvette and an SS Corvette and a Grand Sport. I just didn't seem to hear about them—unless you were close to the industry or reading all the magazines—I just didn't hear about them.*

There's the prototype cars that have been running. At Nelson Ledges in 1984 a prototype '85 was run. The 1986 was run in 1985. Last year and the previous year at one race there were cars run GTO class that were production-based cars.

Editor: *What races?*

JH: *They ran the Daytona 24-Hour last year, the Sebring 12-Hour, Riverside, Watkins Glenn, and ran at the Daytona finale, too. There were a lot of things on those cars that were development-type items, just like they were back in the SS and Stingray days—when they were running those type of cars. They were really developing a lot of things for future Corvettes.*

Ed: *But not quite as publicized now.*

JH: *Not as publicized, although I'm not sure how well those were publicized back then either.*

Ed: *These are run in the IMSA series?*

JH: *Yes. Those had a lot of involvement from Corvette Engineering.*

Ed: *Morrison-Cook?*

JH: *Yes.*

Here's some other cars that I find interesting in recent Corvette history: Remember the car that Ron Grable ran 200 miles per hour on the Indian reservation out in Arizona? It's called Thumper. There's quite a bit of engineering work that went into that—it's a high-performance testbed. We've done a lot of things around that car from a high-speed test standpoint—anything fast aerodynamically and stability-wise. There was another car called Big Foot. The name Big Foot came from the fact that we were fitting bigger tires and seeing what the chassis needed to work with them. We also had some high-performance engines in the car and did some track testing with the car. Both of those cars led into the GTO test that we did. Another car was called Puff—a turbo, the forerunner to the Calloway turbo. We were looking at turbocharged V-6s, which we looked at for a very short time. We decided V-6s weren't what we wanted.

Ed: *What can you tell us about the '88 Corvette? From what we can see, the tires and wheels are new.*

JH: There are a lot of chassis changes on the car as well. Cosmetically, the wheels and tires are about the only thing. But suspension-wise, the front suspension geometries have been all changed to what we call the zero scrub radius suspension. A quick explanation: The king pin axis intersects the ground [somewhere to the left or right of] the center of [the tire meeting the ground]. That affects braking stability greatly, especially with ABS braking systems. In 1988, we reduced that scrub radius from about 75mm, or about three inches, down to zero. So you take all of that suspension and realign all the ball joint angles and king pin axis so that the king pin axis intersects the center of the tire patch. What that does is give you good stability side to side; you don't have any steer effects from braking. It's a very significant change in the stability of the car under braking.

The rear suspension was changed primarily to get an improved geometry for roadholding. The camber curve was changed, and all the other geometries were changed to correspond to this different camber in the rear suspension. And it should work better with the 17-inch tires, too.

There are pretty dramatic changes in the suspension, and they require changing just about every component. Like in front, just to change the king pin axis, you change the knuckle, the upper control arm, the lower control arm; you have to have a different spring, different shock mounts, different length shocks. The brakes are going to change. It's a

real significant change. The same way in the rear. When you change the camber geometry, you have to change just about every component back there. The rear axle castings are different and the lengths are different. Virtually everything is different.

The other thing on the chassis that's changed is the brakes. The whole system is upgraded for 1988. We've gone to bigger rotors on the base car, with dual-piston calipers in front. On the Z51, we have an even bigger rotor—one inch larger than on the base car, with the same calipers. They're impressive looking brakes when you just take the wheels off and look.

Ed: *What's the standard tire size for 1988?*

JH: Still the same—a 16-inch tire on the base model. What we did on the rotor is that we went one inch bigger than in 1987, on the base car. That can still be fitted inside the 16-inch wheel. Then when you go to the 17-inch wheels, optionally and on the Z51, you get a one inch bigger rotor yet. The optional system is fantastic at braking. That's been tested at speeds up to 180 miles per hour on the panic stopping surface.

Ed: *Any engine changes?*

JH: Yes. Engine changes include different heads—a revised aluminum head...It has significantly improved breathing. We've gone to a different camshaft to go along with that head. In-house we call the camshaft an L82½—it's not quite an L82, not as wild of timing, but it's more radical than the L83, which is what the current engine has. We have different rods and pistons. I can't tell you for sure if those rods and pistons go into the '88 or if we're waiting until '89 to do those. But I think our '88 horsepower ratings will be up—it's going to be 245 [bhp].

Ed: *Interior changes?*

JH: I think our interior changes are mostly color.

Ed: *How much of the car's evolution came out of the racing that's going on?*

JH: A lot of the braking, and the suspension work also. Let me give you a "for instance": The 1986 [Morrison-Cook] prototype that ran at Nelson Ledges had the brake system on it that's on the base car for 1988. In the GTO cars that we ran last year, they had the revised rear suspension geometry—as a matter of fact, we played with the geometry a lot during the year. What's in the 1988 cars is the result of that. We ran the heavy-duty

brake system that's on the 1988 cars—the larger rotors. At one point last year, we tested that.

Ed: *Did you do any of the testing on your own racing car? You did rather well last year.*

JH: Yes. I drove in the GTO cars and in the [SCCA] Showroom Stock cars. We came in second in Showroom Stock.

There are other things too that came out of the racing program that are on the production car right now and showed up in 1987—like power steering coolers, improved bearings and hubs, some changes in the braking system—that were a direct result of the Showroom Stock effort. We're yet to see some of the things that were accomplished in the GTO program last year. You won't see them on the 1988 car—they'll be 1989 and '90 items.

I think that the whole thing makes a good story and I didn't know if you were covering that. That's been running through my mind for about the last year that somehow we have to make sure that we get it all documented.

I was the project manager for the Corvette out at the proving grounds from '84 to '86, so I'm intimately familiar with everything that went on. Everything that we did in '84, '85, and '86 when I was out there was incorporated in '85, '86, '87, and '88, because you're working that far ahead, typically. A lot of the things [we're working on in GTO and Showroom Stock] you won't see until 1989 and '90. As we can, we incorporate them right along.

Ed: *Were a lot of the changes that you made in response to complaints on the 1984 model?*

JH: Complaint-wise on the 1984s, we probably took care of those on the 1985s. We hammered on those fast, where they were really significant complaints...We had information out to the dealers as to what they could do for 1984 [on some of the complaints, particularly the ride]. There's a lot of publicity on complaints, but in terms of actual numbers of customers complaining about the ride, there weren't a real lot of them. There weren't but a couple hundred—not 25,000 out of 50,000.

Ed: *Will we see a five-speed Corvette anytime soon?*

JH: Probably not...Maybe you'll see one with more speeds. I mean, we've got one now with seven, effectively. The transmission we have right now is a pretty good compromise for a five-speed.

Ed: *What's coming up in the future?*

JH: *You mentioned the transmission. We're looking at five-speeds. We raced Doug Nash five-speeds in the GTOs. Part of that was working with Doug Nash. Now they're interested in promoting their five-speed, producing for the future Corvette. So it was a joint development program there with Doug Nash on the five-speed. It's become a hell of a good road-racing transmission. Now you'll see Peerless Camaros using it in GTO and Jack Rousch is asking to use it in Rousch-prepared Mustangs. We're looking at five-speeds, we're looking at six-speeds and seven-speeds.*

We also have activity from some of the other suppliers of parts on the cars that are working right with us in the racing programs—the shock absorber people, the axle people, transmission people, [the brake people]. There were changes made in the Doug Nash transmission from '85 to '86, and into '87, that were the result of Showroom Stock racing activities.

The engine and powertrain people right here at C-P-C [Chevrolet-Pontiac-Canada Group of General Motors] are heavily involved in Showroom Stock racing activities. They're watching their cars, making sure they're durable, learning what they can from the engine builders who build engines for those Showroom Stock racing cars—you know, they blueprint them and push them to the limits within the specs. Our engine people are paying as close attention as they can to everything that's going on, because they want to squeak every bit of power out of that 350 as they can, too, for the production cars.

The prototypes give them a chance to run some future parts in the engines so they can get as much knowledge as they can. A 24-hour race is a pretty good test for an engine.

Ed: *Is the 350 engine pretty much it for the future?*

JH: *I think the 350 is going to be around for a pretty long time. Strictly V-8s. Suffice it to say that we're looking at some pretty exciting high-performance Corvettes—things that will make you think about LS-7s and L88s.*

Ed: *Do you receive much feedback from the Corvette GTP car project?*

JH: *It's a little bit hard to derive some of the benefits from it. You have to let things filter down. There's a level in between where you have to let it filter down. You can look at some of the material things—composite brake rotors, things like that. There's some benefit derived from testing that's going on there. From the standpoint of some of the specific technologies, if you look at some of the parts, some of the material technology can be derived [for the Corvette]. It's hard to pick on some of the big things. You might not get a benefit from the transmission or the whole engine, or the suspension in general, but maybe the material technology used in the drive axle [might be beneficial]—if you're looking at some kind of a composite drive axle or special joints that handle a lot of power. We plan on putting more and more power in the Corvette, so we need to look at those kinds of technologies. Composite brakes are another good example of things we need to look at on the Corvette.*

Specific engine things that go along with turbocharging are also good for high efficiency engines. Maybe there's a lot of valve technology and valve materials and piston materials and head sealing. The guy who works on that engine sits right next door to me—Richard Johnson. Richard was the prime development engineer on the 1985 Corvette fuel injection system. So he uses a lot of that original technology in doing the fuel injection system on the [V-6 GTP engine]. The V-6 came from the Corvette technology that he had, but now he's refined a lot of that and a lot of what he's starting to learn from there is filtering into production.

As I sit here and think about it, I [first thought] there wasn't much on the GTP that we use, but there's a lot of things. A lot of things that they learn aerodynamically. We just got a new car here a couple months ago that had some revisions aerodynamically, and also had some suspension revisions.

Ed: *Will we be seeing some Corvette Indy influences in the production Corvettes anytime soon?*

JH: *I think you're bound to. It's like back in the Sixties when you saw a Mako Shark, the original Stingray, and the SSs; there was some influence that came off those cars. So I would expect there to be. The only way there wouldn't be is if there were a total change of people in Design Staff. Because you know that's the kinds of things they're thinking about, so just expect to see some rub-off there.*

Ed: *Are we going to see the present style for the next few years, yet?*

JH: *I think so. Now you'll see some changes, but they're not going to be a dramatic, total new vehicle like you saw in 1984.*

Ed: *Will the changes be primarily to the nose and tail?*

JH: *To the things [that] are easier to change. Although, it's easier to change the Corvette than it is some of the other cars. When you've got a space-frame type of construction, it's easier to change the panels that attach to it.*

Ed: *So it could be just about any body panel that attaches to the car?*

JH: *Right. Look at some of the [prototype and racing] cars of the last couple of years, and that'll give you an eye to the future—transmissions, engines, and so on.*

Ed: *Is there an entry-level Corvette in the works?*

JH: *I don't see doing anything to the Corvette that's going to be de-contenting. When you think of an entry-level Corvette, you think of what you'd have to do to a Corvette to make it an entry-level car. It's an entry-level car right now into the high-performance exotic-car kind of a market. It is the entry-level car of that market. When you look at a 944 Turbo or Ferrari or cars that it really can compete effectively against and beat, it is an entry-level into that market. It is now at what you'd call the top end of the [Nissan] 300ZX market or the [Porsche] 944S market. It's priced right at the top of that market, and it just beats the hell out of that market. Nothing's even close. So if you put that car into what you'd call an entry-level market, you'd probably be talking about 300ZXs and 944s. That's not the market the [Corvette's] aimed at. How would you feel about buying a $35,000 Corvette convertible and somebody else had a $22,000 Corvette entry-level coupe? You might not feel as good about it. The people who know cars would know, but there's a significant number of [Corvette owners] who are very image-conscious, and you've got to be real careful about that image. You can destroy that image so easily by making a couple of wrong moves in the market.*

Ed: *Will we ever see analog gauges?*

JH: *If I'm still around. I defend the instrumentation we have today by saying that I've yet to see a digital instrumentation in a production car that's better. And it was one of the first. When the '84 Corvette came out, it made a bang when you looked at it. And it's been refined a couple of times. Some of the things may seem subtle, but the readability is much better than it was in 1984. I find the gauges themselves to be unbeatable.*

Corvette Racing Highlights

1955
- Stock car record for Pikes Peak Hill Climb

1956
- Record 150-mph run on Daytona Beach
- SCCA C-Production champion
- Ninth overall at Sebring 12-Hours

1957
- First in class at Sebring 12-Hours
- SCCA B-Production champion
- SCCA B-Sports/Racing champion

1958
- First in class at Sebring 12-Hours
- First in class at Pikes Peak Hill Climb
- SCCA B-Production champion

1959
- SCCA B-Production champion

1960
- First in class at Sebring 12-Hours
- Eighth overall at Le Mans 24-Hours
- SCCA B-Production champion
- SCCA C-Sports/Racing champion

1961
- First in class at Sebring 12-Hours
- First in class at Pikes Peak Hill Climb
- SCCA B-Production champion

1962
- First in class at Daytona Continental
- SCCA A-Production champion
- SCCA B-Production champion

1963
- First in Prototype class at Nassau
- SCCA B-Production champion

1964
- First in class at Daytona Continental
- SCCA B-Production champion

1965
- SCCA Midwest Division A-Production champion
- SCCA Midwest Division B-Production champion
- SCCA Southwest Division B-Production champion

1966
- First in class at Sebring 12-Hours
- First in class at Daytona Continental

1967
- First in class at Sebring 12-Hours

1968
- First in class at Sebring 12-Hours

1969
- SCCA A-Production champion
- SCCA B-Production champion

1970
- SCCA A-Production champion
- SCCA B-Production champion

1971
- First in class at Daytona 24-Hours
- First in class at Sebring 12-Hours
- SCCA A-Production champion
- SCCA B-Production champion

1972
- SCCA A-Production champion
- SCCA B-Production champion

1973
- First in class at Sebring 12-Hours
- SCCA B-Production champion
- SCCA B-Stock Solo II champion
- SCCA B-Prepared Solo II champion

1974
- SCCA A-Production champion
- SCCA B-Production champion

- SCCA B-Stock Solo II champion

1975
- First overall SCCA Trans Am series
- SCCA A-Production champion

1976
- SCCA A-Production champion
- SCCA B-Production champion
- SCCA B-stock Solo II champion

1977
- SCCA A-Production champion
- SCCA B-Stock Solo II champion
- SCCA B-Prepared Solo II champion

1978
- First overall in SCCA Trans Am Category II
- SCCA A-Production champion
- SCCA B-Production champion
- SCCA B-Stock Solo II champion
- SCCA B-Prepared Solo II champion

Both as a sports car and a race car, the Corvette
has traveled a long road. It is more than deserving
of its role as "America's Sports Car," and its winning
record on the race tracks of the world is eloquent
testimony to its worth as a true sports car.

- SCCA B-Stock Ladies Solo II champion

1979
- First at Riverside Vintage Car Races (Grand Sport #003)
- First overall in SCCA Trans Am Category I
- SCCA B-Production champion
- SCCA B-Stock Solo II champion
- SCCA B-Prepared Solo II champion
- SCCA B-Stock Ladies Solo II champion

1980
- Second overall SCCA Trans Am series

1981
- First and third overall SCCA Trans Am series

1982
- Second (tied) overall SCCA Trans Am series

1984
- First at Road Atlanta SCCA Trans Am
- First at Mid-Ohio and Willow Springs SCCA Showroom Stock endurance races
- SCCA Showroom Stock national champion

1985
- First in class at Laguna Seca IMSA GTO
- SCCA Showroom Stock manufacturer's champion
- SCCA Showroom Stock SSGT national champion
- IMSA GTP Corvette pole at Daytona 24-Hours, lap record

1986
- IMSA GTP Corvette pole at Daytona 24-Hours
- First at Road Atlanta IMSA Camel GT
- SCCA Showroom Stock national champion

Clubs for Corvette Enthusiasts

National Corvette Owners Association
P. O. Box 777A
Falls Church, VA 22046
Founded: 1975
Current membership: 25,000
Publication: *For Vettes Only*

National Council of Corvette Clubs
P. O. Box 325
Troy, OH 45373
Founded: 1957
Current membership: 10,000

Western States Corvette Council
2321 Falling Water Court
Santa Clara, CA 95054
Founded: 1965
Current membership: 3000
Publication: Quarterly newsletter

Bill Mitchell's 1960 Corvette XP-700 show car.

INDEX

1988 Corvette convertible.